The

FAILURE *of*
NATIONAL RURAL
POLICY

The
FAILURE *of*
NATIONAL
RURAL
POLICY

Institutions and Interests

William P. Browne

GEORGETOWN UNIVERSITY PRESS / WASHINGTON, D.C.

Georgetown University Press, Washington, D.C.
© 2001 by Georgetown University Press. All rights reserved.
Printed in the United States of America.

10 9 8 7 6 5 4 3 2 1   2001

This volume is printed on acid-free offset book paper.

Library of Congress Cataloging-in-Publication Data
Browne, William Paul.
The failure of national rural policy : institutions and interests /
William P. Browne.
p.   cm.
Includes bibliographical references and index.
ISBN 0-87840-857-6 (cloth : alk. paper)—
ISBN 0-87840-858-4 (pbk. : alk. paper)
1. Rural development—Government policy—United States.
2. Agriculture and state—United States.
3. United States—Rural conditions.   I. Title.
HN90.C6 B77 2001
307.1'412'0973—dc21
2001023272

DEDICATION

Dedicated to my wife Linda, whose rare combination of cosmopolitan style and poise along with basic rural values has always kept me going. She reminds me daily of how nice and useful it was to have grown up in Iowa.

ON UNDERSTANDING RURAL AMERICA

As Peter Fonda once said on an entirely different matter: To get it "you had to be there and on something." I was most certainly there, and I was on somewhat of a mission— understanding rural community neglect.

CONTENTS

ACKNOWLEDGMENTS

The greatest thanks for this book go to rural residents, with whom I've spent almost my entire life. If I hadn't been able to personally observe them and their problems over time, this project could not have materialized.

Yet I also have more specific debts. Fred Buttel of the University of Wisconsin always inspired me. So did other rural sociologists and social scientists, such as Lou Swanson at Colorado State. The names are too numerous to list. Two esteemed economists, however, must be noted: Al Schmid and Jim Bonnen of Michigan State University. Their help and ideas were indispensable, as was their ongoing support for my research and intellectual framework. David Schweikhardt, who will soon be an eminent scholar in his own right, provided the same help and friendship. Bonnen, Robert H. Salisbury, and Charles W. Wiggins get added thanks for mentoring me in my slow move from rural thug to productive scholar.

Institutional support abounded. The old Agricultural and Rural Economics Division at the Economic Research Service (ERS) of the U.S. Department of Agriculture housed me and gave me grants. Thanks to former ERS Administrator John Lee for his belief and assistance and to Norm Reid for his great hospitality. Susan Sechler helped wonderfully; she awarded and administered rural funds for the Ford Foundation, and she always expressed intense policy values. I hope this book finally pays them all off, even in some small way.

The Rural Sociological Society Task Force on Persistent Rural Poverty merits more than a word. These scholars kept me involved, challenged me, led me to fill a void, and put up with me as the task force's only real-life political scientist, as well as someone they unceasingly sensed to be a political economist.

One colleague greatly helped by critiquing chapters: Pamela Edwards-Ham. Of all the people I've taught with at Central Michigan University, she is the very brightest, the most energizing, and the best prepared of a very large group. Good colleagues Ted Clayton, Joel Fetzer, and Rick Kurtz also assisted. John Dinse, an old pal and a wonderful intellectual, did even more. Nancy Spragg, who is my best friend in writing skills instruction, provided a lift. Any problems with this book are the fault of these six! Just kidding, I guess.

The usual suspects get rounded up for my gratitude as well. They include my spouse, dogs, friends, physicians, caregivers, other academic colleagues, rural advocates, staff at Georgetown University Press, and clerical help. Jackie Robert merits special mention for her personalized attention to this manuscript. I also must mention the students who worked tirelessly throughout the year to help me complete this book. Janice Booms was far and away most important, but Sonya Frazier, Matt Luttermoser, Aaron Prince, Casey Wilkinson, Anthony Clements, and Joel Zinner also get credit. Cheers to all of them.

PREFACE

This book is written in order to develop a better understanding of rural society in America than now prevails. Yet some readers may regard this analysis as more of an extended essay than a typical policy book. Those potential critics have a point, and I accept it. Indeed, each of the 14 individual chapters is brief and direct in its emphasis. As such, the image of essay purposely prevails throughout the analysis. The reason for this approach is simple: to avoid hopeless immersion in too much theory and too many observations. Readers are best served, I think, by sticking to the essential argument, even if a few academic fine points are glossed over. Such side excursions often simply confuse the presentation, which is far from desirable in an interpretative academic experiment with social history such as this.[1]

What, then, is the essential argument? I contend that some public policies are incompatible with others. As a consequence, incompatible policies that emerge as political ideas at a late date rather than an earlier one get lost. More exactly, they get neglected, ignored, or even discredited—even by their supposed friends. Then they get intentionally lost. As I've said elsewhere, these are bad issues in a political as opposed to a logical sense.[2] Proposed refinements of established policies are maintained for extended periods of time; they are perceived as good issues for government to pursue and "improve upon." That can be the case even as they've outlived their usefulness.[3] Yet they're still good because they have political support.

The result is a distinct bias in United States policy preferences, and that bias has helped structure rural America. This bias has had a dramatic impact on rural society, especially among people who are left without policy benefits. Farm policy versus rural policy is a superb example of one policy (the former) excluding the other (the latter)—perhaps the best in American politics because of its extensive base in time. There are undoubtedly several other examples in policy history, as the theory in this essay implies. What I believe exists on the rural front probably quite nicely explains broader policies of neglect and a seeming policy myopia in American political processes.

The rural policy interpretations presented in the ensuing pages follow three historical stages. First, modern U.S. farm policy emerged in 1862 to make possible other policies that were intended to develop and settle the West. The West would have been little but vacant spaces without numerous agrarians—or what we'd call glorified peasants. Second, farm policies failed to keep all farmers in production. Thousands of farms routinely failed. Yet those policies did lead to an industrialized agriculture that succeeded in making the farm sector collectively ever more prominent and many of its practitioners wealthy, even as many farmers went out of business.[4] Most of those who left the sector were nonadapters of technology and better farming methods.

Third, the process of reconciling individual failure with sector success led to a near-constant but rather narrow public policy search. All sorts of institutions were created and added, in a cumulative sense, one to the others. Thus, an Agricultural Establishment was formed, expanded, and reasonably well-supported by public policymakers.[5] Throughout the late 19th century and into the 1920s, the emphasis was always on keeping able producers in business by providing them with specific but generally available government services for all, from farm education to help in marketing.

This evolution produced a policy paradigm about what was considered proper and appropriate public sector action. As these service efforts intensified, public officials increasingly were wedded to the logic of industrial and commercial farm development or to farm modernization and development. Peasant, or subsistence, agriculture was not really in vogue in the United States. Developed agrarianism and policies to achieve it were regarded as the inherently correct as well as the politically popular means of addressing rural America. This farm development paradigm or strategy had been going on so long, and in conjunction with inspirational nation-building efforts, that it became the only way to see things. Competing rural policy paradigms were easily cast aside as inappropriate. For example, the rural poor and declining local communities were to be dealt with not on their own merits but by fostering a healthy farm economy. The intent was to prevent rural poverty and decline by reaching farmers before they were forced by lagging personal finances to exit agriculture—not to help them after they were gone. As a consequence, the problems of nonfarmers, former farmers, nonfarm residents, and regions without farmers were left without policy attention. Rural society, as a consequence, was left with numerous pockets of neglect.

One simple reason for the neglect explained why it existed: To advocate a rural peoples' policy meant to acknowledge that this pervasive and institutionalized farm policy was insufficient and perhaps even foolish. Such an acknowledgment would have been an admission that the Agricultural Establishment, elected public officials who watched after farming, and farmers as beneficiaries of Establishment services could not countenance. All would have lost too much—public funds, votes, economic help on the farm. Therefore, to preserve the farm policy paradigm and the institutions it had created, rural policy alternatives were simply ignored or even condemned. Institutional momentum meant that there were no real and distinctly unique policy choices from which to select. The farm modernization and development paradigm was too deeply embedded.

This analysis, then, centers on those three interpretive but not distinct lessons. There are, however, two broader theoretical views that are used to advance the logic of the essay. Both reflect, yet deviate from, the traditions of political economics as such thought has evolved into a modern positivism. The first is institutional statist theory, with its focus on the contributions and the constraints provided by existing public policy and organizations. The idea of a sustainable policy equilibrium is central to that explanation.[6] Such an equilibrium of institutions and their own interests is evident in the preservation of the essence of the farm policy paradigm over time.

Change, however, also must be reconciled in the theory. Farm policy and its specifics are constantly emergent and flexible, not cast in specific institutional stone. Thus, within the equilibrium there is a continuing search for policies that better serve the farm modernization and development process. What explains these evolutionary changes and the forces behind them is evident in group politics or the theory of political interests. Interest theory becomes the second theoretical view that structures this essay's analysis.

That theory argues that institutions matter and have consequences largely because their organization and maintenance foster the conditions under which organized interests are created and maintained inside and outside of government. Institutions beget interests; stronger interests, in turn, beget more prominent institutions—and the cycle goes on. The cycle consequently leads to the emergence of a broader array of interested groups and other interested organizations, to protect and, to a degree, to alter the specifics of the existing policy base. Policy thereby expands. Politics, as a result, becomes extraordinarily but expectedly complex.[7] Yet the political process doesn't address just any and all policy options or all emergent interests. There are distinct limits to change. Farming gets extensive attention from multiple sources; things otherwise rural do not. Rural interests are discouraged, even from forming. Rural society then suffers.

At least that thesis provides the framework for why farm policy has historically pushed aside broader rural policy initiatives. I argue for an integrated theory of governing institutions and related political interests. The case to support this integrated theory is made as simply and as directly as possible. It begins in chapters 1 and 2 with a review of why nonfarm rural society could have and can make a realistic and much needed claim for public policy assistance.

The short chapters then turn to an explanation of institutionalism, the farm policy paradigm, and an introduction to a powerful agrarian myth, or an idea that supported farm policy intervention by and within what was once a generally *laissez-faire* U.S. government. Evolution in the constituent benefits of farm policy comes next, followed by a review of proposed efforts to expand these benefits to service nonfarm rural residents. Succeeding chapters explain the fragmentation of farm policy within the Agricultural Establishment as farm services grew, the evolution of public policy turf protection and self-interest, and the resultant difficulties and even improbabilities of rural advocacy. These improbabilities include the institutional failure of rural advocates, the resulting public sector bias in issue selection and information- and intelligence-gathering for rural places, and the unavoidable anomalies in an activist U.S. government that forever managed to neglect rural problems.

Rural policy never really managed to become part of farm policy, as did other types of policy initiatives. To highlight that failure, rural policy is contrasted to environmental policy in a final substantive chapter. Against great odds, environmental policy became integrated successfully into the institutional base of farm policies. I begin to cover all this material by starting with a historical review of U.S. farm and rural problems.

First, however, let's add a warning about what follows. This essay is written in conversational tone and style. The intent is to keep the remainder of the presentation informal, casual, and readable; it's not to "write smart," which often is self-defeating. This issue, of course, has been noted previously by the newly elected 43rd president of the United States. I hope to avoid the formalities of academia and therefore be more appealing and quickly digestible for, as an example, rural and public policy students. Consequently, the essay can also be useful to those in community forums who are organized to understand and, one hopes, later address local rural problems. These people need to know in quick-and-dirty fashion the problems they will face in requesting federal support. Such people, and our contemporary students, don't want to wade through a traditionally heavy tome, however. So please excuse the abuse of formal language here.

Excuse as well the book's bias. The tone is intentionally—I'll admit—irreverent. Why? The purpose of the irreverence is to swim upstream against the overwhelming tendency of agricultural scholars—and others—to hold whatever they like in too much reverence. The entire Establishment is composed of people who revere something or someone: farming, Franklin D. Roosevelt, Henry A. Wallace, Cesar Chavez, the Farm Bureau, Big Jim Patton, farm protestors, Jim Hightower, or whatever. I myself tend to revere the activist farm spirit as it brings forth political responses. But I also often make fun of it. By attacking reverence, I hope to be able to bring greater neutrality to our collective understanding of the political dynamics of agriculture. Let's make way from our diversity of hero worshiping; and let's start here. Then we can see institutional and interest responses for what they were: not necessarily things good or bad, just events, people, and ideas, all shaping reality. So, on with it.

1

A TROUBLED RURAL SOCIETY: Misperceptions of Farming

Four prevailing notions, or social beliefs, get in the way of understanding rural America. These notions are not necessarily closely linked to one another. Nor are they causal in their policy effect. Their combined impact, however, is that there appears to be little social and therefore political utility in advancing public policies for rural communities and places.[1] That, at least, is the policymakers' conclusion.

What are those notions? Surely they become recognizable as apparent truths to nearly anyone who thinks of widespread public interpretations. One is the belief in rural America mostly as bountiful farm America, with timbering, mining, and fishing included for good measure as related production/extraction industries. This belief in the bountiful and in farming is so pervasive that it deserves special attention of its own as this book begins. Second (as I highlight in chapter 2) is the view that rural residents live close enough to urban areas to reap the benefits of the greater productivity, income, and job availability in the city. Third is a tendency to regard rural needs as a function of personal choices to stay isolated and apart from mainstream American life and responsibility. Fourth is a general view that those few rural residents made such iconoclastic lifestyle choices so they could revel in an idyllic, pastoral location where the grass is always green or the snow is fresh and pure. It's like the old stereotype of black poverty: "They like to live that way." "So let'um" is the policy solution.

Thus, Americans conclude, why should government intervene and devote scarce financial resources to these people in those very pleasant locations? The federal government—and the states—should take care of farmers and other production/extraction industries instead because, after all, Americans need these sorts of folks and the products of their labors. Let

1

nonfarm rural residents look to cities or perhaps farm economic successes for their own prosperity or merely economic survival. And let them accept a bit lower economic standard than exists for others simply because it's their quality-of-life choice, not the choice or designation made for them by the majority of citizens who live elsewhere. Besides, in terms of overall quality of life, many people seem to think that ruralites gain the rewards of pastoral glee and tranquility in return for the quite small cost of fewer social and economic benefits. Rural residents are thought to avoid stress and are able to reflect daily on scenic beauty; they avoid nasty traffic, pollution, crime, high prices, and the hectic pace of modern society. This logic has become a prevailing social myth.[2]

The problem is that those conclusions and views are so misplaced, so lacking in fact, that they are dangerous.[3] Because of their inexactness but widespread acceptance, these views lead to a neglect of nonfarm rural needs and a worsening of rural social conditions at many local levels—towns, villages, counties, development regions.[4] This neglect creates a whole set of places in society that are left behind and left out and ultimately are a drain on the rest of America. Any regional neglect of any sort creates not benign conditions but costs that the rest of society will eventually experience. Those costs appear, for example, when rural children fail in their educations, when the rural environment encounters major water pollution, when poverty leads to urban migration, and when social problems of drug and alcohol and child abuse flourish. It's the same type of effect that results from neglect of any specific social class.

Thus, because of the pervasive use of the wrong social and, consequently, political impressions, in the first two chapters of this book I need to briefly examine historical and political reality in rural America. There always has been a seldom commented on but troubled rural society. The farm problem comes first. Nothing else, as we'll see, gets even second place.

RURAL AMERICA REALLY IS NOT AN EVER-BOUNTIFUL FARM SOCIETY

Even a cursory examination of America's agrarian history helps dispel the notion that, over time, *rural* equals farming and ranching. Rural life certainly did start out that way in many, if not most, places. Starting out one way does not necessarily mean finishing in that same way, however. This assertion can best be seen in the development of frontier lands, from upper New York state to the Oregon coast and most everything in between. To a great extent, change has been a reflection of the people who went to frontier places and what actually motivated those pioneers. We must remember that America is a land of dreams, of wishful thinking—and generally inadequate understanding of the physical conditions to which dreamers wander.

Some historians emphasize that settlers and developers were adventurers.[5] These individuals went to the frontier to find excitement and experiences that were unavailable in even somewhat civilized communities. Images of grizzled mountaineers, cowpokes with pistols, and newly rich gold panners readily come to mind. Most frontier folk, however, eventually just wanted to own land, to produce something from it to sustain themselves. As we'll see, a strain of American political thought celebrated and encouraged such attitudes. The point is that frontier settlers were moved less by factual assessment of where they were going than by the thrill of the trek, the search for something new, the promise of a better future on their own.

Most of the people who went to the rural frontier were not going because they were skilled farmers, sophisticated livestock breeders, educated mine engineers, talented banking executives, and the like. Hopes, not introspective insight into their skills, drove them. Thus, when they settled, these adventuresome folks often had grand intentions and drive—but few of the personal talents and resources with which to survive well.[6]

A second set of historians offers a somewhat different explanation.[7] The idea is that frontier folk craved at least a bit of adventure but mostly were led by their own very tangible inadequacies in adjusting to their previous, more populated communities. Call them social misfits, runaways, iconoclasts, lovers of personal independence, nonconformists, in some cases criminals, whatever. Yet again there's a point to their background. Such migrants were always a bit on the edge of social and economic adjustment. They went West or North and up or down the river as a form of escapism. They were escaping from something they hated or with which they simply couldn't cope. They escaped and ran rather than planned their ways, seldom knowing precisely what they could do to live a successful life and with whom they would do it once they got to their eventual destinations. It was like Huck Finn lighting out for the territory so he would never be civilized by Aunt Polly. Again, these people frequently were long on aspirations and short on specific and useful talents. That's not to say that there weren't heroes—the courageous, the cunning, and the adaptive among them. All were there, in folklore and in reality. Rural America, however, was not necessarily built on the foundations of the most able citizenry. These folks were hearty but not as deep in what today might be called executive talents or prized community values. The myth would have us believe otherwise.

Once glamorous interpretations of building America through the efforts of the best and brightest are put aside, we can easily understand why rural places were headed for at least some difficulties. Rural migrants from 1830 to the 1920s were not all strategists, organizers, leaders, or people of great wisdom—or even virtue.[8] We might claim that 19th-century wanderers were the New World inhabitants who were most likely to fail economically, not to mention socially and politically. Their 20th-century offspring and followers fared little better because of inherited and often earned resourcelessness.

At least ethnic ghettos had their own collective support systems in the cities in which migrants to America frequently settled.[9] Italians, Irish, and Jews are excellent ethnic examples of new urban residents who found places where mutual support existed, where a sense of community was easily constructed. Poles, Russians, and various Asian populations later found the same combination of neighborly prodding and assistance.

How, then, did rural frontierspeople survive? Small wonder that Alexis de Tocqueville found what he did in America in the early 19th century. As a French social theorist who traveled and examined mostly rural social settings, de Tocqueville discovered and labeled America a surprisingly intense nation of joiners.[10] Of course rural Americans were joiners: Once the adventuresome and socially miscast settled down—as indeed most of them did—they found themselves in dire need of developing collective social resources, merely to survive as individuals. They had no ready community or ethnic support.

As a result, groups of distinct and always neighborly interests formed all over rural regions. People joined together locally to determine how best to farm or ranch in particular locations—which was what most frontier folk eventually tried, for want of alternative rural jobs.[11] Rural residents also joined in agrarian groups to defend themselves from often-unfriendly Native Americans and hostile environmental events such as fires and pestilence. They joined to bring essential production supplies from cities to the isolated countryside. They joined, as well, to find markets for whatever excess products they raised.[12]

Again, however, these folks rarely formed groups because they were planners, natural organizers, far-sighted sophisticates, or even all that well educated. They quite simply had a pressing need for each other and depended on a few entrepreneurial neighbors to form supportive organizations. Leaders emerged out of pragmatic necessity, not because they were so comfortable at leadership. Later, as groups of interests increased in number and size, the rurally challenged responded to regional, statewide, and sometimes nationally focused entrepreneurs who traveled from place to place to build more extensive organized interests.[13] The Grange, the Farmers Alliance, the American Farm Bureau Federation, and the National Farmers Union were examples. The latter type of organization was not the American rural norm, however. Nor was it the subject of de Tocqueville's wonderment.

Why the organizational frenzy among people who would not in modern terms be expected to join together collectively?[14] After all, today people who have the highest income, occupational status, and education are most likely to join groups. The reason probably was the experience of failure. The fear of imminent failure probably drove joiners: failure in what they had finally settled to do with their remaining lives once motives of adventure and unfounded optimism had passed them by—or simply been given up. These people saw failure surrounding them among fellow settlers (indeed, with great frequency). Therefore, organizing collectively certainly would be rational when no government existed to guarantee settlers any social safety net and no other interactive network of community supporters existed to sustain them.[15] At worst, settlers feared death; at best, they feared a short personal future of more aimless wandering, with few if any of their own resources. They feared poverty and often knew they would likely find it. Organizing locally seemed necessary, even if organization was difficult—even unnatural—and promised no panacea, no guarantee of avoiding the pitfalls that they had seen and feared. Organizing often was the only option, the only thing to do. Nonetheless—and perhaps consequently—organizations flourished in number across American regions; many evolved into more extensive groups with considerable staying power.

Not surprisingly, under such conditions, rural locations were not always great pockets of bountiful farming and ranching success, even if such production was what people mostly tried to do in a particular place. Rural America was not an unbridled horn of plenty where every settler who couldn't keep up the great adventure finally and with relative ease produced a living growing things, even with neighborly help. For many, agrarianism more often was a last resort, after the thrill of the frontier chase subsided. People farmed and ranched because land to do so was available, at least someplace and of some sort—even if it wasn't very productive or safe. Government also encouraged them in various ways, such as through periodic homesteading laws that turned land over to settlers.[16] Government also built agricultural colleges and research centers to improve farming and provided trained experts to visit farmers and try to help them.

Thus, rural America came to be identified as farm America most often by default. That was what most settlers invariably tried to do to live there.

Given the nature of the people and the diversity of the places they settled, initially subsistence or peasant agriculture developed among these predominantly small-scale landholders.[17] What else was there to do? At first, settlers were rarely commercial growers, producers whose successes fueled regional economic growth. Agrarians had few personal resources and almost no opportunities to succeed in this way.

A few examples of failure in the 19th century illustrate what occurred. In Michigan, state officials by mid-century were advertising in Germany for experienced farmers to move there. The earliest farmers were inexperienced amateurs and were failing at too great a rate for emerging national farm policy to help them. Observers in the state learned that those without farm backgrounds were destined to fail when such people unwittingly made poor choices regarding climate and soil selections. Neither settling in places with the longest, most frigid winters nor locating farms on sand dunes kept Michigan's agrarian development and farming hopes alive. As individual farmers continued to do such things, the state's future looked more and more bleak.

Iowa was a different case: more an example of the traditional American farming legend. That state saw many prosperous farms developed in its upper flatland regions, where soil was deep and fertile. Yet failure was endemic elsewhere in the state. Floods plagued those who settled on river bottoms. Northeastern regions produced mostly rocks because those were the dominant soil features to begin with. Southwestern regions were given to infertile soil and, too often, extensive drought. Just settling in Iowa, then, was no magical key to success. Nor was trying to ranch in the dry red rock canyons of Utah, farming in the harsh mountains of Appalachia, or much of anything agricultural near the swamps of Florida—except growing sugar cane like those unfortunate Caribbean islanders. Many people tried, nonetheless, because of their inexperience. Of course, most of those who did failed to hold on to their agrarian experiments, just as they had earlier failed to hold on to their adventurous zeal.

IMPLICATIONS

One might easily ask, "So what?" Why does this rural and agrarian backdrop matter for today's American countryside? One answer to that question stands out. As farmers and ranchers left agriculture in large numbers, the residents who were left behind created social and economic problems. So too did the exodus of those who deserted agriculture and the rural countryside.[18] As we'll see, that answer also points to the rationale for the creation of a national farm policy to modernize farm development before farmers and ranchers went out of business.

The scale and scope of that agrarian exodus were truly astonishing. Until the Great Depression, there was a constant entering and abandoning of production agriculture—that is, farming and ranching. Agriculture was easy to enter; tenancy was an option for many people who couldn't own land; basic skills weren't required—and the failure rate was predictably high. Unfortunately, historians know little about those folks other than that they came and went. Or, we might say, historians know little about them *because* they came and went. It was easier to study those who came and stayed—usually the successful ones. Even population counts of farm numbers were difficult to do and inexact because of this social and economic instability.[19] Relatively modern times are better understood. By the Great Depression, agriculture was moving away almost completely from its subsistence nature and becoming more commercial and even industrial with the spread of mechanization.[20] This was the culmination of a long trend whose consequences would be with us for the remainder of the century. Therefore, the long cyclic flow of easy entry and exit was becoming disrupted. Fewer people entered agriculture. Entry was increasingly costly, with tractors and other equipment replacing much human labor in agrarian enterprises. Moreover, folks had to know how to operate such stuff to enter the sector.

Exit, however, never slowed. It became—or perhaps stayed—devastatingly high. In the late 1930s, farm and ranch numbers averaged what probably was the all-time high mark of 6,631,000.[21] These numbers still defined rural America as farming America. Every subsequent year exhibited losses, however—averaging 88,118 agrarian (farm) units annually. In other words, 1.3 percent of the peak number of agricultural units were lost per year, every year. By 1990, there were only 2,137,000 units—less than a third of those from five decades earlier. That decade saw continued losses; farm and ranch numbers dropped to below 2 million by 2000. All of this decline took place while the overall American population grew considerably.

Two results are clearly evident. America was no longer an agrarian nation where most residents farmed and ranched for their livelihood, even as a last resort. The Census of Agriculture by the end of the 20th century counted less than 2 percent of the U.S. population as farming and ranching. Even that percentage is misleading, however. That annual census includes all agrarian units with product sales of at least $1,000. Most agricultural experts, as well as people with just common sense, call these very small units "hobby" farms, which produce limited second incomes for families that are involved in other businesses and careers.[22] In fact, sales of more than $40,000 annually are the barest minimum required at the turn of the millennium to support a farm family. That earnings figure encompasses only about 600,000 farm and ranch units, which means that far less than 1 percent of Americans live on what would be considered full-time farms and ranches. In fact, less than 10 percent of *rural* residents now live on any kind of farms and ranches. Even rural America is no longer primarily an agrarian environment.

A second result is just as easily comprehended from the foregoing observation: One heck of a lot of people have long been and continue to be displaced from their social and economic circumstances by the ongoing collapse of the family farming community. One way or another, these people, as individuals, have become troubled—often by poverty, not infrequently by hunger and malnutrition, and often by being consigned to substandard housing units. As another example, reports of financially threatened farmers who committed suicide were rampant in the 1980s. Numerous organizations, including some state governments, even set up telephone hotlines to counsel such troubled folk.[23] Calls into these hotlines were plentiful.

Communities as social and economic places were no less troubled. Physical deterioration, local budget shortfalls, neglected municipal main streets, and poor rural roads increased. The decades of the last half of the 20th century, moreover, exhibited one other important continuing community trend: local institutional and human capital erosion. As farmers and ranchers left rural places, few replacement jobs were created. Therefore, public schools, county hospitals, local government offices, community service groups, and the like contracted, consolidated, and often just closed down as rural places lost often substantial populations.[24] As a consequence, there was less institutional and human capacity in much of rural America to deal with the current and future problems of its people and places.

A third result is less evident and not so easily imagined from the decline of farms, ranches, and local settings. Yet it too helps to explain why rural America no longer can be equated with farm and ranch America and why once-agrarian people and places have been so racked with trouble from agricultural displacement. That result is less evident only because nonrural social observers seldom reflect on what's happened to food production over several decades of change. Fewer farms and ranches have *not* meant less food to eat. Most people acknowledge (if prodded to do so) that food and fiber items still appear plentiful in supermarkets and farm markets. Yet most Americans seldom think about the reasons for that plenty. Why? Because the decline in agrarian numbers and rural communities has not resulted in any decline in agricultural production. Quite the contrary.

With the continuing advent and growth of farm mechanization, agriculture continuously came to be more specialized by commodity and further industrialized in production characteristics: Corn here, cotton there, bigger and better equipment everywhere. Over the course of the 20th century, farmers and ranchers may have learned to farm better, certainly to farm bigger, and to do so with generally much greater efficiency. Moreover, national farm policy helped them. Improvements have been threefold: in industrial mechanics, in crop and livestock characteristics, and in the techniques—the "how-to"—of growing. As a result, far fewer agrarians produced even larger yields and more products on substantially less acreage. More meat even came from a single steer or hog. In the simplest terms, there were no longer any economic or practical reasons to continue to think of rural America as farm and ranch America. Nor did Malthusian fears persist that escalating population growth would eventually outstrip food supplies.[25] So what again? Not much of rural America and not many of its people were needed to produce a continuing cornucopia.

SUMMARY OF KEY POINTS

This chapter covers eight key points that are important for understanding today's rural society. All of these points must be understood to appreciate the long-term failure of the federal government to adopt supportive *rural* as opposed to *farm* public policies.

1. Rural America has never been very adequately understood. Prevailing social beliefs held by the public and public policymakers have always portrayed rural America as predominantly an able society of farmers and ranchers. A national farm policy emerged to help farmers help themselves and, in turn, develop strong local rural economies.

2. The emergence of most rural society was about farming and ranching primarily by default. For many people on the frontiers of American development, farming and ranching were last-resort jobs. Robbing stagecoaches and banks had little future. Neither the plans nor the skills of the vast majority of these folks made them likely to be successful agrarians, even at a subsistence production level. People

went to the frontier for adventure and with undefined hopes. Many of them were social misfits. Under such conditions, agricultural failure was high. That dynamic led to a strengthening of national farm policy. (We'll see why later.)

3. Awareness combined with fear led a great many residents of rural America to organize locally. Not surprisingly, most of this organization was for self-help and mutual support. Given the lack of individual agricultural skills, the emphasis of such groups was on farming better and with greater chance of survival. Predictably, farm and ranch groups came to dominate the organization of rural America.

4. The earliest efforts at public policy support for rural needs were to encourage farming and ranching—most directly through homesteading laws and land giveaways but also with direct farm assistance. Dominant farm and ranch groups obviously never complained; they certainly appreciated such assistance—even though it may not have been wise ultimately, as we'll see.

5. Until the Great Depression of the 1930s, entry and exit into agriculture were high and routine. By the late 1930s, however, continuing modernization and industrialization of production made agricultural entry more costly and difficult. Fewer people started farming or ranching as last resorts. Exit remained high and stayed consistently so each year through the end of the 20th century. This trend made the farm and ranch failure problem seem increasingly serious, at least to these agrarians. Well it might: Within six decades, by century's end, less than one-third of the previous number of agrarian units were in production.

6. Fewer than 1 percent of Americans live today on farms and ranches that are even close to being viable economic commercial ventures. Only 10 percent of *rural* residents live on any production places.

7. The exit of farms and ranches from agriculture is about more than numeric decline. Those who have exited agriculture and their rural communities have endured hardship and troubles as a consequence.

8. Much of the agricultural decline and most of these troubles are long term, not temporary. A hungry world no longer appears to be waiting for food and fiber demands to increase inexorably. Improvements in mechanization, biological capability, and production

techniques allow fewer farmers and ranchers to produce more and more crops and heavier livestock on fewer acres. Therefore, rural America is never again likely to be truly farm and ranch America, even if prevailing social beliefs miss that point. The effect is that this mistaken notion creates more rather than less harm over time as public and policymaking observers fail to adequately understand rural conditions. Observers seldom target for correction any problems apart from those still identified as mostly about failures in agricultural production and agrarian unit losses.

2

OTHER SOCIAL MISPERCEPTIONS THAT MISS RURAL PROBLEMS

Other important misconceptions exist, even when Americans come to recognize that the rural countryside isn't entirely covered by farms, ranches, mines, lumbering, and commercial fishing. The three other most important social beliefs, as I note in chapter 1, that disadvantage a realistic understanding of things rural can be easily summarized by three oft-repeated questions: Why don't those country bumpkins just commute to the city to work? Why worry about these people, given that they chose to live there? Why do anything for these people, given that they live in far better circumstances then those of us who put up with the urban rat race?

These questions are fundamentally different from any thoughts people raise about food production and agriculture. How so? Actual experiences—though misinterpreted and mythologized—seem to drive these three questions; not many Americans form opinions from direct involvement with agriculture. As generations of Americans are further removed from what are very likely to be their own family's farm and ranch roots, they tend never to see and experience agricultural places or agrarian work. Where do they get their ideas? They've seen calves and lambs in a petting exhibit at a municipal zoo, perhaps. Corn and wheat are merely some things flaked into cardboard boxes for them to eat at breakfast. Meat must be in precious short supply because prices appear much higher than they were 20 years ago—inflation not being considered. Obviously, agricultural issues are driven by long-held and generalized social beliefs rather than because people regularly are challenged to seriously reflect on the decline of farm and ranch America.

At least for developing some degree of awareness, far more Americans do have direct experiences with other aspects of rural America. These experiences, however, develop skewed views of an unreal world rather than realistic appraisals. They reflect a mythic bias about how nifty it must be to live in the country. In particular, given the greater likelihood of their traveling, upper- and middle-class Americans have had the pleasure of country visits, maybe routinely at their very own cottages. Moreover, these economic classes constitute the citizens who are most likely to hold public office, belong to various political groups, vote, and otherwise express vocal opinions about what government should do.[1] Their views matter most in generating public policy support. For various reasons, however, even many lower-income city folks conjure up the idea that the rural environment must be a better place to live. Maybe it's because Mama told us about "back home"—perhaps in songs about that old country home.

The great difficulty for a widespread and realistic understanding of rural America, however, is the collectively and most commonly shared nature of rural visits. Rural travel is far from random. The Atlantic shore and the Great Lakes are common destinations. The mountains also get plenty of visitors. Western Kansas and the High Plains of Texas do not. They're too hot and too windy; there's nothing to do there. Nor do visitors regularly frequent inland northern Maine; Hibbings, Minnesota; west Texas; the desolate parts of the Southwest's Four Corners region, with its large Navaho reservation; the dry eastern plains of the state of Washington; most of Appalachia; the Mississippi Delta; or any part of North Dakota at all. Not much recreational fun is to be had in those places: no beach, no Six Flags Over Wherever.

Such selective visitation and travel are attitudinally important. Because vacationing rural travelers from the rest of America go to places they really hope to enjoy, they experience the countryside very selectively, even as they tend to generalize about living a high-quality rural lifestyle.[2] Thus, the three questions reappear as they were posed in this chapter's opening paragraph. Why? Somebody drives from New York City to visit the nearby rural Hudson Valley and believes with some degree of accuracy that people can live there and commute. These same dreamers forget, however, that you can't realistically drive daily from Cochise to Phoenix, Arizona.

The rhapsodizing urban visitor to the northern coast of Lake Michigan may chat with the semi-retired antique storeowner who moved from Farmington Hills to Crystal Lake near Frankfort, Michigan. Ah, the visitor sees a person of choice who consciously selected the arduous but charming Northland! Yet that dreamy visitor never meets the far more frequently found lifetime resident of Frankfort's rural Benzie County. Those folks likely have no skills, no high school degrees, no capital assets, frequent if not chronic unemployment, substance abuse problems, and at best a summer job in fast food distribution and an off-season unemployment check. What would these people gain by packing up for Detroit or Grand Rapids? What resources do they have to do so? They have no realistic choices about places to live, so they stay at their old homes out of habit. Wandering is less in vogue today than during frontier times.

Visitors also forget that the idyllic Lake Superior coast of summer gives way to excessively long and cold winters. Paradise, Michigan, is far from the real place of paradise. They don't realize that prime winter entertainment for the hangers-on is a trip to the faraway bowling alley or a cold-weather sojourn to illegally poach out-of-season venison. Nor do they understand that wood stoves are used because they're inexpensive and not just cozy, that the beaten and rusted pickup isn't driven merely because it's rustic, nor that the quaint family that sells tomatoes by the side of the road in August doesn't do so to winter in Miami Beach. Yes, experiences often are teachers—but not necessarily accurate ones with regard to knowing all about rural America.

WHO CAN DRIVE TO CITY WORK?

It should be apparent at this point that one place rural is not necessarily much like any other place rural. Nor are rural places likely to be equal or comparable. Indeed, the term *rural* is very general and imprecise. In conventional wisdom, it connotes a great deal in that it explains a countryside America of general but variable contrasts to urban locations. All the same, however, the term is hopelessly confused even by government statistics and definitions, which are defined so rigorously that they cause actual meaning as portrayed above to be obscured. This difficulty adds to the problem of selective observations and public bias in drawing conclusions about countryside places.

Let's briefly look at government definitions. In the most recognized government parlance, *rural* is that which is not "urban." *Urban* is specifically defined, most prominently by the U.S. Bureau of the Census. Without rhyme or reason—nor explanation—the Census Bureau in 1906 began calling urban entities places that were home to at least 2,500 residents.[3] Thus, a rural resident lives in the countryside or in a small town or village with fewer inhabitants. Those people account for just less than one quarter of the nation's total at millennium's end.[4]

As urban sprawl and suburbanization led to adjacent urban places sharing larger and larger physical spaces, the Census Bureau coined another pair of terms at mid-century. It was looking for greater accuracy of description. *Metropolitan* and *nonmetropolitan* areas also were rigidly defined—again without explanation. Metropolitan areas were a collection of places within either a county or contiguous counties where 50,000 or more people lived.[5] Nonmetropolitan areas were all other areas. Generally, of course, there were less densely populated green spaces included in metropolitan areas that often looked like the countryside. Under such generous terms, approximately 80 percent of the total U.S. landmass is still nonmetropolitan. A little more than 20 percent of all U.S. residents live there. People living in such places may or may not be able to conveniently drive to the city—or anyplace else—to work. And the United States, especially in the hinterland, is notorious for not providing mass transit.

In an aggregated statistical sense, the terms *rural* and *nonmetropolitan* fail to explain much because they don't mesh or match. They quite simply are not meant to be the same. For example, as of 1990, 44 percent of rural residents lived in metropolitan areas, whereas 56 percent lived in nonmetropolitan regions. Furthermore, 37 percent of nonmetropolitan residents lived in urban places. Moreover, more than 20 percent of nonmetropolitan folks lived in cities of more than 10,000 residents but fewer than 50,000. That's hardly countryside. For metropolitan places, about 15 percent of residents were technically rural.[6] They obviously didn't think of their residential circumstances as city places. They were in the countryside. Nonetheless, data about the two pairs of terms are all we have to use in commenting on that countryside. Thus, regardless of the imprecision, I use them throughout this chapter to illustrate key points.

Small wonder, though, that generic use of the term *rural* often ignores or forgets statistical definition.[7] Rural generally comes to mean what people want it to—or what they know and understand. Americans intuitively know what's the countryside—that is, those less populated places. That intuition is what they follow. Even government agencies do the same. A quick review of definitions of *rural* for federal programs shows great variability; few agencies state the same criteria for eligibility for whatever benefits each provides. Some agencies even define rural differently for different programs they administer. *Rural* means what each agency says it means for the unique bureaucratic and political problems that each one wishes to address on its own terms. And more than one agency has designated an area as rural when a local congressperson complained of its need for federal grants in aid.

As a result, we have real problems in answering specific and vital questions. So who, then, can drive to city jobs? The U.S. Department of Agriculture (USDA) had tried to figure that out in different ways—to little intellectually satisfying avail. USDA started its analysis by recognizing three possible factors that made it more likely that extended rural regions rather than small rural places such as villages are the appropriate units for understanding who goes where to work. First, the population of a region is larger than that of a single place, so a larger pool of skilled or semiskilled workers is available to work for and, therefore, enhance local rural employers. Second, when several rural counties or towns work together to encourage jobs, they can at least theoretically combine financial resources and have more available means of support for employers. Third, economic health in one rural community—again, theoretically—benefits adjacent places that share lifestyle factors such as housing and providing shopping options for workers.[8]

What USDA found regarding who went where was interesting, even if it unlocked no mysteries. Two ways of looking at things were of particular interest. One was the idea of industry clusters, which are a mix of typically low-technology, routine performance employment enterprises that do pretty much the same type of business. Most are in manufacturing. Therefore, to gain employees and across-firm interaction, such businesses locate in geographical proximity to another. USDA found these clusters distributed in widespread fashion throughout rural America.[9] Obviously, such clusters attract workers from considerable distances within regions as these personnel find the most satisfying and affordable housing. Interestingly, 283 of 2,270 rural counties had more than 40 percent of their workforce commuting outside of other counties. How many of these rural counties were really metropolitian? Who knows?

A second way of examining who went where explored the idea of even more broadly identified clusters—specifically, late–20th-century shopping and employment clusters.[10] Sociologists observed that, within extended regions, nonmetropolitan urban cities have emerged and grown, dominating commerce in each of those countryside, nice lifestyle areas. These areas are not the "big cities" of popular lore—the scary Chicagos and New Yorks of the world. Workers within those regionally dominant cities frequently traveled as far as 50 miles for jobs. More commonly, workers came from within a 20-mile radius around those cities. So there really were two employment zones that defined each cluster. That description, however, was an overgeneralization. The size of such zones and clusters varied with the individual states and national regions.[11] Northeast regions, and states such as Vermont and New Hampshire, had smaller zones at the outer and inner rings. Travel was more difficult in such places. In the wide-open Rocky Mountains—for example, in Wyoming and Montana—workers tended to be willing to drive farther (and, of course, at faster speeds). The clusters were not only fewer in number but larger in scale, as jobs were harder to find in less densely populated places.

What do these findings suggest about rural jobs? Only a bit, and obviously not without some uncertainty about who actually can go where. For instance, who goes to the big city, and who gets to work in another far-away rural place? However, those who can drive to the big city probably fall in one of two aggregate categories. First, the 44 percent of rural residents who live in metropolitan areas seem likely to be able to drive to city work. In addition, less than 20 percent of nonmetropolitan residents who lived in rural places in 1990 were adjacent to urban locations. They too likely could commute to the city. So we can claim with some limited confidence that more than 60 percent of rural Americans can indeed work in the city if they are able and if they want. Yet that high percentage is unassuring to the widely held social belief that rural residents should all find their livelihood where everyone else works. More than one-third of those in rural America—nearly 10 percent of all Americans—still are effectively isolated in employment from big city jobs because they are just too far away. They may, however, work in rural lifestyle or employment clusters. Maybe not, though. Obviously we have inconclusive data.

CHOOSING TO LIVE IN THE COUNTRY

Population trends indicate that many people continue to live in the country. Yet it's quite hard to say that it's by conscious choice, except perhaps for those who can work in some city setting or another. What are those trends? Quite simply, population in the countryside has steadily declined since 1930—in many places since 1920. That was when the Great Depression began for U.S. agriculture. There have only been two brief periods of exception.[12]

In 1950, 44 percent of the U.S. population lived in nonmetropolitan places. Decreases in actual numbers occurred in each decade, although some of that statistical loss was the result of a few metropolitan areas emerging through growth from their previous nonmetropolitan status. By 1990, however, only 22 percent of the population lived in nonmetropolitan places. Choosing to live in such locations clearly was not a widely favored lifestyle or employment strategy.

Is there a reason for these losses? Of course—and again, employment and income prospects largely account for them. What do people do in rural

America when they live and work there? If people want to farm, ranch, timber, mine, and fish as their work, more than 57 percent of such jobs are in
nonmetropolitan areas. Only 22 percent of manufacturing jobs are there,
however, and these jobs are mostly at the low-technology and low-paid industrial end. Moreover, only 19 percent of construction jobs and 18 percent
of service jobs are nonmetropolitan.[13] Most manufacturing, construction,
and service jobs cluster as close as possible to urban locations. Thus, we
should conclude that employment opportunities—or the lack of them—su-
percede choice as a reason for people to live where they do. It's just like for
poverty-ridden inner cities, right? This logic explains why rural American
youths who are well educated quickly export themselves to urban areas
with greater job choices after graduation.[14]

That conclusion about lost opportunity is reinforced by two additional
trends. First, the rural and nonmetropolitan places that lost population at
the highest and most consistent rates in the last half of the 20th century were
regions where farming, ranching, and other extractive industries dominated
local economies. Such jobs offered declining opportunities.

Second, the two brief times during these years when rural populations
increased were short-lived—for very practical reasons.[15] From 1970 to 1980,
nonmetropolitan growth was greater than metropolitan population increases. Then, in the 1980s, the population loss returned. Nonmetropolitan
growth recovered, however, from 1990 to the decade's end.[16] This period
was another era of great economic growth nationally. In both cases, increases—on the one hand—tended to be among people who were white,
male, and elderly. People were retiring in the countryside, especially in attractive retirement communities where they became a rural economic elite.
Even retirees did so mostly when favorable national economic conditions
prevailed, however. Opportunities to increase income through part-time
jobs and to lower personal living costs were greater. Expanding retirement
savings accelerated those moves as well. In contrast, when the national
economy slowed or personal costs rose, even retirement moves to rural
places declined. Personal retirement nest eggs were threatened. Others, who
wanted jobs, moved almost solely to the city. Staying at the old urban homestead, or even setting up a new city home, apparently seemed less risky than
moving to the uncertain, less opportunistic countryside.

This is where the other hand of rural immigration comes to be important.
In the 1990s, with national economic opportunities surging, younger Americans also moved to the countryside. Rural places added 2.7 million jobs by
1997. Unemployment in many rural countries dropped to unprecedented
levels, even though average job earnings remained constant. And constant

meant low: about 25 percent less than urban wages. Perhaps that wage dis-
parity explains why 20 percent of 1990's rural immigrants were foreign
workers; they were more inclined to take available lower-paying jobs. Lower
levels of education and job skills characterized these younger immigrants,
who placed an increased strain on already distressed schools, health care facilities, and community services. This gravitation to *any* available jobs explains why only 40 percent of rural counties grew in population in the 1990s.
The rest had no such job opportunities. It also explains why a dispropor-
tionate number of working rural residents still lived in poverty. Two-thirds
of the rural poor were in working families.[17] Low wages equal being poor.

ARE RURAL PLACES REALLY BETTER THAN URBAN ONES?

Better? One thing makes many rural observers and residents say no, they
are not. That factor is the existence of persistent rural poverty throughout
most, if not quite all, of the countryside. The residents of 23 percent of all
rural counties (600 counties) are in persistent poverty. Yes, just as in many
inner cities. Rural poverty extends to all racial groups; the majority of the
poor are white. This poverty also creates common social problems that
plague and prove costly to local public service providers. These problems
include high rates of personal abuse, crime, school dropouts, and drugs.
Rural youths are more inclined to use marijuana, cocaine, crack, and even
heroin than urban youths.[18] Several conditions contribute to this poverty: a
lack of basic resources such as education, cross-generational cultures of
poverty in rural areas, restricted opportunities for jobs and personal development, community decline, low wages in these regions, and the absence
of any systematic attempt by the federal government to correct rural poverty
problems.[19] The countryside, then, is far from idyllic.

    Several economic factors make that conclusion clear. Many of these fac-
tors are linked, of course, to the existence of rural poverty. These factors include businesses, business conditions, and jobs. Metropolitan job creation
and business investment have consistently outstripped those of nonmetropolitan places, even when rural areas grow.[20] While the national economy
continued to expand in the late 1990s, nonmetropolitan economic growth
dropped after 1995.[21] Historically, rural manufacturing economies have
fallen into recession before those of urban places. That observation should
hardly be surprising because rural industrial investments have continued
to lag behind those of urban areas, even as rural manufacturers gained (or
stole?) many of the lowest-wage urban jobs in the 1990s.[22]

Manufacturers that moved from urban to feasible rural settings have done so precisely to escape higher urban wages, to seek part-time workers, and to discard worker benefits such as disability and health insurance.[23] They've accepted lower rates of worker productivity to make these moves. They may find workers disappearing when the fish are biting or deer season starts. Workers often go on the Mountain states' "bush time" or the Gulf states' rum-driven "Cruzan time" rather than by standard clocks. Nonetheless, this strategy obviously succeeds because, with the exception of rural industry clusters, rural manufacturing jobs are the lowest-paid industrial jobs in the United States—perhaps rightly so. Nevertheless, they are cost-efficient for employers. Compounding this income problem for rural communities is the shift in the nature of prevailing U.S. industry. This shift creates instability for future employment. While manufacturing nationwide changes almost exclusively to high-technology production and a reliance on high-technology workers, rural places have gained the same type of routine performance jobs that have moved to Mexico, South America, and the previously nonindustrial Pacific Rim.

A future shift to a healthier and more stable rural economy as well as a higher-technology industry doesn't appear likely. Although rural schools often provide superior learning environments for students, they lack the best-trained teachers and the quality special programs—including job training—to move students into high-technology jobs.[24] Moreover, the best-trained and best-educated young people continue to leave rural places for better-paying urban jobs.[25] That trend creates a shortage of the best and most competent workers to fill potential jobs—and it makes for social losses for rural communities and families. The most likely and best-prepared future local leaders are leaving. Many older family members are seriously troubled by a lack of career opportunities at home for their children. Too often, the parents then also hope to leave.

All of this data indicates a general American rural setting that is far from overly pleasant. Persistent poverty, low prevailing wages, the least stable industry, less-competitive schools, and a benefit-poor labor base that hardly encourages health care and other local personal services are not very attractive community features. We hardly need mention that local cultural events are rare in these places, as are opportunities for fine dining, continuing education, and a variety of consumer product purchases. Rural solitude and an escape from hectic urban conditions come at a high cost that few but the most iconoclastic U.S. residents are willing to accept. Even if they are locked away in retirement villages, they need to come outside at times. From a modern perspective, these places tend to be incomplete communities. One can fish and hunt and golf there, but can one really do such things all of the time?

One can also operate a high-technology telecommunications business in such places—and become another type of rural elite. Again, however, that businessperson sometimes has to leave the nest. Moreover, she faces service inadequacy and community hostility. This hostility increases as such business operations cluster together in desirable outdoor settings. Not only are clear class lines obvious to other local residents; resentments also occur because such outsiders lead to an escalation of local housing and consumer goods prices. Younger and far less prosperous workers in traditional or tourist occupations are priced out of housing markets. They also are charged with the costs of paying more for necessary consumer products such as food and clothing. Such community schisms lead to "bad blood," local political challenges, confrontations, crime, and even violence when the "outsiders" go *outside* their narrow confines—as they sometimes must.

All of this bad news for rural places is further compounded by the matter of which places are the most economically troubled ones. Rural areas with manufacturing economies are least bothered by poverty and low and shifting wages. Agricultural and service economies, such as tourism and tourist places, face even worse conditions and have become even less complete communities.[26] Many of the places with the highest and most chronic poverty rates are in the American South.[27] Poverty rates often are 25 percent there; 10–20 percent unemployment is typical. That's even after a decade of economic prosperity nationally. These locations, not incidentally, often are where most Americans seemingly would prefer to live if they had choices. Certainly cold-weather rural places have not been the priority full-time choices for retirees, vacationers, and urban escapees.

No, it seems, sympathetic rural public policy—as opposed to the current policy of neglect—would not just be a subsidization of an already grand rural lifestyle. Most countryside places are far too economically troubled and much too lacking in generally preferred social benefits for very many urban escapees to have wandered to them with foresight and having made selective choices.

IMPLICATIONS

Despite what appear to be widely held public opinions about rural America, things were never as easy and as pleasant there as they seem (at least, in general). With poverty rates high, employment prospects limited, and agriculture in decline as a local economic support, rural advocates and experts can quite logically claim that a need exists for a coherent national government rural policy that is independent of national farm policy. In fact, rural advocates and public-sector analysts have long made that claim.[28] Moreover, since early in the 20th century the federal government has routinely advanced promises of a national rural policy.[29] None, however, has emerged—probably because analytical wisdom confronts conventional wisdom and potential political loses.

The outlines for such a policy seem clear from this chapter. A national rural policy goal should be economic and job development for the most isolated communities and residents of the real American countryside. Metropolitan areas are far more able to combine resources and generate their own and adjacent rural industries and jobs. Considerable government support, primarily through education and job training, exists in urban settings to facilitate jobs and income advantages that most U.S. citizens can reach.

Any national rural policy for the American countryside can't be too generalized and overly systematic, however. Developing a set of government programs that are brought in—in similar fashion and with similar goals— to each isolated region would be of little use. A coherent rural policy to deal with the most pressing problems that inhibit local growth would necessarily be tailored for individual places.[30] Generic stuff of a one-for-all-and-all-for-one nature won't work. Rural regions and communities are unique places that are not well described by statistical definitions of their populations. Traditions, terrains, climates, and resident characteristics vary greatly. As a consequence, economic potential varies from one rural place to another rural place. Businesses and industries that can be successfully introduced in each one vary as well. The same is true regarding the types of jobs that can be created in each place. Some places will have no manufacturing job potential; others must develop less well paid service economies or economies that depend on extensive and already existing agricultural production. The important thing to remember is that a sensible rationale for national rural policy can logically be advanced—and, despite conventional wisdom, one is arguably needed.

SUMMARY OF KEY POINTS

Eight key points are included in this chapter. All are intended to better describe the social and economic conditions of rural America and to convey an understanding of the logic of a national rural policy.

1. Rural America is composed of highly varied regions, communities, and places. These places range widely, from highly desirable locations to very austere and often troubled ones.

2. That variability is not well understood, particularly by the U.S. public. Most Americans who have traveled to rural places and enjoyed their experiences have gone to the most desirable and entertaining locations. They've skipped the rest. The policy elite, for example, goes to the Finger Lakes region of New York or the Gold Coast of western Michigan and believes that this is rural America.

3. That variability also is obscured by looking at government definitions of *rural* and *nonmetropolitan*. These terms not only mean different types of places, they also fail to communicate differences in the characteristics of varied rural places.

4. If there is some usefulness in government statistics—as there seems to be in what we've found here—about two-thirds of rural or nonmetropolitan residents could indeed drive to some sort of city jobs for work. They may have to drive 15–20 miles or even longer distances to do so, however. Fifty miles may be an outer limit for most. Bad roads and bad weather persist, of course.

5. That barrier still leaves more than one-third of countryside residents—or 10 percent of all Americans—isolated from city employment, with its greater variety of higher-paid jobs. These people may well be better off if new rural elites move in. Maybe.

6. Most Americans do not choose to live in rural places, for very logical reasons of economic opportunity. Only about one-fifth of manufacturing or service economy jobs are rural. Moreover, these jobs tend to be located as close to cities as possible. Only agricultural jobs, which are in decline, are found mainly in rural places.

7. Two other factors tend to make rural residency less appealing. First, poverty rates are high. This factor creates social problems and provides poor resource bases for rural as opposed to urban places—yucky for living. Second, the jobs and businesses that tend to be located in rural places are characterized by low wages, low technology, and an unstable future. Rural communities, moreover, likely lack the financial, educational, and manpower resources to correct their conditions. This factor, of course, brings the potential for community splits when business leaders bring their investments and managers to these places.

8. These conditions mean that few rural places, especially among the most isolated, are places of preferred living or candidates for likely indigenous development. That, in turn, makes it logical for advocates and analysts to argue for a national rural policy that works to enhance rural communities. Any national rural policy, however, must be tailored to the array of highly variable local conditions, not to a set of average conditions. This requirement certainly also points, as we shall see, to the difficulty of advocating for and creating such a rural policy. It just seems easier, perhaps, to ignore it.

3

AN INSTITUTIONAL
PERSPECTIVE

In this chapter I argue that institutions matter a great deal in politics and government. They not only order what the public sector does for its citizenry, they also do a great deal to determine what that sector does not do. The point of this book is what doesn't get done. That's its focus. Reduced to its simplest, the argument is that the national emphasis on a very logical farm development policy has excluded a careful consideration of a no less defensible rural policy.[1] That direct comparison, however, is the subject of chapter 4. For the present, this chapter first explains what governing institutions are and what they do. It then delves into what organized interests are and what they do.

Essentially, institutions are rules.[2] They have a specific emphasis on some among the many social goals, a bias in favor of what they each are most capable of doing. This chapter addresses why institutions, once established, are so difficult to reform, or to fundamentally alter and change. That explanation focuses on what political economists regard as transaction costs.[3] Transaction costs are merely the price placed by the political process on governmental reform—or any other decision, for that matter. Those costs include such things as arranging the many deals and tradeoffs that must be made for change to occur.

That's where interest theory comes into play. In the United States, transaction costs are especially cumbersome because so many complex public organizations in different branches and sometimes in different federal levels must be partners for any such deals to be effective. Privately established organizations whose essential interests are defined by public institutions raise these transaction costs higher, especially in the United States. The U.S. government is nonauthoritarian, with powers divided between three branches and two federal levels plus local jurisdictions, and resplendent with checks and balances. Lots of tradeoffs are needed, and they can hardly be forced on any participants. The tradeoffs, of course, affect the practices of policy implementation or delivery, not just the passage of laws.

Problems with transaction costs complicated reform and made it more difficult because of the actual and expected rise of organized political interests that enter the bargaining process from the private sector[4]—or at least for privately held reasons. These special interests—which often are groups but may well be single corporations or even churches or Boy Scout troops (or the offices of individual members of Congress)—organize protectively to guard the benefits their members or supporters have obtained from existing public policies (not to mention their work in making new policy demands). Because of the open and democratic nature of the American electoral process, such interests effectively enter into bargaining. That process provides opportunities and incentives to bring like-minded people to gather freely, express even narrow policy demands, and organize to influence institutions. For those reasons, interests become *de facto* policy partners or participants (or, as some prefer to say, players). As I argue subsequently, the numerous farm groups that evolved on the frontier for self-help reasons played that partnership role as they matured. They defended existing farm policy, continuously asked for more public support, and opposed any federal efforts to pass a national rural policy. Farm and ranch groups perceived rightly that adequate funding of rural policy would come at the expense of farm policy success one way or another: financially or through lost reputation.

WHAT ARE INSTITUTIONS?

Contemporary political economists see institutions as very specific and tangible entities.[5] Institutions are indeed the formal rules of living—at least those embedded in society by government. Rules, then, are public policies. They include, first, laws that govern behavior, such as those passed by states outlawing toxic waste dumping in public forests. Second, rules are public programs.[6] Programs include legal steps to define who gets to use the products, or the constituents; who funds and delivers the services; and who enforces use and how they do it. An example is a program that specifies who may and may not use public forests and for what purposes, allocates state dollars to set up and operate specifically equipped campgrounds for public visitors, and establishes state park rangers who are to ensure public order and accord with state laws on these public premises. As this example implies, rules are, third, public organizations—like the state park rangers or (for most of the purposes of this book) the U.S. Department of Agriculture.

Organizations are rules because they too are specified in law and have operating jurisdictions over individual public programs. They decide who gets what treatment and how they get it. Like laws and programs, public organizations are institutionalized.

Where do institutions come from? Simple. Institutions are created by a combination of three things: tradition, some type of governing consensus, and—most necessarily—formal political action. Institutions are not regarded by most political economists to include the products of tradition and social consensus that societies informally adopt. Thus, watching National Football League games is not truly institutionalized each fall for all American males over the age of nine. It's simply a habit.

What do institutions do? They govern behavior, for one thing. The behavior of all those who live, work, and play in the public arena, or society, is affected: public officials, users of public program benefits, all other citizens, and even people such as undocumented immigrants who work in the United States.

Institutions do more than merely govern behavior, however. They also specify who will bear the monetary and nonmonetary risks and costs of transacting life and business in America.[7] Let's simplify that last comment. Rules also specifically define who pays for providing laws or services or public officials—such as amounts of taxation. Then the rules define what will happen to those who violate legal convention—such as the penalty for someone who fails to stop her truck for an oncoming school bus with flashing red lights. In that sense, institutions determine what one pays if one doesn't play by those rules—at least if one gets caught.

Obviously, all institutions have a bias. They favor some things or some types of people in society, but not others.[8] Consider, once again, the case of state forests. People who like to camp under relatively cramped conditions are winners. Businesses who want to dump their radioactive wastes there are losers—they can't. Because of state income taxes in some places, however, all citizens who don't camp or prefer to camp elsewhere also are losers. These people pay taxes, but state park rangers neither come to their doors at home to offer services—such as, for example, lighting the barbecue pit—nor do they visit individual wilderness camps or private campgrounds to provide a comfortable and convenient wood supply.

The bias that this extended essay deals with is no less easy to understand. From at least 1862 into the 21st century, the U.S. national government spent vast sums of money to provide for improved rural conditions. Yet it established these programs mostly to develop and eventually modernize the lands and facilities of farmers and ranchers, or American agriculture. These folks were winners, or biased favorites. In the same period of time, that government did very little for rural communities, the rural poor, the unemployed, or nonagricultural rural businesses such as commerce and manufacturing—even when many of its administrative officials thought it should. These people, their places, and their work were the losers. They were, as ensuing chapters explain, those who were biased against.

THE IMPORTANCE OF TRANSACTION COSTS IN OPPOSING INSTITUTIONAL REFORM

Transaction costs exist because, in the focus of this book, policy reform proposals benefit some people but impose new, or previously unborne, costs on those who have been winners before or at least have been content with the old ways. These kinds of decision-making costs can best be understood by applying them within the context of American national government. What must be understood at the onset is that policy decisions under the U.S. Constitution were not meant to be made easily. Quite the contrary. Whereas proponents of centralism, such as Alexander Hamilton, wanted a relatively hierarchical structure of government with clear and final authority vested to take leadership, others did not. Centralization made decisions on policy too easy and quite possibly tyrannical—bully like. Concentrated power was regarded as the very definition of a tyranny that might well work for the worst in America.

Federalists, or decentralists—epitomized by James Madison—wanted a complex structure of government in which numerous participating institutions had to be brought together for a consensus before any policy was passed.[9] Bullies and tyrants were not to be tolerated. Federalists were very concerned with avoiding the authoritarianism associated in American minds with the dictates and whims of the English crown. They also were concerned that one part of a quite diverse America—such as southern plantation owners—could be victimized by, for instance, northern industrialists. After all, the American Revolution was largely a battle against the crown; it was fought in favor of diversity of all represented interests.

In general, the Madisonian view prevailed in drafting and institutionalizing a constitution as the fundamental or basic set of American political rules. Because government decisions were not to be made easily and quickly, the transaction costs of making deals and tradeoffs accordingly were designed to be quite high. Powers were separated among three branches: an executive, a generally dominant legislature, and a judiciary. Each branch was given checks over the others: executive vetoes, implied judicial authority to rule legislation unconstitutional, and legislative override of executive vetoes are all well-understood examples of things that mandate careful negotiation and compromise for policy to be made. The division of power between national and state government also added transaction costs.

Other innovations, many of which were post-constitutional, only added to raising transaction costs. For example, the legislature was divided into two houses, with essentially equal authority; the executive and legislature each exercised some controls over administrative organizations; and constituent units in the lower legislative house won considerable authority by being regularly able to elect, reelect, and even toss out existing members of that Congress. The list goes on, but the point is made: This was not an efficient, economical, or business-like way to run a government. It led to massive obstructionism—or heavily imposed transaction costs—within and across branches. Governing was to become a constant and pitched series of battles, not a matter of genteel policymakers reasoning together.

Moreover, there are additional, extra-constitutional transaction costs that are unique to policy reform efforts. If previous government programs are reversed in favor of something else, the public sector must fund and operate the replacement policy. At the very least, it must pay for dismantling old programs, their facilities, and their staffs. It also must assume the learning costs of putting any new programs into operation and developing knowledgeable administrators to make them work as intended.

In addition, previous facilities and program materials that had fixed purposes will now be largely obsolete or wasted. The result is that political decision makers, who already have a hard time achieving a consensus, also will be skeptical of the burdensome task of policy replacement. They'll need exceptionally persuasive information that what is to be changed really needs changing. Policy reform, in other words, is far harder than the always-difficult assignment of merely passing policy. More than constitutional structure is involved. So too are behavioral costs of time, energy, and effort.

Let's put all this in perspective by looking at the example of reforming farm policy in favor of rural policy. Context in all cases helps understanding. Only a few transaction costs among many need be mentioned to provide that context. First, if the president as national leader favors rural policy, Congress must react skeptically. That's its constitutional—not to mention electoral—expectation: guarding against a power grab. Second, congressional representatives of agriculturally dependent local and state rural economies will act defensively on behalf of their farm and ranch voters. This imperative will pit these congressional members against representatives of manufacturing and tourist-dependent rural economies. Nonfarm-district representatives will want to win for their rural constituents. Initially, they won't think of the costs of that victory. They'll just yell for a while. In contrast, urban and suburban legislators will not think kindly of the president's proposed reform. Rural policies won't benefit their constituents; moreover, those home folks will be taxed for the budget costs of dismantling and replacing farm policy. Other structural problems abound: Third, policy must be written so that the judiciary will not find either the policy itself or the treatment of farmers unconstitutional. Fourth, a reform bill must pass both houses of Congress in identical fashion. Fifth, the president must consider the tradeoff of rural benefits for the budget costs imposed. The idea of reform may be fine, but is it worthwhile to be labeled a "big spending liberal budget buster"?

A raft of practical transaction cost problems then come forward: Sixth, what will become of colleges of agriculture and agricultural research stations that rely on considerable federal appropriations? Seventh, will economic growth in rural communities offset economic losses from having, for instance, less agricultural research? Eighth, can federal farm extension agents be converted economically into rural development specialists or prison guards or national park rangers? Ninth, will there be a farm and ranch interest revolt against the reforms? Tenth, will nonfarm rural voters even appreciate the changes? Will agencies respond? What will state governments do? And on and on. In other words, will previous policy winners raise too much of a fuss? And will new winners really see themselves as winning anything of value? There, perhaps, lies the weightiest transaction-cost dilemma of all. All of this, of course, explains institutional inertia.

THE MANDATORY ANGER OF PROTECTIVE
POLITICAL INTERESTS

One of the basic tenets of political science is that the number of organized interests continues to grow.[10] It does indeed, even if many organizations actually die. That's followed by a second truism: Organized interests have a political advantage when they defend against change. They do indeed, as we shall see.[11] Not surprisingly, given these long-standing observations, public policy generally is in a state of equilibrium or stability.[12] New protective interests always seem to enter the process. Modifications or alterations of programs may occur as a result, but broad-based reforms of any arena of encompassing public policy—such as commerce or transportation or agriculture—are rare.

Policy equilibrium can be broken, however. In fact, policy stability is disrupted in America, though not very often. Some political theorists note that such punctuated equilibrium—or busting of the *status quo*—occurs at a time when focused public and policymaker opinion gains attention in national politics.[13] Three interrelated factors are credited with this new focus of opinion: the rise of numerous emergent organized interests, especially grassroots or local homefolks groups; the rapid growth of national media attention; and a stirring of previously neglected congressional attention. Events such as multiple Washington committee hearings, a series of locally held investigatory hearings, appointment of special committees, introduction of several new legislative bills, and the rush of previously uninvolved congressional members to cosponsor such bills or add their own issues to them are among the many things that clearly indicate likely legislative reform. These activities lower institutional transaction costs of reform because they provide real incentives for many people to decide in its favor.

Other policy theorists offer supportive explanations for what prompts those rare reforms. These scholars note that when a sizable national network of reform advocates organizes intergroup coalitions and generates general public interest, major policy change results.[14] That analysis makes sense, of course: Such strong advocacy movements are seldom seen, but when they do occur they do gain society-wide attention. The media and Congress then exhibit flushed and hectic concern. The women's movement, the Civil Rights movement, the anti–Vietnam War movement, and the environmental movement are major examples of late–20th-century advocacy coalitions that punctuated prevailing policy stability. The transaction costs of not changing, or accusations of being politically unresponsive to what may be a majority, were heightened by movement momentum. Almost by definition, social movements that don't generate such attention fail to gain policy reforms.

A factor forgotten by scholars pertains to what effective groups want. This factor influences whether a movement actually evolves. Certainly, not all issues and public programs are capable of being of widespread public interest. Some issues are too abstract or removed from daily reality for people to comprehend, such as the fundamental rights of rocks—or the fundamental rights of migrant foreign workers? Others seem like good ideas to many people but offer no strong incentives for individuals to work for them. Improved accounting standards are a good example. Such issues usually offer collective, or public-wide, goods to a broad range of beneficiaries who are personally only marginally and very indirectly winners in any potential reform legislation.[15] Why should the marginally involved pay the transaction costs of participation and mobilization? No damn reason. In contrast, some issues and proposed laws and programs offer special, very directly personalized benefits to specific people, at least symbolically—women, blacks, civil libertarians, students who fear war, dedicated pacifists, and people who want to protect and save their threatened planet.[16] These individuals will pay very high transaction costs not only to participate but to see their issue through to a win.

The first type of issue generates "diffuse interest advocacy," with sincere but generally lukewarm support from all but a central network of policy entrepreneurs as the core of any emergent movement. Those almost stillborn issues obviously have long odds against going far legislatively. The second type of issue, however, creates intense interests. Lots of people can be made to feel as if they have a very specific stake in policy reform. It means something to their hearts and souls, so these intense, reform-type political interests diligently and nervously pay attention to media coverage, and they enthusiastically pressure congressional attention from the grassroots. Groups, reporters, and legislators then see policy windows of opportunity and go to work to climb right through them.[17] Intense issues, therefore, dominate the policy process.[18] They easily grow in number and can overcome by sheer strength of their offensive any presumed and expected advantage of the defenders. Diffuse interests can't do either; therefore, they maintain a social and political marginality—or just disappear. Public policymakers, in effect, pay little or no transaction costs as they generally ignore diffuse advocacy. At best, the advocates win a few minor and relatively inexpensive programs to call their own. This outcome typifies rural policy.

What does this analysis mean for that logical farm policy and any efforts to adopt a broader and no less defensible national rural policy? Transaction costs imposed by organized interests are heavily weighted against passage of substantive and substantial rural policy. Rural interests, as we've seen, are hard to define nationally. Who, exactly, would win from a federal rural policy? Business? The poor? Tourists? Retirees? Those in the Southwest? The North? Never has there been a nonfarm rural movement, as we'll see in chapter 10. Thus, it's difficult to say who would win. Accordingly, because rural lobbies are developed individually they compete politically in policy reform as diffuse and poorly attended interests. Who among the foregoing list will rally and bring intensity? And why would they, given the uncertainty of reform benefits?

Farm organizations, in striking contrast, are very intense interests. These groups grew from an organizational base of very much needed rural joiners or self-help neighborly associations (see chapter 1). They evolved into effective grassroots national groups that lobbied for farm assistance in the late 19th century. Others also regularly recurred in slightly different form as short-lived protest groups of politically angry and immediately persuasive farmers.[19] By 1921, a four-group national farm lobby was established and active in Washington.[20]

Moreover, farmers no longer identified themselves as just farmers. Throughout the 20th century, farmers specialized and industrialized by crop and by type of livestock—sometimes even by breed. Nearly all of them organized interest groups. As they did, these commodity and livestock groups soon moved into national politics for selective policy benefits of their own, such as a swine center. No longer was there commonality among the diverse. The farm groups, then, were not only increasingly intense, they were many in number. Still other farmers always held out the promise of another farm revolt to inspire lots of sympathetic media attention and resulting congressional fear and positive reaction.[21]

Farm groups were further advantaged as, for all practical purposes, they grew up and matured along with what became a very extensive national farm policy. Farmer participation in establishing programs and laws was expected and eventually welcomed openly.[22] Farmers were of major influence in deciding the structure of farm institutions—from the Grange fighting for farmer assistance with the railroads through winning extension help to fighting battles for rural mail delivery to the American Farm Bureau championing and winning price support legislation in the 1930s.

Thus, farm groups evolved as intense about whom they represented. They were no less intense about protecting a seemingly ever-expanding base of what they regarded as uniquely farm-oriented institutions of government. Indeed, they actually were so intense as to be involved in the frequent identification and creation of new public institutions to add to existing institutions to do something else to ease the ever-present annual numbers of farm losses. These losses in the future might include them, if nothing were done. Thus, when farm interests saw proposals for an alternate rural policy as potentially limiting farm power and farm program benefits, they imposed such high transaction costs on pursuing policy reform efforts that major proposals for change never advanced very far. Farm groups said that policy for rural areas sounds good, but it should be to improve agriculture and not divert attention to towns. To an important extent, American politics maintained a 150-year-long farmers' movement. By golly gee, rural America was farm and ranch interest turf. Keeping that social belief alive was the agrarian message.

IMPLICATIONS

There's more to the politics of institutions, interests, and transaction costs than the mere lesson that public policy reform is extraordinarily difficult and usually unlikely. That doesn't say much. The important implication is this one: Because of that politics, some of society's important social and economic conditions can be ignored over time, so that festering conditions are overlooked and even get worse. Conditions in nonfarm rural America appear to be an excellent example.

American government, as portrayed above, does not do long-term planning on the basis of forecasting the future very well. The multiple institutions that would need to plan together to accept projections make even strategic goals improbable to set. That government also doesn't make short-term adjustments to new conditions very well either. It finds it hard to seriously reconsider existing institutional arrangements, even in light of new information. That's a policymaker's worst headache.

As a result, national farm policy and new programs emerged with very little information about long-term food needs or what for many, many decades would be an escalating capacity of farmers to grow more. Knowledge was simply imperfect. These things weren't understood well, nor could they have been anticipated. Policymakers, in consequence, responded instead to the presumed needs of national development by helping move more agrarians further to frontiers and underdeveloped rural regions.

The creation of so many agricultural institutions meant something important, however. Government kept making fixed social investments in agriculture and thereby encouraging—if not mandating—a resulting political momentum on agriculture's behalf. Over time, it was hard not to unhesitatingly fund and protect farmers and their policy institutions, from the land grant colleges in the American states to the Department of Agriculture in Washington. Like NFL football, that too became a habit, albeit a rather formal one.

Policy change became incremental and always focused on doing more for agriculture. One farm institution was created on the base of previous institutions. Determining what to do better and differently for rural America was not easy. Deliberations regarding potential programs took place within a maze of largely farm-oriented institutions. Madison undoubtedly envisioned such a maze, if he could only have thought that the federal government could ever have created such a thing as this. Even Madison, however, in his wildest dreams, probably couldn't have seen the extent of the institutions' prevailing biased orientation or what very high transaction costs they placed on decision makers. Thomas Jefferson (a close confidant of Madison) probably would have appreciated the result because he believed in the need for a kind of chaos in government—but not necessarily of this sort, dominated by public officials. Policy institutions through their organizations became wedded to the ways that each did business, or simply the prior performance of their own programs. So did farmers and ranchers as institutional clients and selective program users. They liked getting something, and didn't want it jeopardized. Accordingly, deliberations over policy were not to be based on good governors reasoning together or on up-to-date and comprehensive reviews of rural America's social and economic conditions. Instead, past and general social beliefs about agriculture's importance captured rural governance.

SUMMARY OF KEY POINTS

This chapter provides an institutional explanation for the neglect of non-farm rural policy needs. The explanation is based on institutionalized political momentum and the high transaction costs associated with institutional reform. The following seven points summarize in a simple way the concepts as they are important to future chapters.

1. Institutions are government's policy rules—laws, programs, and the organizations to promulgate them. There's a necessary bias within all institutions, based on preferences on behalf of those they long have served. Rural institutions in the United States have always had a farm and ranch development bias.

2. The starting point for that agricultural bias resulted from previously established beliefs that national development could result only from encouragement of agrarian expansion.

3. High transaction costs imposed by the multiple Madisonian-type institutions of the United States made it extraordinarily difficult to ever reconsider or question that agricultural bias. However, the appropriateness of a Hamiltonian, centralist vision still prevailed in American politics. As we shall see in chapter 12, this paradox

undoubtedly provided some complexity and complications even to agricultural policy.

4. Other factors, such as the existing fixed governmental investment in farm policy, made already high transaction costs of policy reform even more pronounced.

5. A wide array of farm and ranch interests organized to protect and promulgate a farmers-first policy. These groups and organizations regarded rural policy as their own co-opted part of farm policy; they strongly resisted any extensive and independent nonfarm rural programs. These intense farm interests further raised the transaction costs of any policy reform in this arena.

6. Nonfarm rural interests have never been politically or organizationally strong anyway. Given the diversity and complexity of rural American social and economic conditions, it's hard to determine who would win and what would be won from a national rural policy. That includes even the identifiable losers. Any emergent rural interest, from among those losers, has had a diffuse focus, inherent political weaknesses, and a resulting marginality in public policy deliberations.

7. Because of the intense and high transaction-cost nature of American agricultural policymaking, policy officials generally govern on the basis of past institutional investments. They neither plan for the future very well nor respond well to short-term conditions that suggest the need for severe policy change. Agricultural policy—like its products of corn, cotton, and wheat—grew essentially as more of the same old stuff, but always packaged differently, for increasingly numerous and varied farm needs.

4

RURAL POLICY *as* FARM POLICY

This chapter looks at what types of farm and nonfarm rural policies have been passed in the United States, or institutionalized. The emphasis is on the explicit content of who benefits—and how they benefit. Because new laws and programs are filtered through structures established within older ones, the lack of specifically rural institutions early on severely disadvantaged the creation of any later ones. In particular, this chapter traces the historic evolution of farm policy as a necessary antecedent of rural policy. What happened, as a consequence, was that whatever rural policy evolved was always regarded as merely a subset of that dominant farm policy.

Two things are emphasized here. First the institutions themselves are covered, with an emphasis on explaining how one led to another (each as kind of a logical guess). Public policymakers and business interests closest to them as lobbies generally believed that agricultural modernization and development was the key to extensive nation-building and frontier settlement. To a great extent, it was odd that these proponents emphasized the creation of an activist government. After all, the structure of government, with the great difficulties attendant with passing legislation, was essentially *laissez faire*.[1] It was not only Madisonian. People and businesses in this capitalist society were generally expected to provide for themselves, which of course made it quite likely (if not inevitable) that the rural poor and underemployed would be left to their own devices—and preyed upon. They were hardly important enough to that special task of nation-building to be treated as policy and social belief exceptions.

Farms and ranches as family-owned and -operated enterprises were unique, however, as the perceived cornerstones of national expansion and growth. Moreover, this reality was regarded as a practical, not an ideological, matter. Importing food to feed a nation that refused to fill its own continent was never a question. Therefore, when agrarians kept failing, rulemaking players—albeit reluctantly and rather slowly—added more and more assistance for them. Despite the slowness, so many institutions eventually were created that they surrounded farmers and ranchers with nearly every possible service—as it was said, helping them help themselves.[2]

Economists finally looked at the range of these comprehensive services and, as noted in chapter 1, called it an Agricultural Establishment.[3] It was that huge. Their intent was to descriptively identify the singular farm-development purpose of what became an immense set of interrelated and interdependent institutions. Because of their sheer numbers and common workload, Establishment officials became politically powerful in their own right. These institutions were inoperative without them giving advice and assistance to agrarian producers, as well as to policymakers about agrarian needs (to forwarn them).

That point leads to the second emphasis of this chapter. With more and more agricultural services available, farmers and ranchers and their families (even in the South) became increasingly dependent on service providers. Such dependence brought grassroots support and loyalty to high-capacity program and organization administrators who had not been constitutionally anticipated to be a significant part of American government. Thus, agrarian dependency and the political noise it created were two important factors leading to nonfarm rural neglect.

They were not the only factors, however. With very limited political control in their own right, administrators have never exercised their own political power.[4] They combine with other driving policy forces, which in agricultural policymaking have been twofold. These other forces were the cultural justification for doing exceptional things for farmers and the growing intensification, and thus the shrill noise, of emergent farm and ranch interests from the grassroots private sector. These issues are the subjects of chapters 5 and 6—which, with this one, complete the explanation for prevailing farm power and the resulting bias of public policy for rural America.

BUILDING TOWARD AN AGRICULTURAL ESTABLISHMENT

The 1860s were an ideal time for farm public policymaking. With the secession of the southern states to the Confederacy and the resulting loss of Washington influence for plantation agriculture, the Civil War opened an important window of policy opportunity. The principal spokespersons for large-scale farming—not to mention slave labor—were removed from policy debates. After 20 years of trying in the face of southern obstructionists, proponents of development finally gained passage of an authorizing act for what became the U.S. Department of Agriculture (USDA). The Act of Establishment of 1862 set forth, under very broad guidelines, a relatively minor federal agency to take comprehensive—as well as open-ended and potentially expansive—action to find and disseminate any relevant information on improving agriculture.[5] From the outset, this organization had a scientific mission: the discovery and fostering of new and better seeds and plants. In particular, USDA was to emphasize distribution of goods (seeds and plants) and services (information on how to best use them) to agrarian producers. In addition—and of equal importance—it was to promote the scientific enterprise of ongoing discovery to farm users.[6]

What was institutionalized within USDA's original mission was this applied scientific enterprise (or, as the logic of inquiry would call it, empirical positivism). This was science for the people: farm science to farm people. Although policymakers at the time may not have foreseen it, this scientific emphasis brought social and economic development to the forefront as a new and significant political force. The actual public policy product of dealing with agrarian improvement wasn't just giving farmers seeds, as many of them saw things. That product ultimately was to be nothing less than modernization and commercialization of traditional subsistence agrarian practices.

There was more to development as directed through public policy efforts in 1862, however. Freed from southern state obstructionists, Congress moved almost simultaneously to pass three other, though independent, bills. The Homestead Act (actually the first of what became several) legitimated squatting on designated tracts of open frontier land—generally federal property that was not sought by private investors and western developers such as railroads. There was a common, logical, yet unplanned tie between this initial homesteading and USDA's creation. Land was made available while USDA engaged in research and outreach to alleviate the problems of the people who settled there. This was more than a short-term dream, obviously. Even more 1862-style agrarian assistance was forthcoming. The Morrill Land Grant Act provided still other tracts of public land to each of the states for educational institutions that would teach the latest facts and findings—the science—in agriculture and mechanics. Finally, the Transcontinental Railroad Act hastened farm and supply movement West, as well as the exchange of farm products to markets. Giving land to railroads, which could then be sold to existing homesteaders, was one key to raising capital for construction. As revolutionary as it was, however, this fourfold policy effort proved to be only a first stage of development and farm modernization efforts. It remained to be built on, as insufficient to its task.

Several important policy innovations followed to hasten the modernization task. Federal experiment stations were added to assist the agricultural development work of USDA and the land-grant colleges in 1887. They were set up locally, usually adjacent to the agricultural colleges, to undertake scientific solutions to the unique problems of nearby farm and ranch producers. Their intent was to generate more applied scientific research to solve production difficulties than USDA or the land-grant educational institutions could muster. As a result, modernization took a giant leap forward. Black schools were added in 1890, mostly in the South and primarily because the vast array of tenant farmers were ignored by still all-white land-grant colleges. Agricultural constituencies increased as a result of all of these developments.

When it became clear to agricultural observers and policymakers that education and research were not being sufficiently promulgated, USDA and the colleges sent out local—or extension—workers to assist producers directly. These uneven, rudimentary, and often ad hoc efforts were standardized and centralized in 1914, becoming a truly federal Extension Service. The national and state governments were actual structural partners in Extension. In the meantime, a growing USDA was elevated to full Cabinet status.[7] This development meant that, as farm groups forcefully insisted, a farm and ranch advocate served as presidential advisor on at least formal institutional par with advisors such as the Secretary of War.

This collective set of organizations was the "Agricultural Establishment." It was at least effectively and efficiently organized to provide centrally unplanned yet interrelated and comprehensive services. Its total responsibility was to provide for farmers as modernizing cornerstones of agrarian and national development. The only problem this Establishment faced was how to get all agrarians to use and understand what agricultural professionals were saying.[8] Nonetheless, modernization of the agrarian sector inexorably moved forward—along with the increasing skills and professionalism of agricultural administrators. Farmers moved from sticks as hoes to sharp steel plows and then to tractors. They moved from subsistence farming to, for more and more farmers, producing for the market economy.

By 1916, this federal Agricultural Establishment and U.S. policymakers were forced to reconsider and once again expand on what they had done. The existing agricultural professionals were not enough. Farmers and ranchers were still failing and exiting production agriculture. A Federal Farm

Loan Act (FFLA) was among the first laws that moved to do a far broader range of things for failing producers. The FFLA also was a new approach in that direct government financial assistance to producer cooperatives was appended to the farm self-help approach of the existing Agricultural Establishment.[9] The FFLA established a precedent of giving money to producers and only to producers, although funds actually went through the cooperatives.

More of these highly selective (some farmers-only) public policy benefits followed. A credit system provided direct-to-farm loans to improve production operations—that is, to further fix up and modernize the old homestead.[10] Agricultural market agreements, which used additional direct funding for farmer-owned cooperatives, brought the cooperatives a capacity to deal forcefully with processors and commodity handlers. The intent was to remove producer isolation from price-setting decisions.

Farmers-only benefits went even further, treating producers as unique people in this otherwise free-enterprise society.[11] The cooperatives, for example, were exempted from antitrust laws, allowing joint marketing action among what were otherwise inherently competitive growers—competing, of course, against only themselves. Then regulation of middlemen was established on farmers' and ranchers' behalf. The goal was to ensure that producers' economic failures did not result from corruption in stockyards, railroads, and other agribusinesses as food moved through them to consumers.[12] The policymaker message was: Don't meddle with our much-needed modernizing forces of national expansion and development—the farmers, that is (those who alone got these sweetheart deals).

Clearly, through this new legislative assistance, farmers moved to a status as even more special Americans in a *laissez-faire* land. They gained the sort of policy benefits that were unavailable to others, even in earlier agricultural policy. After all, others could find ways to use education, research, and even extension services to aid them as secondary food suppliers or middlemen. Private farm service providers, such as millers, also could benefit from the old but not the new. This flurry of institutional creation clearly transformed—and certainly expanded—the Agricultural Establishment by moving it from the provision of only collective social goods to, in addition, offering selective ones, though only for certain growers. As a consequence, producers intensified their institutional interest in the Agricultural Establishment and moved politically even closer to those providing public services to them.

Yet public policymakers were far from finished with altering market relations and bringing producers further into the Establishment fold.[13] The collapse of farm prices after World War I—with its high wartime demands on U.S. farm production—was the motivating reason. Farming quickly went from a golden age of prosperity to a depression. The result was another policy innovation that provided farmers with a distinct buffer from the effects of the free market. Even with all that had been done for producers through the now multifaceted Agricultural Establishment, the 1920s saw a depression in rural America that brought a resultant and distasteful slowing of agrarian modernization and rural development.[14] In response, a divided and unsure government created new programs for (at first) the six most politically significant basic crops.

Producers were given direct cash benefits for what they grew to keep them in business.[15] The Agricultural Adjustment Act of 1933 (AAA) and its rewritten version in 1938 were not in keeping with any of the then 70-year-old traditions of U.S. agricultural policy. This legislation certainly was not self-help for farmers, nor was it merely the creation of more organizations to financially and legally assist producers in specific facets of their operations and marketing.[16] The AAA, in essence, simply gave checks to some farmers, who in turn really liked and often depended on this financial remuneration. It also provided loan guarantees. The Agricultural Establishment, however, regarded payments and loan guarantees only as temporary, until the Depression ended.

Not surprisingly, price supports and the loan guarantees that were added to them became the real foundation of U.S. agricultural policy throughout the remainder of the millennium. The intense political interests of farmers were far more focused on the financial assistance of the AAA than they were on other and earlier, far more indirect, benefits. Love for the collective goods of the agricultural colleges and experiment stations could never compete with the farmers' tremendous gratitude for special federal dollars. Nor could selective financial support for marketing cooperatives be as satisfying as government checks in farmers' very own pockets. This way, a farmer could buy her own new tractor, for example, to modernize with federal dollars that were now in her own possession. Nobody was able to gather the political will to phase out what were planned to be temporary institutions.

The result was that primary attention to farm policy after 1938 meant tinkering with direct payments and loans. For instance, the number of eligible crops was soon extended beyond six (and counting). Market orders were extended to other crops, to limit supplies and keep prices from bottoming out. These programs were of the greatest intensive farm interest, even in 1995 when price supports were replaced by even higher Freedom-to-Farm payments. This initiative was a hoped-for but hardly assured phasing out of direct payment programs—finally.[17] By 2001, however, Congress was raising caps higher for various programs than anyone envisioned in the 1995 farm bill. When emergency weather programs were added to payments for environmental additions, international trade losses, farm contributions to rural community well-being, crops that weren't grown, and losses on crops that were grown, the largest-scale producers were each eligible for $288,000 in federal payments. This was, as USDA proclaimed, the year of the farm safety net, or a policy of ensuring farm survival one year at a time. Does this actually sound as if "finally" is here? Other Establishment institutions, such as the colleges, were tended to, of course—although with declining revenues in the face of rising operational costs.

Much of the reason for the rising costs of original Establishment institutions was very simply explained. Agricultural policymakers and farm supporters knew they had to do more for others within Establishment programs to keep political support for price policy alive.[18] Accordingly, ranch, labor, poor people's, consumer, environmental, and several other interests were gradually and slowly given a stake—and specific benefits—in farm policy. Yet that stake was always modest and usually provided through farm institutions.

This, of course, is where federal rural policy entered into what was a base of farm public policies. All rural residents gained a share of the rural mail system and parcel post in the 19th century. Rural electrification later went to small towns as well as farms and ranches, especially organizing as user-owned cooperatives (which, incidentally, became big businesses). After the mid-20th century, small units were set up in the land-grant colleges, the experiment stations, USDA, and extension to provide services to rural communities. These efforts had to be small because any extensive policy initiatives would have acknowledged farm policy failure and brought resulting policymaker skepticism about this assistance. Thus, the limited size, funding, and means of evolution of rural programs always made clear that this sort of farm policy accommodation did not bring forward a decisive national policy for those left behind by farming. This strategic decision was important, of course, in keeping community development efforts down. Within the Agricultural Establishment and its institutions, rural efforts remained little more than filler, rounding out what seemed to be a public relations package emphasizing that agriculture policy was for all Americans, rural neighbors included.

THE INSTITUTIONAL DEPENDENCY OF PRODUCERS

Why did farmers and, to an extent, ranchers fight so hard for Establishment assistance? One reason stands out: As federal agricultural policy expanded, market-driven producers became increasingly dependent on its many benefits—for very good reason, apparently.

As the post–Civil War era saw agriculture spread west with proliferating numbers of agrarians, the early returns on farmer innovations brought forward by education and outreach began to gradually increase productivity. Subsistence agriculture began to decline. A combination of public and private investments started and then continued to transform the farm sector into a market-oriented, capital-intensive industry. An expanding number of farms and ranches were coupled with an ever-escalating use of improved means of production. This result, combined with general social conditions, made for a modernization paradox: Producers came to be able to continually feed more consumers, but consumers were not demanding that much more in food and fiber products.[19] People weren't eating more to bail out farmers—or to keep up with them.

Agricultural professionals and policymakers believed that they had a strategy to combat that paradox by doing more and more of the same work through the Agricultural Establishment. Over time, however, they proved mistaken in what they did. By promoting a farm policy that was tuned almost singularly to further enhancing the productivity of each producer as well as the general efficiency of production, they expected to lower food costs and increase commodity purchases by consumers. Presumably, with cheaper food, people would eat more and eat faster. Although this ideal never quite worked as anticipated, farm dependency certainly increased because of the plan. With new and complex methods, producers needed continuous professional assistance.

Three things happened. First, there was an ongoing if uncertain expansion in farm and ranch numbers. Because of Establishment assistance, going into farming always looked like a possibly best-chance, last-chance occupation to souls who otherwise didn't know what to do with their lives. Expanding farm numbers gave agricultural professionals more to do and more people who used them. With expanding use came a greater degree of dependency. Finally, expansion and service brought a renewed commitment to the by-then established goal of transforming American agriculture further away from its peasant roots.[20] New institutional initiatives were always being passed, it seemed, to better cope with and, it was hoped, finally solve the modernization paradox.

Underlying price circumstances also furthered dependency. By the 1870s, producers found even greater price and income vulnerability. In the short term, neither farm product consumer demand nor the supply of products was responsive to frequent price savings. With time, however, fluctuations in farm production did bring changes in price. Moreover, because more and more usually was grown, rather than more and then less, prices usually were on a downturn. Consumers, therefore, paid consistently less of their income for food; previously, that set of prices was only a relatively small part of their total overall expenditures anyway. These folks, in that sense, considered America a blessed place: Eat more, pay less (but never enough of either).

Producers had no such good fortune. The investment assets of money, time, and energy were sunk into farms and ranches and the means to be producers—and only producers. That is to say, assets were fixed, not easily transferable to another investment. A farmer couldn't easily switch to a petting zoo or divest and build a manufacturing plant on the Dakota plains. In consequence, producers had few incentives, but they had imposing personal costs, including debts, if they cut back on the amount produced.[21] The implication was clear: Individual control over personal asset use was lost for all but the most impractical farmer or rancher. The rest just kept growing at maximal rates. Where was (what we'll see later as) that presumed yeoman independence of Jefferson?

Modernization, commercialization, and national development created an easily answered dilemma for producers. They could choose to take advantage of practices advocated by the Agricultural Establishment, or not. Not doing so, however, meant failure. Poverty was ensured, unless they chose to leave production agriculture. Given the frequent exit and entry of farmers and ranchers in the 19th century, many obviously opted for this pathway.

As an alternative, others often reluctantly adopted technology and produced more of what were already oversupplied commodities. Of course, by producing at lower cost even with the same price, only the earliest innovators among the still numerous producers gained a market advantage or made money by paying attention to the professionals. Late adopters of professional advice struggled in vain to catch up with their more farsighted neighbors.[22] Excess production, of course, kept escalating. Prices kept dropping. Furthermore, the seeds of future farm and ranch exits were well planted. In that sense, public policy, the Agricultural Establishment, and its advice and technology brought more rather than less inequality to rural America. This time, it was on the farm, not just between farm and town. Yet these things surely also created even greater Establishment dependence on the part of remaining producers. They understood that they were compelled to heed professional recommendations to have any chance at all, even if they were in the worst economic shape of all their neighbors.

When 20th-century commodity programs were passed, their side effects induced even greater inequality in rural America. There simply wasn't enough money to bail out all producers with prices so low. Ranchers didn't gain price supports, so they lost. Smaller-scale farmers lost because commodity programs paid out on the basis of amount grown. Even with limits that eventually capped payment levels, larger-scale growers gained bigger federal checks. They were the big winners.

There was somewhat more to it than that, though. Commodity programs reduced the risks of expansion of the homestead by establishing floors under prices. This factor kept total income to individual program-crop farmers guaranteed through a combination of purchase price and supplemental government payments. What happened? Those with the largest payments— and with risk minimized for them by government—had additional incentives to buy the nearby land of less-successful farmers. As demand for the neighbors' lands increased, prices increased (artificially, of course). Two things ensued: Many putative producers, such as young people, were unable to afford property, or they paid too much to make a profit if they did buy.

In addition, many farmers who were on the margins of successful operation could not afford (or, faced with a good offer, did not wish to afford) to retain their property and farming rights. Bigger but fewer farms remained, unintentionally, of course—really the opposite of what was intended. Production, nonetheless, still increased. Dependency on the Agricultural Establishment prevailed. It was useful to send the kids, as likely inheritors, to an agricultural college to make them better growers. Support for cooperative marketing was even more valued when only a few farmers could manage and control a large crop. Most important, however, almost no one could turn down that federal price support check. It was the real means for keeping many farmers in business, and in intense support of farm institutions.

IMPLICATIONS

The implications of creating a well-received Agricultural Establishment are easily understood in just a few words. What is most clear is that institutional farm policy gained high status in American government and politics. That status elevated farm modernization above social justice as a policy goal. It facilitated national development for many years. Later, the fixing of so many public-sector assets into an Agricultural Establishment created high transaction costs for any proposed policy reforms. Only the amount of assets fixed within the U.S. military could have come close to that fixed into farming and ranching assistance and the technological modernization of that sector. Moreover, it was fixed into agriculture first, before anyone else got public goodies in an otherwise *laissez-faire* era. Anyone who later proposed a differently focused rural policy obviously was not going to be well received by those with this power. In fact, they would be attacked forcefully as a threat by a large array of intense farm policy advocates and administrators. That had indeed happened to the Federal Farm Board (FFA) in 1929. The FFA provided the collective benefits of theoretically higher prices at the cost of (God forbid) reduced production. It also was voluntary—and farmers with fixed assets obviously resisted.[23] So did Washington farm groups, who helped bring about the FFA's quick demise.

Obviously, administrative influence alone could not have entrenched American farm policy power. Administrators and other professional staff certainly assumed great institutional prominence in American politics. One reason was that their numbers and their professionalism were far greater than in any other policy area, at least early in agriculture's formative years. Other forces, however, also were at work over the decades to ensure that farm policy persisted, even while it sometimes accommodated many new social demands and values.

The other vehicles for farm policy persistence were of two types. Farm policy, as chapter 5 shows, kept riding into Washington and around the nation in a supercharged yet fundamentalist myth of agrarianism. That myth preached farming's inherent social value in America, democratically and socially. Society tended to believe that message—which, of course, was carefully though subconsciously crafted by agricultural advocates and professionals.

The second type of vehicle provided an intense and highly concentrated, even intimidating, organizational ride. No industrial sector in America was ever more organized into highly protective groups than the farm sector. Nor has any sector consistently won more policymakers as its friends and allies than have farmers and ranchers. Of course, no other sector has had a greater institutional dependency to protect. (Those are the subjects of chapter 6.) Together the Agricultural Establishment, the myth, and the interest group frenzy have been the basis of U.S. farm policy and the bane of a broader and more equitable rural policy.

SUMMARY OF KEY POINTS

The conceptual ideas raised in chapter 3 are applied in context in this chapter. The major focus traces the development of an extensive array of farm institutions and the emergence of farmer dependency on those institutions. These phenomena vested considerable political influence in agricultural administrators and service professionals. They also led to a rational resistance to political consideration of a national rural policy.

1. Farm policy, in its contemporary form, was initially enacted in 1862. This was stage one. This contemporary policy approach emphasized national development through agrarian modernization and farm commercialization.

2. As farm modernization and development continued to flounder throughout the rest of the 19th century, more and more policy institutions were created in an ad hoc, unplanned fashion. Most provided collective, public-wide policy goods. Their intent was to assist efficient and economical production through a comprehensive range of professional agricultural services to clients; their methods ranged from education to help in the field.

3. By the end of the 19th century, enough farm-directed organizations and other institutions were in existence that the term Agricultural Establishment was appropriate.

4. After the collapse of farm prices at the end of World War I, agriculture entered into yet another crisis period of overproduction and low prices. The result was more policy intervention and more farm-oriented institutions—this time with a greater though not exclusive emphasis on selective policy benefits for producers.

5. Those policy additions, however, solved few problems. As a consequence, an entirely different tack—only somewhat explored in earlier legislation—was added with the AAA of 1933. This time, price supports and a buffer from free markets formed the cornerstone of farm policy. Agricultural policy was no longer simply helping producers help themselves. Government would just do part of it. The rest of the 20th century saw continuous tinkering with price policy as well as accommodation of many nonfarm interests to ensure support for, primarily, the strange phenomenon of farm price programs.

6. Over time, farmers and farm groups came to develop more intense political interests in farm policy. The primary reason for this intensification of interest is easily explained: Farmers became more dependent on direct farm payments and loan guarantees than they had been on the earlier and always useful services of the Agricultural Establishment, with its emphasis on helping to enhance farm modernization.

7. Within this institutional structure, an alternative national rural policy was regarded as far from a good thing. Passing it might bring cuts in farm program funding and even skepticism about the whole of the policy base. As a result, resistance was always intense—just as it was to organizational innovations such as the Federal Farm Board, with its emphasis on voluntary production cuts and potential but unintended income losses. Farmers understood the problems of their own asset fixity and the unrealistic expectation of voluntary cooperation in reducing production, so they tended not to do it. Nor did they intend to redirect their Agricultural Establishment to rural poor people and declining communities.

5

THE AGRARIAN MYTH
as FUNDAMENTALIST
VISION

Ideas have power. That's how an old lesson goes, as this chapter explains. That lesson can be seen first by looking at the conclusions of a veteran agricultural professional hand, or long-time employee. In the 1930s, the USDA's Bureau of Agricultural Economics was an administrative unit with considerable influence, based on its staff's analytical expertise regarding the nuances of farm policy operation.[1] One of its most notable employees was John M. Brewster, a philosopher working and contributing among a staff of what were mostly economists. After watching the politics as well as the analysis of agriculture for some time, Brewster drew from his own intellectual traditions and concluded that established ideas drove much of the decisional process within government. Brewster felt that human behavior was conditioned by conscious and unconsciously held principles that merged within people to bring them to favor certain policy approaches and alternatives and ignore others. As he wrote, people "act on beliefs and first principles whether or not the principles can be shown to have metaphysical truth."[2] Modern academics might rephrase that heady language and say that societies create paradigms and that these paradigms at least help structure public actions and preferences. A regular person might simply note that, if an idea seems like a useful one, just let it be your guide and keep following it in one form or another.

What Brewster became acutely aware of was a first principle of American social theory known as agrarian fundamentalism. Or Jeffersonian democracy. This ideology expressed the simply held belief that the hardworking and self-dependent farmer who toiled on the land was the basis for a good and maybe even pure society. The independent farmer, or yeoman, was free from the frequent corruption of cities; left to his own devices, he would properly steward, or caretake, his land. This stewardship, extended to the multitude, would make for a well-cared-for and very protected nation. Agrarian landowners, as stakeholders, would preserve democratic rule. Such a vision later was used to easily justify a national farm policy, particularly as it provided a basis for nation-building and westward expansion and development. This ideology did not emphasize the need for food and fiber production. Instead, it promoted the hope of creating producer landowners as a large and stable social base. Thus, as 19th-century policy proponents expressed it, the costs of encouraging farmers and ranchers to multiply were worth the price of unique government action in an otherwise *laissez-faire* era.[3]

This chapter first looks at the content and force of that message. Next, it turns to the promulgation of this mythically held ideology. That is, what did agricultural professionals and other farm interests do to promote and keep their fundamentalist vision alive in policymaking circles?

THE FUNDAMENTALIST MESSAGE

The power of the idea of agrarian fundamentalism was derived through its accuracy at a point in time and the status of the man initially behind it: Thomas Jefferson. Jefferson was an idealist who valued individual freedoms far more than he did general social good—and, certainly, far more than the ease of government decisions.[4] As such, his was a perfect complement to the prevailing Madisonian institutions. Indeed, Jefferson and Madison were close friends of often like minds. Because Jefferson saw the virtues of rural agrarian life as it was lived out in his new republic, he preached and praised that lifestyle. Family farmers were needed to preserve democracy because of their tendency to be farsighted and committed. Often Jefferson made this argument from positions of authority, such as his presidency. In so doing, he told a true story of what existed in much of early America. That is, he created what philosophers call a myth as well as what policymakers call a social goal for government. Jefferson's message about agrarians was not to be understood as a fable, or a false story of what did not exist. Fables survive only as legends to tell in lesson-giving or as entertainment. Myths, however—as stories that were true at least at one time, or as objective reality of a moment in time—persist as people in circumstances they hold sacred point to their cherished if idealized past.[5]

Agrarianism, as we saw in chapters 1 and 2, was actually alive and indeed a norm in Jefferson's time. Even as it was later eclipsed by astonishing urban and manufacturing growth, agrarianism was always present in America. It also was politically well if enough prominent people told truths about its glory and its history and if they always linked that past to a present that still was at least marginally existent.

As a consequence, there was always a great deal of political rhetoric in praise of U.S. farmers, farm families, and their virtues. As a flip side to the virtuous, the truths of the shame of American cities were always recounted as well. Those wanting to keep Jeffersonian agrarianism alive as a fundamentalist vision for how America should be structured could always add to their story's validity by recounting city horrors. The portrayals were mostly of what trapped urban Americans let happen to their morals, their children, and even the food produced on farms but adulterated in city processing industries.[6] Thus, America had its agrarian and, not unimportantly, its original first principle, linked intrinsically to an early hero and a proverbial wise man of constitutional stature.

The important idea expressed in this chapter is that the primary values of society are learned in the crucible of human experience.[7] Those values are as politically and socially real as what took place in agrarian times. Older generations pass them on to subsequent generations. Therefore, these values are long-lasting and patterned belief systems that are useful to and considered first in public policy debates. To an extent, at least, they establish a nation's character and enhance stability in at least one applicable economic sector.[8] That is, they help bring policy equilibrium, or stability, and don't allow for its easy punctuation, or reform.[9] The public good in this is simple: Without shared social values, problems cannot be collectively addressed. There's no sense of appropriate policy direction.[10] Thanks to Jefferson and America's agrarian past, however, a policy direction most certainly prevails in a steadfast way on farm and rural issues. It exists partly because people believe it, partly because others use the myth for political manipulation.

Why not use myths? The social value of farming and its preservation simplifies what otherwise would be complex and competing policy conflicts.[11] A specific course of action is justified—in this case, for supporting farmers and ranchers through Establishment services and cash payments.[12] Few people ask: What the heck is government doing? Why? Most Americans at least subconsciously know the reason.[13] Yet they do not understand or know how much modern and commercial agriculture has changed since the yeoman agrarian days of largely subsistence production by families. Nor do they care, even about what government does and spends.

Few people, as we saw earlier, have any direct knowledge of contemporary farming (see chapter 2).[14] Most rely on opinions from but a few people who, as friends and neighbors, influentially provide policy information. Perhaps as few as 5 percent of Americans are actual opinion leaders.[15] These are the same people who know and usually articulate first principles. In this case, they know and experience much about farming or farm policy. Their ideas, however, are influential in simple form because most of the public doesn't want to process large amounts of policy-relevant information and sort through it.[16] Especially about farming. Those data aren't useful to the daily lives of most Americans. Moreover, the media reinforce symbolic, mythic, and simplistic public knowledge.[17] Television and newspapers endlessly report prevailing social beliefs: The suffering farmer and her economic woes over agriculture are dominant and recurring themes. Related entertainment events preach the same theme in movies, Farm Aid telecasts, and barroom country songs. Few intellectual or analytical concerns are reported on actual farm policy content or the details of agriculture's problems.

No wonder this outdated and no longer accurate myth of agrarian virtue has driven leading agricultural scholars crazy for more than 60 years. Brewster was not a lone soul noting this first principle's disastrous effects in producing and maintaining outmoded agricultural policy.[18] Others argued for years that a once-objective reality had lost its contemporary realism.[19]

Why, various scholars asked rhetorically, doesn't government intervene economically on behalf of other threatened independent businesspeople who operate convenient services? Small neighborhood gas stations, dual-isle Main Street dime stores, and local hardware stores in which the proprietor himself helps each customer find proper plumbing or yard care parts and solutions: These businesses are at least as endangered as family-operated farms—and just as socially useful. Alas, however, neither philosophers nor parallel business comparisons drive farm and rural policy decisions. Few of either are sought in political debates. It's always the carefully crafted and preserved image of hardworking family farmers that prevails.

What can be summarized about that image, or the myth's substantive content? After all, that substance has been discussed only in a general way, as a hint. Let's have a checklist of the components of the modern but carefully preserved agrarian myth as they enter into policy debates.[20] What follows are its often articulated central points.

1. The values of agrarianism are simple: preserving the independent family farm and its family operators.

2. Farming (as family-run enterprises) economically dominates and sustains rural America.

3. There is an average family farm that represents American agriculture. It's what farm policy struggles to maintain.

4. Modern farm production is highly productive, economic, and efficient. That belief differentiates agrarianism somewhat from the past—much to the better.

5. As farm prices decline, farm income declines as well.

6. The world economy depends on U.S. agriculture, and vice versa.

7. Good farming brings good stewardship of a farmer's land and the surrounding environment.

8. Farm programs, with their low price emphasis, take care of food programs for the world and for the domestic poor as well as for farmers.

9. Past farm programs have accomplished their goals very successfully. However, they are inadequate, and more assistance would produce greater farm stability.

As Brewster would argue if he were to magically reappear, none of the foregoing points represents the whole of contemporary truth. Their articulation is only a cynical use, with guile, of Jefferson's first principle as it's been applied to farm policy, or public policy benefits for farmers only. In reality, all of these points are accurate in very small part.

Modern commercial agriculture has many goals, from farm preservation to greater technical specialization and increased farm size. Much of rural America is inappropriate for this intensive production. Therefore, farming isn't rural America's business in all places. Although family farms still dominate production, they are so diverse that, by crop and around the nation, no average family farm can be detected. Even size and income vary dramatically—as does the degree of family control over the farm's operation.

The goals of modern agriculture, as it promotes gradual agrarian evolution, are themselves subject to question. More production does not necessarily mean more efficient productivity. Farm incomes are not necessarily reliant on farm prices as producers grow and raise, and then sell, more at lower production costs. Agriculture has never meant sound environmental practices. It is by nature a destructive means for bending prevailing ecologies. Farming is the nation's worst source of pollution and land and water degradation. As farms grow in size and use more technology, stewardship becomes more difficult.

U.S. agriculture does not sustain the nation's economy, nor does it primarily depend on a world market. Food programs for the poor are small, incidental, and inadequate by-products of farm program benefits. They are good for public relations, however. Finally, farm programs have never met their goal of preserving and protecting farm and ranch producers, as the large numbers of annual exits attest. Their net impact instead has been bigger farms, fewer farms, higher land and production equipment prices, and resulting rural community stress, as well as even more corporate and banker control. At best, one can argue only that national farm policy, once so logical, must be seriously rethought—as the perpetrators of the AAA intended in 1933.

PRESERVING THE AGRARIAN MYTH

How, then, does this myth prevail? Who keeps it alive through the present, and why? What guileful parties are influential enough to successfully employ such manipulation? Who's conning us now? Although parts of the answers to those questions are discussed in chapter 6, the institutional structure of users of the agrarian myth should be outlined briefly here.

The first part of the answer lies in the Agricultural Establishment itself. Bureaucracies present problems, not just valued services on which farmers become dependent.[21] One such problem is that of representation in policymaking. Bureaucrats who have unique programmatic jurisdictions and responsibilities tend to function as much like organized interests—or politicians—as like neutral evaluators of their clients' needs and the effectiveness with which they serve those needs. As another old USDA hand (and one of Brewster's contemporaries), Paul H. Appleby, concluded, politics and administration are indistinct in that both are part of the same continuing policy process.[22] Bureaucrats must play politics and administer—and they can't separate the two. In part, they even purposefully create farmer dependents because they need such clients politically. Therefore, bureaucrats become advocates, or public-sector interests, on behalf of their own programs.

As advocates, they portray most favorably what they do—which, of course, brings forward messages about policy benefits that they provide for the family farm and for keeping agrarians in business.[23] Few bureaucrats say what elected officials don't want to hear, especially in some confusing and drawn-out analytical fashion. Simple messages are best, and what message is more simple than some short version of Jefferson's myth? Two leading agricultural observers concluded that USDA is not a monolithic bureaucracy and that USDA bureaus respond in policymaking in their own ways, as fairly autonomous.[24] This observation brings forward numerous messages among bureaucratic agencies that are competitive yet still commonly focused in their annual chase for federally allocated dollars. At least 10 such autonomous agencies have traditionally joined the chase—from Extension to the Farm Credit Administration to the ever-changing organizations that oversee direct farm payments.[25]

The result is that elected officials and USDA leaders receive a cumulative, many-faceted message about what great things are done for now-dependent farmers—but more could still be accomplished for these needy denizens of virtue. Another factor enters when bureaucratic messages are constructed for the money chase. Local farmer committees have been part of the process for delivering almost all USDA programs. In many instances, USDA program operation also has been shared with education, research, and even state government officials who work routinely with local producers.[26] Incentives for cooperation with farmers and other Establishment institutions mandate that decentralized USDA officials who deliver services seek common ground with farmers and other bureaucrats in finding policy and financial support. Praising farmers is the most common and least contentious ground available. Few, if any, successful bureaucrats publicly criticize farmers as a group. Hence, the agrarian myth gets annually reconstructed but not updated and refined by politically minded agricultural professionals.

Bureaucrats don't act alone to preserve the myth, however. Organized private interests do as well; indeed a raft of them do it. Moreover, despite the subject of chapter 6, they must be mentioned here as well. Policymakers describe a burdensome cacophony of private-sector and privately intended organizations articulating farm needs and the image of needy and socially important farmers.[27] The diversity of these interests and their lobbyists make Washington seem like a theatrical experience replete with "surround sound."

What goes on? What are the surrounding sounds? On the left, farm groups clamor on behalf of their needy and deserving members. On the right, agribusinesses plead the virtue of production agriculture as, for example, providing supermarkets to the world, through (of course) their own corporations. To the rear, environmental groups praise farm programs as mechanisms for significant, but recent, environmental delivery. They could work better, however. World food groups join them, noting America's role in feeding the world's hungry and, certainly, asking for greater support in regularly renewable multi-purpose and accommodative farm bills. Other social cause groups voice their own modified farm legislation support from further to the rear.

The front of the theater matters most, however, because, in addition to noise, the front also provides the visuals. Farmers themselves are talking, visiting legislative offices in their work boots, carrying signs about country woes, and encouraging Willie Nelson to sing about their trials and tribulations. In all instances, these omnipresent modern agribusinesspeople come off looking like descendents of Jefferson's image, wailing away about their importance to America's present and its heritage.[28]

When elected officials and USDA executives escape the Washington Theater, the noise and visuals accompany them. Farm interests and their fellow travelers have mastered the numerous means and tasks of lobbying, especially locally at the grassroots.[29] Radios play ads. Network anchors interview weeping or overly stoic farmers. Corn producers show up at a congressman's home. So what happens? American politics gets a loud, diverse, and also professional articulation of the important and longstanding need to support national economic—and governing—strength through assistance to the still-deserving descendents of heroic agrarians. No wonder myths live, prosper, and produce policy successes.

IMPLICATIONS

The persistence of American national farm policy demonstrates that ideas, as ideals, are as important to politics as the politicians themselves and those who seek to influence them.[30] All matter, of course. Ideas are the vehicles, the horses, that the riders come in on to lobby. A society and, therefore, a government needs its first principles to order and stabilize its public policy. Policy areas that lack first principles, social beliefs, or once-true myths probably meander considerably in form and content.

The problem with first principles and myths is that they become outmoded, or at least in need of being reformulated (or let's say rebunked).[31] When something like agrarian virtue makes its way into policy rhetoric, difficulties in proper analysis and consideration come forward. It's really difficult to ascertain whether the myth is present because the advocates believe in the principle and its value or whether they're just cynically manipulating it. It's probably a little of both. In the case of farm policy, the agrarian myth appears to live because it can still be applied to a very different, very modern, and now-industrialized farm sector than was true for the days of yeoman subsistence. Moreover, the myth does help deal with the agricultural dilemmas that bring forth arguments over the modernization paradox and the long-term farm overproduction problem.[32] That is to say, a debunked and recast myth, as contemporary truth, might help deal with those dilemmas—the ones relating to a 5,000-acre wheat farm in the Dakotas or a spread with 4,000 hogs in the Carolinas. After all, modern farmers share the overproduction trap with those early agrarians who first looked to national development as a positive social good.

The one real warning in this chapter is that policymakers must look carefully at the substance and implications even of beliefs that many people seem to ardently hold. If they don't look carefully, major policy reform probably will never puncture the outdated policy stability in some issue areas. Rhetoric will rule. Myths, as we will see in chapter 7, can hold back the formation of alternative interest groups and congressional attention to competing programs. It's also unlikely that reporters, who are moved first and mostly by caterwauling farmers, will see the largely unrelated needs of rural communities and their residents. The logic of farm policy, then, will always overshadow that equally defensible rural policy.

Thus, some myths need to be stopped, or ground to a halt. Texas politics provides an example in a state with an increasingly diverse population of whites, Hispanics, African Americans, and many other ethnic groups. Racial tensions often are high, especially between whites and Hispanics as the two politically dominant populations. These tensions seem unlikely to abate until some very traditional rhetoric is cast aside—in other words, until old-timers and new Texans "Forget the Alamo."[33] Mythic discussions are certainly excitable, and so need purging—or at least modernizing.

SUMMARY OF KEY POINTS

It's far harder to envision ideas that affect policymaking than it is to imagine power in the hands of specific and resourceful people. Nonetheless, when a society invests certain ideas, such as agrarian fundamentalism, within powerful institutions, such as USDA, those ideas take on their own life.

1. Ideas have the greatest amount of power when they are idealistically wrapped in a society's widely believable first principles or myths.

2. Myths such as agrarianism are meaningful because they represent an objective reality, or a truth, about some socially significant moment in time. These myths are not fables. In this case, Jefferson's era was certainly agrarian, and his vision of the independent yeoman stabilizing society and democratic government was very romantic

and lifelike. Given American experiences, Jefferson's vision was far more romantically appealing than that of his and Madison's nemesis, Alexander Hamilton, who quite reasonably foresaw an industrializing American society best served by a strong central government.[34] The image of working in a factory while the monarch rules holds out little romance.

3. Agrarian fundamentalism became a reasonable and believable cultural justification for national development and, of course, its proposed settlement. The myth was believable and easily manipulated by guileful interests that could use it to their political advantage.

4. The Agricultural Establishment was built on the myth of serving a farm and ranch nation. Ironically, though, that Establishment in many ways worked against the myth of agrarianism. It quietly came to follow principles of scientific, positivist discovery, and it worked hard to modernize and commercialize the agricultural sector. Family farming has become less believable.

5. The power of agrarian idealism, or the myth, was largely undiminished, however, by sectoral change. The notion and belief always remained that government should do more to help independent farmers help themselves, and so in turn help the nation. The entire set of agricultural institutions was constructed as this mythic rhetoric went on. Institutions also promulgated it. Thus, institutions and myth became ironically intertwined and inseparable in politics.

6. In time, the substantive content of the myth was badly inaccurate and outmoded, on several dimensions. Nonetheless, agrarian beliefs persisted even as they failed to communicate to policymakers and the public exactly how American agriculture had matured and what it had become.

7. The myth persists at least partially because of those who have used it for political gain and institutional protection. By now it's been heard so often that it is ingrained. There are two of these preservationist forces. The first is bureaucratic service providers—or institutional caretakers—who have power because farmers and ranchers rely on their advice and assistance. These providers believe in the need to keep established institutions alive. The second force is a wide variety of social interests, including farmers and ranchers, who simply keep resurrecting the myth to protect and expand their own

extensive public policy benefits. These are the institutional clients. Both forces, through their obstinacy, impose heavy transaction costs on any proposed legislative reforms.

8. This persistent use probably can be attributed to two factors. First, those closest to agriculture and agricultural institutions seem to seriously believe at least rudiments of the fundamentalist myth. They use it so often that it's somewhat real to them. Second, these interests also find that the myth, even if it's cynically applied, can be effectively manipulated in federal farm and ranch program appropriations and legislation. Therefore, what seems real often is also approached with knowing winks and nods about how a silly old story still pays off.

6

COLLECTIVE VERSUS SELECTIVE BENEFITS *and* FARM INTERESTS

As the preceding four chapters explain, two driving social forces helped bring about an Agricultural Establishment of farm services and, eventually, direct financial producer support—that is, money. Agricultural professionals grew in number as farm institutions proliferated. As empirical positivists with an orientation toward scientific and factual discovery, these agricultural professionals provided extensive advice and assistance to farmers and ranchers.[1] These market-oriented clients gradually became more dependent on grassroots professional services, including dollars. With a growing demand for their institutional contributions, administrators of USDA, the land-grant colleges, the experiment stations, and extension gained considerable influence as farm policy spokespersons. Policymakers listened to these newly popular officials.

What the professionals often spoke about was the second driving force in doing ever more for producers. The vestiges of agrarian fundamentalism, as forcefully advocated by Thomas Jefferson, became a sweeping political rhetoric that was handily applied as a rationale—in this case, for taking unusual government action on behalf of a single class of citizens. The message was that farmers were better than the rest of society: responsible for democratic political stability, national development, land stewardship, and feeding the public. Therefore, unique treatment was in order for those unique Americans. This very believable myth, manipulated as it was by producers and agricultural professionals, helped drive policy. It gave a proper reason for moving in the direction of greater and more intrusive government in a country where people were otherwise expected to help themselves succeed.

Myths by themselves don't move an unusual type of public policy along. Nor do administrative professionals have that power to successfully articulate and force through public policy recommendations on their own. Without an independent farm and ranch voice speaking on its institutions' behalf, the Agricultural Establishment never would have existed. Farmers and ranchers and the organized interests they formed were the third driving force. They were important because of the political—and thus electoral—momentum they created, first at the grassroots and then at the Washington, or governing, level.[2] These emergent groups together formed a strong lobby—or, more accurately, a set of lobbies allied only on the general principle of Establishment protection and enhancement.[3]

What was most significant about these lobbies was that they were recurring, or routinely in the face of public policymakers.[4] Producers gained power by exercising their prerogatives as laid out in the U.S. Constitution's Bill of Rights. They gathered; they spoke out. Their assemblies were frequent, forceful, and directed toward anyone and everyone who would listen. They were a bit intimidating, in fact, even frightening—especially, at first, in a physical way. As Iowa's Senator Guy Gillette once said, "I'd rather have President Roosevelt going after my hide than I would supporters of the old Farmers' Holiday. Those bastards might have taken my hide, literally."[5]

This chapter looks at the origins and social development of this third driving force in creating so many and such complex Establishment institutions. It explores why they mattered. It examines these lobbies in two stages; each stage reveals a symbiosis between what was organized and what types of public policies were being created. The producer lobby emerged and grew along with and out of the laws and programs that were institutionalized on its behalf.

In a very rough sense, this development of a lobby and laws took place in two stages that were different in form, style, and substance. They led, in turn, to two different forms of agrarian power as continuing voices in driving at least agricultural public policy and at most the policies of other economic sectors. Stage one, as the first section of this chapter explains, emphasized collectively distributed public policy benefits, grassroots political movement, and general social intimidation. This was "outdoors" politics. The second stage (which is examined in the second section) moved in the direction of winning selective public policy benefits for distinct types of producers, developing producer power through ongoing Washington offices, and winning policy results through insider political maneuvering within the nation's capital. This was "backroom" politics. Obviously, the second stage evolved from the first as lobbying refinements were made and the lobbying environment changed.

Yet the two stages must be examined separately to understand how agriculture's political and policy fortunes grew and persisted institutionally within the nation. Had farmers and farming not been different by stage two, farm politics would never have been able to repeatedly and successfully restrain a national rural policy. This power is covered specifically in chapter 7, but first let's move on once again to farmers as America's ever-active joiners.

COLLECTIVE BENEFITS AND THE FARM THREAT

It's important to note the context in which farm policy first emerged. What, for instance, kept national development and settlement interests focused on agrarian needs? And why did farmers receive so many unusual policy goodies—oops, benefits—over so long a time? The answer has two parts. First, farmer organizations kept forming, loudly protesting economic conditions, and disrupting the larger political process. Second, periodic drops in farm prices and income created a rural economy that was always in crisis, despite—and often because of—increasing farm productivity.[6]

Those groups, the conditions they faced, and what they did will be explored sequentially over time. First came the Grange—or, as it was formally called, the National Grange of the Patrons of Husbandry.[7] This first of the almost nationally organized general farm groups began in 1870—just as agricultural expansion grew at the Civil War's conclusion. High war prices were lost as production increases rose when farmers went back to business; Grange membership increased dramatically. That increase is hardly surprising in that corn prices had fallen 32 percent between 1866 and 1878. Those same conditions brought the radical Greenback Party and the Free Silver Movement to rural America from their urban birthplaces—to prey, of course, on farm and ranch discontent. The latter two organizations argued for national economic reform, not on behalf of farm institutions. In particular, they were proponents of the Bland-Allison Act and the coinage of silver as the means for expanding the money supply.[8] The hope of farm protestors was that silver coinage would bring more money to rural America from what was seen as the urban monopolies. When Bland-Allison passed and the money supply failed to increase, farm protest turned ugly, violent, and threatening to the enemies who were believed to purposely repress farmers.

Yet it was not the Grange that led economic reform protests. The Grange generally was a low-key lobby; it was especially attuned to railroad reform in hopes of controlling exploitive rate structures. Grange members weren't against or necessarily even believers in the monopolists. Not all groups were so reticent, however. The South led the way, with that era's "big three" mass farm protest organizations: the Texas Alliance, the Louisiana Farmers Union, and the Agricultural Wheel. All were groups that threatened to disrupt southern economies by attacking credit providers that farmers relied on annually to finance the year's crops.

Southern farmers, more than their northern and western counterparts, were financially strapped because of credit costs and were dependent for life on lender goodwill. This was a more recent family farm agriculture—and one not yet in possession of capital equity. It also was an agriculture with its own class conflicts. Farmers who were increasingly in contact with agricultural professionals came to favor a market economy to support their businesses. Most farmers, however, were yeoman subsistence types, still economically and socially smarting from the Civil War. Added to the mix were freed black farmers, who (unlike the whites of Reconstruction) were able to participate in state and local politics. Many issues of basic and traditional farm rights such as cattle grazing on common grounds were being reestablished in law. Black freedmen threatened the yeomans' farm survival far more than they did those who were moving to a market economy. Yet the freedmen also threatened these development proponents. Freedmen wanted law to give them land, but not an impersonal reliance on the market. Freedom, in Jeffersonian ownership terms, was their goal.

Turbulence of this sort spawned a complex rebellion.[9] The three protest groups merged in 1888 to form and expand as the National Farmers Alliance (NFA). The NFA grew, in part, by being much more militant and overtly threatening than the Grange, which the NFA labeled too slow and misguided in forcing political reform.[10]

The early 20th century saw more farm organization momentum and even more anti-capitalist sentiment and plans.[11] The National Farmers Union (NFU), which still lives, formed from the ranks of the declining NFA. The NFU's intent was to build alternative and competing institutions to market cotton. Its plan for getting them was a farm withholding action, to force policymaker action. It did not.

Almost simultaneously with the NFU, the American Society of Equity (ASE) was created in Indiana. The Nonpartisan League (NL) grew in North Dakota somewhat later, in the aftermath of a debilitating dry season of increasing farm exits. All three groups expanded to neighboring regions until a troublesome farm force constituted a militant national threat, at least in its rhetoric, to economic and financial institutions. The ASE also was organizing a withholding action, announcing plans to form its own farm-controlled trust, or centralized monetary source held in farm hands. The NL was no less intimidating to public officials and banking institutions. It sought to elect nonpartisan but League-allied farmers to take over state governments and, once in office, shift responsibility for farm income losses from loan recipients to lenders. Holy geez: Bankers, not farmers, would fail. By 1918, the NL controlled North Dakota's governorship and both its legislative houses. The NL also created what became a permanent Minnesota Democratic Farm-Labor Party, separate from and often flaunting national Democrats.

Farmers of this era also intimidated policymakers and nonfarm lobbies by direct actions. The NFU used marauding nightriders as enforcers to "recruit" nonparticipating producers. The ASE set fires and dynamited the machinery of tobacco marketers and middlemen. At the movement's most frightening, farmers supported nearly every populist, people-praising, antigovernment politician who appeared. At least the dominant yeomen types did so—and they existed nationally, not just in the South. As a result, rural residents became the backbone of the national populist movement and its efforts to win control of government.[12]

The same dynamic occurred with the Progressive reformists in Wisconsin. Populists demanded that close ties between public officials and business leaders end abruptly, bringing politics and government back to the masses. Progressives agreed. They hoped to rely on good-willed public-sector professionals to help the masses. The professionals, of course, were to be on a short leash of people power. This combination of violent behavior and ongoing antigovernment sentiment created fears that the demonstratively worst and least educated segments of American communities might rule, fueled mainly by their own anger and the emotional pressure of peers.

In this context of farm failures and organized opposition, public officials kept accelerating the creation of those unique farm institutions. Policymaking sentiment was simple: Modernize and educate that very necessary and expansive agricultural sector to create a supportive national middle class and thus stabilize politics. That is, roust the rabble. To serve such sentiments, the addition of more service institutions and the creation of a "help-farmers-help-themselves" big government was widely perceived as a small price to pay: Forget *laissez faire*.

Noisy farmers who idealized farm life and its contrasts with the rest of America's miserable society may not have gotten what they wanted, which was economic reform. Collectively available policy benefits were abundant, however, especially for the use of those who committed to a market economy. Farmers did see USDA and scientific research strengthened and the nationalization of an expansive Extension Service that offered greater personalized hands-on help to struggling agrarians of all sorts in even the most isolated places. There also were more homesteading opportunities to open up more productive places. This American public policy oddity was far better than a radical takeover of government. That, at least, was what national development interests and their policymaking allies concluded. Moreover, perhaps locally placed, wise agricultural professionals could even quell some of the radical sentiment that seemed to be pervasive in farm areas. Professionals could be voices of reason as well as forgers of a new, modernizing farm middle class. That was the hope, but it too badly overlooked the cultural splits between modernizers and yeomen in the farm community.

So what happened during this first stage of farm policy creation? The repeated formation of angry, hostile, and threatening farmer organizations at the grassroots level led to collective public policy benefits to at least placate if not satisfy the otherwise mythically esteemed agricultural sector. Government was able to point to all the wonderful things it did for farmers and ranchers, not city folks.

THE SECOND STAGE OF GROUPS AND POLICY

The second stage of farm lobbying was as different from that of the populist, anti-capitalist protest groups as was the movement by government from emphasizing collective public policy benefits to providing specific and direct payments to farmers. Yet there was some continuity of groups, old to the new style. In truth, the two moves were intricately related. By the 1920s, a professionally staffed farm lobby was ensconced in Washington, and most of its groups sought to exercise influence through direct contact with and persuasion of policymakers—often, though, by relying on ideology for communications, or on the diverse principles articulated by many of that day's members of Congress. Taking noise to the dusty roads of rural America was out, or at least it was held out as a secondary strategy. Group members instead were told to contact their congressmen (what women?) and comment, often to district voters, on the local, back-home appropriateness of their support of farm issues.

Four groups that sought to represent all types of farmers opened those early Washington offices.[13] Three of them were the fraternalistic and decades-old Grange; the more radical Farmers National Council (which also spoke for the NL); and the National Board of Farm Organizations, which was sponsored by the still overtly populist NFU and was the lobbying agent for the closely allied National Milk Producers Federation as well. Each group represented a unique regional constituency that their staffs sought to inform and make electorally responsive to legislative votes. The Grange was strong in the Northeast and the Pacific Northwest. The Council had its members in the western upper Midwest, and the Board was a concoction of western Great Plains farmers. The fourth group, the American Farm Bureau Federation (AFBF), had a true national following because its locals were organized at least in part by government. Farm Bureaus usually had offices adjacent to those of their institutional sponsors. Who were those sponsors? They were the obviously nonneutral and hardly moderate agents of the Extension Service.[14] Not surprisingly, with its national voice and its institutional support from informed agricultural professionals, the Farm Bureau was the most aggressive farm interest group, as well as the most successful at direct lobbying. The group excelled at activating the grassroots in many states and in numerous congressional districts. The other, more ideological, groups also turned like-minded congressional heads, however.

The 1920s were consumed principally by the matter of creating and consolidating farm group power, especially by the Farm Bureau. Because Washington politics entailed rhetoric and persuasion rather than violent protest, that consolidation involved four things: convincing legislators that farm economic problems would not soon just go away, getting legislators to realize that an informed grassroot's interest in individual congressional votes was also permanent, creating at least the impression that activated farmer grassroots sentiment translated into electoral wins and losses at home, and cultivating the support of Southern farm cooperatives as allies to Midwestern groups in policy matters.[15] Those successful efforts led to the internal cooperation of farm state legislators through a formal and later informally organized farm bloc. As a result, farm policy changes and additions were no longer dependent on national partisan leaders. The grassroots was by then truly present—and at least semi-institutionalized itself—in Washington, especially in 1933, when the controversial AAA authorized cash payments to farmers. Farmers were all but actual lawmakers.

What was going on? It's easily explainable. When farmers thought of themselves first, organized around immediate relief satisfaction, and demonstrated grassroots unity, government in a rare display of deference to political power rewarded them as individuals. Moreover, policymakers did so with the persuasive institutional support of those seemingly omnipresent agricultural professionals.[16] These service providers, with their great capacity to inform, had already realized that the farm problem was persistent and chronic. So they generally were more sympathetic to farmers than to policymakers. So much for the wise-and-moderating theory of calming those agrarian animals.

Professionals, perhaps more than individual farmers, realized as well that production agriculture was changing in ways that public policy had to address. Farm group leaders also understood and politically preached about the changes. Yet the grassroots were wedded to the past, although no longer to a dominant rejection of a modern farm market economy. What was the transformation of the sector about? It involved several related changes. First, farmers were increasingly specializing by crop. Second, specialization was aided by modernized and industrialized production, which made it easier to care for 1 or 2 crops per farm rather than 6 to 12, including Ma's chickens. Third, specializing farmers and their agricultural professionals selected and promoted crops that were best suited to certain regions. Thus, the "corn belt" meant a Midwest emphasis on large corn crops; the "wheat belt" meant the same for the western Great Plains; there also were dairy belts, the extensive southern cotton belt, three distinct peanut belts, and a host of other places that championed regionally grown crops and commodities such as barley, cattle, and hogs. Grandmas were no longer growing chickens on every American farm.

Because heavily grown commodities each had their own production and marketing problems and needs, individual commodity groups and cooperatives gradually took on a new significance. The general farm groups that were composed of all farm production types mattered less. Specialized groups also set up their own staffed lobbying shops in Washington, generally adopted the principles of modernizing agribusiness, made public policy demands about their own regional problems and needs, and mostly cultivated political support through alliances with congressional members who were from their regions. After mutually accommodative alliances were set forth between regional interests, farm policy fragmented.[17] The philosophy of farm policy attention was simple: We'll support what you want for your home turf, you do the same for us. No longer was the Farm Bureau—troubled as it was by the 1950s with its own partisan alliances, problems, and conflicts—the best voice for a holistic (though not necessarily manageably comprehensive) farm policy.[18] Farm policy and its representation increasingly became an amalgam of regionally oriented dairy programs, corn programs, wheat programs, tobacco programs, hog programs, cattle programs, honey programs, wool programs, and on and on.

Farm sector changes, as a consequence, also transformed public policy for agriculture. These changes shifted the fortunes of farm and ranch interest groups from the general to the even more intense commodity policy benefits. Within Congress, commodity specific subcommittees with their regional representation assumed more power than did the full House and Senate agriculture committees.[19] The White House, of course, had a far more difficult time than before successfully intervening in the traditionalized policy grants of bits and pieces of assistance to agriculture.

The only thing that could break the sector's fragmented political control over Agricultural Establishment institutions was a threat from nonfarm interests. Because late–20th-century farmers are such a small part of the population and the electorate, farmers and ranchers look like nice and easy pickings in annual battles over program appropriations—as well as the renewable authorizing farm bills. What the agricultural sector won in those battles, other interests didn't win for their constituents. Budgets weren't infinitely expandable, after all. An alliance of farmers and laborers was tenuously put together to share support in the 1950s; the first successful outsider challenge came in 1973.[20]

Labor and welfare advocates had traditionally supported pro-farm congressional votes, primarily because of attractive fundamentalist rhetoric about farmers as needy souls. In 1973, however, they withheld farm bill support. Although these advocates did not attack the way in which the omnibus, multipurpose farm policy was put together as a fragmented whole, they wanted their own piece of that noncomprehensive and thus potentially wide-open policy base. They insisted on the policy reward of food stamps gaining permanent legislative status. Not much of a problem, except for bruised congressional egos. Accordingly, food stamps were added to the 1973 farm bill, and labor and welfare lobbies became active coalition supporters in several future farm bills.

In those subsequent farm bills, however, other types of intense nonfarm interests imitated the behavior of food stamp reformists. Environmental, consumer, agribusiness, and alternative agriculture proponents found their own allies and sometimes won benefits in Congress. Throughout the 1980s and 1990s, those allies threatened to oppose farm bills that failed to include benefits that their lobbyist friends specifically desired. As a result, agriculturists became ever more accommodative, gradually expanding the content and intent of farm bills as well as the purposes of budget appropriations for USDA, agricultural research, the land grants, extension, and so forth.[21] Those institutions took on added responsibility to work on behalf of the hungry, food safety and nutrition, more serious water and soil quality, organic production, and new product research. New, specialized, and selective benefit programs for each set of advocates were set up.

Because farm bill and appropriations debates also frequently alluded to nonfarm rural problems, rural programs and responsibilities were brought legislatively still further into the reaches of the Agricultural Establishment— for co-opting, it turns out.[22] Because rural advocates were diffuse and few and because these few were lacking in extensive political support, however, nonfarm rural policy gains were always minimal.[23] Certainly the full range of rural community needs was never successfully addressed by Congress (see chapter 7). Such proposals were political—and thus public policy dead ducks, dead on arrival. To use a more subtle metaphor, they were precooked geese, done in long before policy debates began by agricultural profession-als and congressional members, farm and ranch interests, and their sup-portive nonfarm lobbies. Rural proponents never became a part of the new and inclusive politics of food or of any old farm politics either.[24] Rural areas brought no new supporters (and thus help) to federal farm policymaking. Rural advocates had nothing with which to exercise even blocking power on farm bills. So why share scarce federal dollars with them? Ha: Guess again, you guys. Even if we farmers sound like your friends and recognize that rural communities could use more money, we'll support it only if lots more is allocated to the farm-rural sector.

IMPLICATIONS

Conventional wisdom portrays American farmers and ranchers as politi-cally powerful. That premise is based largely on the amount of public pol-icy benefits that go their way. Yet, as the preceding analysis has made clear, agricultural power is in this context more situational—a matter of existing conditions—than it is an absolute. That is, agriculture conceivably could lose its power today under several sets of changing political circumstances (for example, campaign finance reform).

Agricultural institutions owe their existence to the political forces of na-tional development and settlement, not to farmers themselves. These insti-tutions, moreover, were easily accepted as part of a political rhetoric that emphasized the linkage between national development and America's agrarian base, or its highly believable small family farm heritage—its yeomen. Thus, when farmers of the 19th century engaged in noisy protest and demonstrated severe income problems, more institutions were easily and frequently, if rather reluctantly, created on their behalf.

The prevailing idea was that government intervention could modernize the farm sector, create a stable agrarian middle class, and make farmers less interested in basic economic reform or financial redistribution. After all, such reform demands had been the goals of most intimidating farming protests in that era of collective agricultural policy benefits—that is, institutional services. Although the Grange had worked hard to demand USDA's elevation to Cabinet status, protesting farmers were not saying that what they really badly wanted was an extension agent in Cherokee, Iowa, or a new horticulturist at Iowa State University.

The increase in agricultural institutions, up to and beyond the AAA, occurred because professional establishment employees recognized the farm and ranch dependency that they had created, especially among market-directed producers. They also recognized that even more public policy was needed for long-term sector success. Modernizing and industrializing those solid agrarian citizens had made it increasingly necessary to find ways to lower and improve food prices to consumers and otherwise market what seemed to be a chronic surplus in commodity production. By the 1930s, government responded to bureaucratic urging and the frequently articulated agrarian myths of fundamentalist American virtue. Farm interest groups only did their part in escalating the importance and presence of rhetoric and economic reality. Protest politics in the form of the 1930s Farmers Holiday Association and increasingly radical but often nationally affiliated state and local farm groups became evident as well, with intimidation of other farmers and politics-as-usual policymakers reappearing.

When more intensely focused but generalist farm interest groups settled in Washington, they also were important. They could better monitor the behavior of members of Congress, better inform farm members about which members of the legislature were their friends, and then mobilize a grassroots political response for friends and against enemies. The Farm Bureau, in the history of U.S. lobbying, pioneered the intensive use of specifically directed grassroots pressure rather than the mobilization of diffuse grassroots anger.

As a result, farm interests gained a semi-institutionalized, almost legally established position for themselves in American governance. They were at least handy for blame by policymakers if farm policy ever blatantly failed.[25] "They made us do it" would have been the congressional cry. As these interests grew increasingly intense and farm programs were tailored to highly specific, or very selective, user needs, semi-institutionalization could only increase. Even as more diverse interests forced agricultural policy to accommodate their own intense and specific programmatic demands, cattle interests and corn interests and cotton interests and such retained their positions of semi-institutional and widely accepted influence. They were almost inside government and almost written into law—almost, but not quite.

They were expected to be players, though, even desired in policy debates as necessary (and moderate) participants.

What came about from 1970 until century's end was an expanding notion of farm, or what came to be seen as food public policy, as well as increasing competition for scarce financial support among now numerous participants. At first thought, that should have been an opening for organized rural interests. In that context, however, it was useful for all of the intensely focused private-sector players, as well as public-sector agricultural professionals, to exclude or at least minimize costly and limited establishment services to those who could generate only nominal political clout. Because rural advocates by nature formed a small and diffuse lobby with nonspecific wants, they therefore continued to lose, long after rural policy was a real threat to the credibility of farm policy.

SUMMARY OF KEY POINTS

Farmers and ranchers were never solely responsible for the widely accepted notion of farm power.[26] Their considerable political influence must be shared among the historical forces behind nation building, Jefferson's vision of agrarian fundamentalism, early farm protest, the later establishment of an innovative and sophisticated lobby, and the often stressful but successful accommodation between farm interests and various social cause and business groups. This chapter reviews the accumulation of farm group power over time. Key points include the following:

1. Farm interests were only one of three forces that drove the continuing establishment and evolution of agricultural institutions. The myth of agrarian fundamentalism and the actions of agricultural professionals shared center stage.

2. Nonetheless, farm policy grew in a symbiotic way with the changing farm lobby. Both emerged quite compatibly in two stages.

3. Nineteenth- and early-20th-century farm protest supported agrarian development efforts but was more directed to economic reform movements, including Populism and Progressivism.

4. The creation of more Agricultural Establishment institutions for farm services was directed primarily to placating farmers rather than meeting actual and expressed public policy wants. Nonetheless,

farmers—even the remaining yeomen—slowly became dependent on such services.

5. Farm politics shifted abruptly in the 1920s as a farm lobby became established in Washington. The generalist Farm Bureau was the most influential of the lobbying groups for several decades, building its influence on effective grassroots mobilization of many types of farmers and with institutional Extension Service assistance.

6. Beginning in the late 1940s, general farm groups gave way in influence to more intense commodity groups that adjusted to but also helped shift the focus of farm programs to specific crops and critters. Cattle interests, for example, became more concerned with western grazing and water rights than with any of the collectively available service features of agricultural policy.

7. In time, with an annually declining farm population and a reliance on electoral performance for influence, farm interests were successfully challenged for control of agricultural policy. Outside interests from labor to environmentalists wanted and gained bits and pieces of what was still legislatively acted on as farm policy. They also gained shares of services of Establishment institutions, from Extension to the land-grant colleges to USDA. Only some types of groups had such power, however.

8. Rural interests shared little in this accommodation. They lacked sufficient supporters and a generally agreed policy intent. In short, their focus was too diffuse in public policy terms, their advocates too powerless, so they were unable to compete with intense and very specifically directed organized interests.

7

BASIC RURAL PROBLEMS GAIN ATTENTION— ALMOST

From a policymaking perspective, it makes little sense to attribute political power to any groups or ideas that had no impending threats to beat back. Or to mute, at least. On the face of things, that might be expected of rural policy. Perhaps proposals and position-taking never emerged in national government for advocacy of a comprehensive national rural policy. After all, numerous rural scholars have suggested that obvious rural neglect and even the creation of rural inequalities by government have been great.[1] In a dramatic way, a 1990s Rural Sociological Society Task Force on Persistent Rural Poverty concluded that its members saw "a near total inability on the part of U.S. governing institutions to deal successfully with the wide range of American rural needs."[2] In fact, only two relatively modest bills were ever passed: the Rural Development Acts of 1972 and 1980. One was the initiative of a Republican president and the other of a Democrat; both followed years of liberal administration welfare programs.

Doesn't government carefully check objective reality or develop analytical measures of rural needs to jog public policymaking minds? Even when it's so difficult? Perhaps there's already been a hint in chapter 2 that it doesn't. Thus, maybe there have been no serious ideas and advocates to attack. From the outset USDA's mission was to develop and thus be responsible for all of rural America, but that obviously was never its priority.[3] Moreover, as other federal administrative departments such as Commerce, Education, and Transportation took on a few rural programs, USDA was designated to coordinate efforts.[4] Did it do so fairly or seriously in the search for a logically defensible rural policy?

Most of the evidence suggests that it did. Some does not. Yet there definitely were numerous high-visibility, high-stature policy proposals to rou-

74

tinely beat back. These proposals all favored a far more balanced approach than mere reliance on farm and ranch development. Moreover, most proposed ideas were widely publicized presidential initiatives, drafted with careful preparation by ranking rural spokespeople from USDA and later from other departments and the White House. Therefore, the ideas to beat back by those who wanted to keep rural policy as merely a small part of farm policy do appear formidable. As the next section explains, a formidable enemy did recurrently appear, among what could have been friendly farmers. As the succeeding section notes, however, nonfarm rural America never developed an alternative rural lobby to fight back, even in 1972 and 1980.

Apparently, advocates felt that any national rural policy alternative to a national farm public policy would have little chance of success. Nor did it seem likely, probably, that an influential lobby could be crafted out of the multiple and divergent needs of so many and such dispersed nonfarm rural interests and places. It would by necessity be terribly diffuse and generally unfocused in its immediate goals, hardly able to deal adequately with the ever emergent and increasingly intense farm groups.

HOW EXTENSIVE IS THIS HISTORY OF RURAL PROPOSALS?

The answer is simple: It was most extensive. Moreover, it began early, in 1909; even earlier analysis was done by what were becoming experts on rural life. The initial Report of the Country Life Commission was inspired by Theodore Roosevelt's interest in quality of rural living, conservation, and natural resource use.[5] The Report suggested, in strong language, that persistent problems in rural areas were independent of farming and agrarian development needs. That is to say, government shouldn't mix and match rural and farm policies.

Later, during the Great Depression, a newly created Resettlement Administration aimed at removal and relocation of the rural poor so that they could find work.[6] This effort was small but highly touted. All through that Depression and later years, however, leading federal agricultural economists with substantial ties to Franklin Roosevelt openly advocated attention to micro- and macroeconomic rural conditions.[7] Secretary of Agriculture Henry A. Wallace became a strong proponent of rural policy and of farm policy reform—to no avail.[8]

The Eisenhower administration proposed its Rural Development Program with an initial goal of creating off-farm jobs. Rural poverty and hunger were addressed in highly visible fashion during the Lyndon Johnson era.[9]

The National Advisory Commission on Rural Poverty was especially prominent in those years.[10] Johnson, a rural Texan, gave it substantial attention.
Rural development acts were central advances of the Nixon and Carter administrations. Both were tied successfully to reforming federal policies to
allocate funds directly to the states and local governments for their own use.
President Bush (the elder) later proposed a federal Rural Development Administration as part of his failed Rural Development Act of 1989. The Clinton administration once again emphasized more centralized rural policy
attention by forcefully advocating—and then all but completely abandoning—its multifaceted farm, rural, and research proposal, the Fund for Rural
America. Thus, public policy opportunities existed aplenty on the national
political agenda. Each should have encouraged policy-attentive proponents
who might want to organize their interests and advocacy around nonfarm
rural problems.

Although these and other rural policy proposals were always laced with
at least some farm-related concerns (such as agricultural research), agenda
opportunities frequently existed for nonfarm rural advocates to at least attempt to direct discussions to alternative policy wants. There could and
should have been incentives at those peak agenda times for organizing advocacy. Apart from very small attempts, however, such organization never
happened. At first glance, that fact defies academic wisdom, even presum-
ing the imperfect nature of the mobilization of potential interests. The
agenda literature, for example, notes that when a political stream of discussion opens up, groups with a stream-related interest organize and enter
the flow of activity in most policy situations.[11] Why, then, in the midst of so
many apparent chances was there never a resourceful rural lobby? Almost
all of the foregoing initiatives were either very short-lived in their impact or
failed to pass. Why didn't rural activists emerge to press their advantage?

WHO LOBBIED FOR RURAL AMERICA?

Did rural lobbies emerge and merely fail to move rural issues beyond the
early political agenda stage? The answer is a complex "no." To an extent, a
very strong rural lobby came about. Unfortunately, it was composed entirely
of farm groups with competing agendas, such as the AFBF. In actuality, a
real rural lobby of nonfarmers did not emerge. Very few rural groups independent of farming were ever evident. From another perspective, rural lobbying power was extensive. Lots and lots of farm policy was continuously
passed—"by the bucket," as a former Secretary of Agriculture said.[12] In

more objective reality, an independent, alternative, and coherent rural policy voice was all but meaningless and invisible. Rural policy benefits were few and far between, if they were passed apart from farm programs. Let's unravel those two contradictions of interest and policy over time.

In a rural agrarian society, organized interests were more than plentiful. That must be understood. Thousands of U.S. farmer associations organized in the 19th century, many of which exerted grassroots influence over members of Congress and local public officials.[13] None were more successful than locals of the Grange, who organized into a once-formidable national lobby.[14] In addition to the Grangers' highly acclaimed successes on railroad regulation, they scored other policy victories. A rural mail system, parcel post delivery, and elevation of USDA to Cabinet status and a mission greater than just advancing plant and seed science were important Grange accomplishments. These successes did take care of wide-ranging rural needs and wants of that still truly agrarian era: Nonfarmers, for example, got rural mail delivery.

In the process of achieving such victories, farmer organizations quite legitimately acquired reputations as rural spokesgroups. Well they should have, in a society in which "rural" tended to mean mostly farm and ranch. There were, in effect, not many other rural advocacy organizations.[15] Even nationally, the highly significant populist movement was a farm movement rather than a general rural phenomenon.[16] That status as the rural lobby was enhanced by the narrowness of nonfarm rural residents. Farm policy demands usually were ignored by small-town businesses, local organizational leaders (for instance, in churches and banks), and national business interests that wanted successful farm development. They simply let farmers do the politics. Public-sector professionals employed in the rapidly developing Agricultural Establishment of education, research, and extension all encouraged the notion that their grassroots farmer clientele were the rural spokesgroups before government.[17]

By the time a national farm lobby was firmly established in Washington in the 1920s, the rural representation of these groups was at least semi-institutionalized, or almost written into law. It was city versus country in Washington, urban versus rural—but not farm versus rural. Farmers were *the* country rural folks of American politics. That reputation grew firmer still as farm groups were given an active and respected voice in designing Depression-era rural relief programs in the 1920s and 1930s. Most of that effort led to federal commodity price supports as farmer payments in the AAA. Added to the work of Agricultural Establishment specialists who were assisting farmers in developing an industrialized and more economically efficient agriculture, direct farmer payments and related production controls placed the federal government squarely in the midst of improved farm management practices as the intended means for developing rural America.[18] Government policy eggs, so to speak, were literally all placed in one paradigmatic basket: Help farmers grow more, bring them industrial capacity, let them produce more efficiently, have them prosper, and then depend on that prosperity to provide for all the rest of rural people and problems. The institutionalization and promotion of farm development—and of those very influential farm groups who appreciated public-sector farm development assistance—effectively closed the door to alternative rural advocacy.

As a result, American politics came to have a strong, multi-group rural lobby. This lobby always spoke with a heavy farm accent—particularly the accent of large-scale industrializing producers as opposed to smaller-scale subsistence agrarians. Nonetheless, this rural power was strong. Many more newly emerging farm groups quickly came to lobby on behalf of their favored commodity programs and other well-used USDA programs of the 1930s such as credit, electrification, and conservation.

Proliferating groups all shared the same farm industrial accent and claimed as well to be able to provide, through trickle-down economic effects, for all that was rural. Because none of these interests wanted to see any of their favored programs' funding lost, all of them organized to defend their existing policy advantages against any advocacy interlopers with alternative and competitive policy goals. The expected and semi-institutionalized status of farm groups within several policy networks generally made that easy work (at least until 1973).[19] Thus, farmers became that strong but biased rural lobby. Their advocacy was simple: Give more farm assistance, sympathize with community-based rural problems, reject proposed rural policies as too costly, ask that such proposed financial initiatives be folded into farm program funding, and apologize for not being able to win both farm and rural programs. Farm groups, in effect, were the best friends and worst enemies of rural community interests. For example, rural development funds during the Clinton era earmarked funds more easily to farmers than to small communities. Farmers whose crop practices contributed to value-added product development received cash allocations as rural policy budget items.

Yet nonfarm rural problems persisted. Accordingly, several observant and capable public-sector experts within the small rural parts of the Agricultural Establishment always saw them. The goal of these experts was to design a consistent, coherent, and comprehensive rural policy that balanced national farm goals with the national needs of other rural residents. This goal led to that aforementioned spate of frequent and recurring public policy initiatives that advanced to—but not far into—the political agenda. Ironically, however, it did not lead many policy-attentive rural advocates to form organized interests around neglected nonfarm rural problems. Nonfarm rural organizations that actively sought to influence public policy were always extraordinarily small in number, even after farm populations declined more and more into lower single-digit percentages. Before the welfare-oriented 1960s, in truth, such groups really never organized at all. So there was no real nonfarm rural lobby that addressed the wide range of rural problems at an early date.

What emergent post-1960 nonfarm rural organizations shared, in contrast to the many longstanding farm lobbies, was a very small surge and decline. These surges followed the experts' introduction of national, all-purpose rural policy proposals or programs that otherwise proposed benefits to all rural residents as part of the general population. Declines followed policy failure.

Examples best explain. For all practical purposes, Rural America was the single national nonfarm rural interest group that worked on the Johnson administration's Great Society programs. It succeeded in gaining a distinct rural focus to a few poverty programs; this focus on behalf of rural residents was largely won from gains made across the board in all welfare programs.[20] By gaining status as the rural expert within the large advocacy network of liberal welfare rights and labor groups, Rural America helped bring federal dollars and assistance to the rural poor. Those people otherwise might have been ignored in a period in which the focus was on the urban crisis and on disadvantaged and rebellious urban people.[21]

By the mid-1980s, however, Rural America was no longer an active lobby, although it was still around. It died from lack of philanthropic patronage contributions. Yet rural initiatives still reappeared on, for instance, the omnibus farm bill policy agenda of 1985. A few new lobbies predictably appeared to take advantage of that renewed policy stream.[22] Not many did so, however. The Rural Coalition, the Rural Governments Coalition, and the National Rural Housing Coalition (NRHC) each independently brought together their own diverse range of member organizations. All favored continuing "new federalism" budget allocations to and through the states. These coalitions won very little, although they did gain increased funding for Native American reservations, local government public works programs, and construction opportunities for rural builders and contractors.

By the end of the decade, however, when a separate rural development act was proposed, all three coalitions had dissolved, and most of their former group supporters were absent from the policy process. Only two small organizations, managed by two very visible and politically prominent entrepreneurs, attempted to orchestrate the bill from the lobbying side.[23] One had directed the old NRHC; the other was a foundation executive. Both individuals, quite expectedly, were subject to extensive attacks by farm interests for assailing the farm-connected rural policy base. Who would dare say, they seemed to claim, that farmers weren't true rural advocates? The bill died, not surprisingly, only to have some of its provisions attached later to the 1990 omnibus farm bill. Rural water systems gained the major funding victory at that time. They were in vogue because of rampant media reports of nitrate-based pollution of private wells held by numerous farm and rural residents.

The mid-1990s saw more of a surge of new players and a decline of those who had been active in the previous farm bill. Even an academic association, the Rural Sociological Society, lobbied actively for federal research support for its members, as well as for more general rural attention. So too did the land-grant universities, another set of irregular but knowledgeable rural policy players. Better-funded lobbies of the 1990s included the newly formed National Rural Health Association and the one organization that had been always present and active since the 1960s: the National Rural Electric Cooperatives Association (NRECA)—an organization lobbying on behalf of big member-owned utility businesses.

As should be clear, policy proposals by their simple existence have not necessarily encouraged an extensive array of lobbies. The two are not always intricately linked. Items on the political agenda, even with extensive support from public-sector policy experts, did not translate into success. There were no dramatic policy opportunities created by or for the many potentially favored rural interests. Political theorist E. E. Schattschneider was correct: Latent interests often ignore what others presume to be seemingly obvious policy opportunities.[24] Some issues—such as rural ones—apparently are just not regarded as attainable, or as winning ones. Therefore, potentially favored organizations and interests avoid them after examining their prospects for victory. Lobbyists call these "bad" issues.[25] As the next section concludes, factors other than farm group power and institutional policy status are important reasons that nonfarm rural issues tend to be bad ones.

IMPLICATIONS

A basic tenet of political science is the belief that as policy opportunities—or windows—arise, policy-attentive individuals form organized interests.[26]

Some political observers see this dynamic as automatic. The intent of these attentive interests is to win benefits from within the new opportunities. Proactive lobbies, it seems, come about when policy-attentive individuals study a policy situation and then organize and advocate to deal with it.[27] It's a classic case of learning and adjustment, organizing around what can be politically defended.[28]

So, with the plethora of policy positions taken on behalf of nonfarm rural needs, why are rural lobbies so small and so few? The problems of nonfarm rural lobbies apparently begin when a possibly wide range of policy-attentive individuals note their own lack of ties to the institutions within the agricultural public sector. They learn that they and other rural interests operate at a political disadvantage, if they choose to operate at all. So why bother? No reason, they probably say.

Despite the presence of capable and sympathetic rural experts within the Agricultural Establishment, such individuals and their agencies are not a critical mass. They have long held a minority nonfarm status. Their very expertise and knowledge of rural society developed over the past century as an add-on to USDA and service providers, mandated by the Establishment's claim that rural America was farm America's responsibility. As a result, although rural experts can get things on the preliminary policy agenda of a national leader, by themselves, they apparently can't keep them there as those agendas evolve. If the institutions don't care, interests won't bother. There's no real opportunity—or so it seems.

This analysis, of course, is consistent with the explanation of the Rural Sociological Society as its task force once sought to explain rural policy failure.[29] Farm power and extensive farm networks take over rural agenda proposals.[30] The acquiescence of the rural poor and powerless comes into play.[31] Farm groups then dump their rural proposals.

Still other factors are at work. Much has been going on within this process that also explains even more about why persistent nonfarm rural interests have not developed in the face of plentiful opportunities to organize. Indeed, there is a linkage between public policy debates and who organizes to participate in them. This relationship is not always random or illogical.[32] The answer lies in who really cares about rural policy. Appearing before a joint committee of Congress, a leading rural expert once observed that things are easily explained. In all his experiences, he simply never found a true constituency for those rural policy experts' goals of consistent, coherent, and comprehensive national rural policy. [33] Supporters can't be found when government looks. They can't be encouraged if government tries to encourage them with promises of increasing attention.

Yet many specific or selective types of rural interests have been and are advantaged by gains made by their representatives on nonfarm rural policies. It's just that their efforts and their gains are logically and satisfactorily minimalist, not comprehensive.[34] Successful rural interests periodically organize, form loose associations or coalitions with one another, surge and decline—or come and go—within the policy process as they want, and extract minimal (but for them consequential) policy victories.[35] They get a little that they like, and then scoot. They fail to pursue the experts' oft-advanced goal of broader or wide-ranging rural policy, though. And these policy-attentive individuals don't pursue that goal with vigor because they understand full well that their loose institutional linkages, as contrasted with those of farm groups, mean they won't likely win anything on such a large scale anyway.

Organized interests that lack any strong institutional ties must pursue political gains and relationships in different ways than those who have greater insider status.[36] At the same time, though, these interests and those who represent them seldom conclude that their own highly specific goals—or desired selective benefits—are invalid, inappropriate, or implausible.[37] Instead, as these lobbies become politically attentive, they seek to find ways to get as much as they can for their own very selective, narrowly focused supporters: reservations, water systems, rural construction. For the National Association of Counties, for example, it's always been rural roads and bridges. Interest groups shop around, so to speak. As a consequence, they play a more restrained political game, sticking to a set of—for them—basic rather than generically national rural demands.

What have rural interests typically done? Three strategies stand out: the pursuit of limited, or selective, policy benefits; little commitment to national rural policy; and frequent involvement with nonrural interest coalitions. First, they've generally sought their own noncollective or selective policy benefits. The goals they advocate selectively reward those who support each lobby or otherwise share specific characteristics with the supporters. More accurately, those who have had the substantial resources required to lobby have followed this strategy. Water systems, rural electric cooperatives, county governments, contractors, and a large assortment of other, better-funded, interests have won tangible rural policy benefits of this sort since the 1960s. Even Rural America, with its limited funding, more or less followed this strategy by sticking to poverty issues. Idealized policy abstractions about things rural as opposed to very specific rural needs are avoided. Rural interests individually keep to the core of what their members or supporters want and will use. In a sense, they imitate commodity farm group strategies (i.e., doing what different types of crop farmers want). They look for bits and take available pieces.

Second, rural interests that do organize seldom concern themselves with furthering such encompassing policies as the oft-advanced national rural development legislation. That's too abstract and diffuse. It means nothing. Instead, as their policy-attentive representatives shop around politically, they attach their own unique goals to other legislation—bills that are more likely to pass. Farm bills, which recur every few years because of legislative requirements, are the most common such vehicles.[38] Other bills work as well, however: A Clean Water Act can provide opportunities for conservation goals or for rural parks; welfare legislation can assist the rural poor; a health care reform proposal can be the vehicle for providing more stable rural health care facilities (if it ever passes).

Third, attentive rural interests, as a consequence, develop multi-interest coalitions wherever they can, on whatever bills they can. They don't restrict themselves to coalitions with other actual or potential rural groups. Nor do they stick to rural policy bills only. No one sits around and ponders whether all rural problems are being represented. That is, these groups, like many others, pursue short-term coalitions when they can do so—with whomever they can do it.[39] Encompassing rural coalitions of several rural groups (but only rural groups), in fact, seem unlikely to be favored. They appear quite unlikely to accomplish policy goals for the participating partners. In all likelihood, their proposed policies lose. Although this behavior negates the long-term potential of any singularly strong nonfarm rural lobby, it matters little. And it ensures that some rural interests may win at least a little on some legislation or another.

What, then, are the results? As the Rural Sociological Society observed, this form of strategic policy adaptation means that the wide range of America's rural needs continue to be ignored.[40] Most rural problems can't be adequately addressed in this fashion because they require a comprehensive, interactive, and system-wide rural vision or because they are representative of poor and powerless rural interests that are least likely to organize.[41] Thus, persistent nonfarm rural problems are not simply the fault of farm power and the powerlessness of the rural poor. The strategies of the most resourceful and successful rural organized interests are to blame as well: They give up on the rural vision; yet they do so without much choice.

SUMMARY OF KEY POINTS

There have been numerous national rural policy challenges for farm interests to defeat. Most, however, have been administration proposals and positions rather than the threat brought forward by strong rural lobbies. What seems unusual at first glance is that those many proposals have not evoked strong rural interests. Certain key points explain why:

1. Since the Report of the Country Life Commission in 1909, and particularly since the Great Depression, most presidential administrations have advanced nonfarm rural programs toward the national political agenda.

2. Those programs have rarely advanced very far beyond the agenda-setting or preliminary policy stage. When rural items have passed into law, they have been only secondary parts of presidential administration initiatives, or they have been short-lived.

3. A rural lobby, independent of farm groups, was never evident until well after World War II. After that, few organized interests articulated nonfarm rural policy.

4. Most of the resourceful nonfarm rural lobbies that emerged and found a modicum of success were groups that desired specific selective benefits for themselves, such as rural water systems, housing construction contracts, or Native American reservation benefits. None of these groups was much concerned with a consistent, comprehensive, and complete nonfarm national rural policy for the rural poor and their declining communities. That goal was too abstract.

5. That goal also was regarded as likely to be unattainable given the weak institutional ties of rural folks as compared to farm groups. Why fight the likely winners? No damn reason.

6. Policy-attentive individuals who organize groups came to that conclusion as a result of learned political responses. They observed and studied politics, came to suspect farm group motives, and generally shunned rural advocacy.

7. As a consequence, policy-attentive individuals did jump into rural policy debates. Yet they generally did so through limited opportunities and on behalf of selective policy benefits. These folks and their organizations gained a few things as a result.

8. This opportunistic, fragmenting behavior also can be cited as a reason that a comprehensive rural policy never found much favor. Self-interested behavior and limited opportunities were as much a problem for serious policy reform as were farm groups and the acquiescent behavior of the nonorganized rural poor and powerless. Rural interests were content with striking out on their own, for but a pocketful of silver coins.

8

CONCENTRATED *but* FRAGMENTED PUBLIC INSTITUTIONS

So, how *are* the agricultural institutions organized? That comes next. It's been argued that political change has a way of forcing alteration in a bureaucracy's original intent and mission. That's true, even as proponents of that change insist that the alteration merely works out the true purposes for which that bureaucracy initially was designed.[1] Such a justification certainly describes the evolving expansion of interests served by the Agricultural Establishment. The poor and hungry receive nearly the same allocation of federal budget dollars for food programs as farmers receive for farm programs, so policy change indeed has occurred. Regulation also has come to USDA as a major responsibility, for areas from nutrition to environmental quality.[2] However, legal scholars who note USDA's new regulatory focus also claim that the Department best exemplifies bureaucratic resistance to change in its basic, most valued mission.[3] Even while it spends large sums on food needs, USDA still responds primarily and in many ways to farmer constituencies and their promotion. Organizationally, moreover, USDA and other establishment institutions are designed around farm needs almost exclusively. Those organizations have been only marginally altered to encompass service to other interests, including those of rural communities and nonfarmers. That's certainly a concentrated effect of emphasizing farm services. Farmers came and come first. Rural America becomes a public policy stepchild.

For rural interests and problems, that alteration of institutions was particularly marginal and ineffective over time. Farm prosperity was still equated with eventual rural prosperity, if only farm products could be efficiently and economically marketed. Some myths never change, or change in their impact. At least, that message of farm-equals-rural persisted within these evolving and altered institutional designs and their organization within the Establishment. This point also has been made before—perhaps too often.

This chapter's basic intent is to specifically examine the institutional designs that bureaucratically organize to serve and promote agriculture—and neglect nonfarm rural interests—within the American nation-state. The purpose is to show how farmers prevail, albeit in a fragmented public policy sense, and how basic rural problems of poverty and decline receive minimal attention. Rural needs other than farming are institutionally disadvantaged by bureaucratic structure, from Congress to USDA to the land-grant colleges. Within the organizations of governance, rural policy means little because it has few proponents and planners apart from those with a farm mission. No institution within the Agricultural Establishment is neutral and objective about serving farmers first (though some may not be enthusiastic about it).

The first section starts with Congress, the next looks at USDA's structural arrangements, and the third examines other selected and locally active Establishment organizations. In all instances, the following observation is clear: Although agricultural governance and service was originally intended to have both a farm and a rural mission, the rural mission gets short shrift in organized rulemaking even today. Institutions that have been established or operated for generic rural problems are relatively few and underpowered. They get sucked up and overwhelmed in an institutional whirlpool of attention to farm policy needs and farm wants and farm regulation.

CONGRESS DECIDES

One very informed and very senior member of Congress once made a very telling request: "Don't talk to [my constituents] about that rural policy business. We're here to inform them about and get their feedback on the proposed dairy program."[4] His meaning was obvious. It was more than the fact that his wasn't a natural constituency for promoting rural policy. That very popular congressional member was getting the electoral populace—his voters—fired up about farm policy and what he could do with it for them. He wasn't about to solicit grassroots information about general rural needs. Nor was he interested in putting voters in the position of thinking about rural community decline as something the federal government and he should address more carefully.

From his perspective, why should he? His dairy-dependent district had immediate problems that an existing congressional committee was institutionally well organized to address. On the other hand, Congress was not well organized to deal with any hoped-for rural policy. Nor was this member positioned to actually do anything about rural community decline if the issue (God forbid) came up. As that member noted, "What you can do depends on where you're situated, what issues you're assigned to review and recommend."[5] Left unsaid was the member's belief that a congressional representative also tried to get situated in a position that resulted in district votes. Dairy did; rural didn't seem to.

It may be a stretch to think of Congress as a bureaucracy. Usually the term is reserved for public agencies and departments—the administrative state of numerous professional experts, managers, and their associates. Administrative units of government collectively formulate public policy designs, deliver program services, help determine who gets their benefits, and find out whether policy succeeds or not. In short, the administrative state—along with others—*develops, implements, and evaluates* specific public programs.[6] "With others" is the key phrase. Congress also plays a very formal role in each of these three stages, which puts it constantly at center stage among elected politicians in policymaking. More importantly in thinking of Congress as bureaucracy, that legislative institution has structured a complex and evolving organization of its own to do its work.[7] Members of Congress *do* believe that they occupy a single and constrained niche—or situation—in a large-scale and rule-bound organization.[8] Actually, they exist within a series of not well-coordinated organizations: parties, caucuses, committees, subcommittees. They are simply parts of parts within their own institution. Nonetheless, all components, or at least parts of them, must work collectively to produce any product, or law.

That, indeed, is bureaucracy: formally organizing to work jointly to produce a product. At the turn of the 20th century, the organization of Congress was strongly top-down, or hierarchical. Congressional leaders ran the show. The show was concentrated in their hands. They directed legislative business. In the 1920s, congressional leaders were able to halt internal legislative discussion of farm relief programs. Their pragmatic focus was elsewhere, on other types of public policy—notably tariff legislation.[9] Their time and energies were spent in getting enough votes to form majorities on those other prioritized matters. Member careers, therefore, were most affected by leadership conclusions drawn about each individual.

That institutional organization gradually changed, however. So too did the matter of who within Congress directed the course of legislation. Farm issues led the way for this reform. It became apparent in the 1920s and 1930s that voters would express their opinions on legislative performance by voting for and against farm-state members of Congress. As a result, the leadership mattered less to members. Members from nonfarm states began to see similar electoral dynamics applying to them on different issues. They were worried first about their own electorate as the people who would most affect their continuing in office. These ambitious members increasingly regarded Congress as a professional career for themselves; staying around was the key to having a career.

As a result, reform of congressional organization—the institution itself—became the rule of the day. The congressional rank-and-file moved to give more institutional power to a series of decentralized and thus fragmented legislative committees. The committees would respond to specific public problems, such as agriculture, commerce, and transportation. As a practical matter, jurisdiction over those policy areas was permanently assigned to the committees. Committees would organize to design policy, structure implementation rules, and evaluate past and future program needs. Members gained the right to get committee proposals on the agenda of both houses of Congress.[10] They no longer needed to suck up to the leaders to get agenda status. A renewed legislative bureaucracy emerged, more reminiscent of the mid-19th century after the demise of strong Senate Whig Party leader Henry Clay than of the early 1900s era of dominant partisan leaders.

Individual members gained more policy responsibility and influence along with these changes. Thus, the aforementioned congressional member—the one who avoided rural policy discussion—was situated on the agriculture committee. The niche or situation he occupied there was for rank-and-file review and recommendations on dairy programs. His suggestions often, if not always, were definitive in rulemaking on dairy matters. Rural programs, however, were not within his niche. Nor were formulating dairy or rural programs the responsibility of the leadership of the modern era, as they were in that earlier turn-of-the-century period of strong leadership. So it's no wonder that The Honorable Dairy-Dependent District wanted discussions back home of dairy programs. Bureaucratized congressional structure—the federal legislative institution—allowed him to do something about those issues, but not unrelated ones. He was regarded as an independent legislative island of power for dairy policy.[11] He was just a fragmented part—the dairy part—of concentrated farm benefits and services. His home district needs came easily to the political organization of his Washington, a perfect fit. So he served within two institutions of two establishments: Agriculture and the Congress.

That's the way things were generally within the bureaucratic structure of Congress in the mid-1960s and early 1970s, especially for agriculture. The agriculture committees of both houses were made up overwhelmingly of members from rural districts and states. This was in a time when 203 of 435 (47 percent) of all House districts were rural.[12]

The specific result was important, particularly for rural communities. Not all rural districts and states were represented in agriculture committee seating. Such was the habit that had emerged within the congressional institution. Nearly all rural committee members came from heavily farm districts and states, not from the woods of the Great North or other nonfarm rural areas. They were selected because they came from places where single types of crops were dominant. Moreover, it was expected that these selected members would be spokespersons for the unique, specialized, and economically important crops on which their constituents depended. Again, there is a single reason in this long essay for an important question: Why? Pro-agrarian philosphers have said that political theorist John Locke posthumously mentored Americans in the design of their organizational structure—at least for the institutional Congress.[13] If he did, it was with a very Madisonian intent. Citizen power was to be directed though one's own elected representatives, the ones from back home, who then were to gain positions of home-relevant influence in national government. So all this seemed just fine. The congressional institution bent to the will of the agricultural institution, on policy questions if not always finances.

Representatives from unique and limited geographic areas were then to serve those different and varied constituencies—that is, the home folks. This arrangement truly fractured the notion of a Congress directed to the national public interest. So rural America had dairy congresspeople, corn congresspeople, wheat congresspeople, and the like. Eventually there were even food stamp congresspeople. There were no rural generalists, however, to include on the House and Senate committees that also controlled rural policy initiatives. General policy for all of agriculture, including rural programs, was to be worked out, or negotiated, by those very different committee members. They worked out the not-so-easy task of governance in America. That is, things on the two committees were *theoretically* as Locke supposedly intended. The entire committee of farm commodity spokespeople was to develop a national plan, as a negotiated compromise among crops. That ideal, however, was as far as philosophy went. Pragmatism took over, as it usually does.

As Locke and Madison probably did not intend, the compromise served only a narrow farm interest. It compromised only on those exact crop wants and needs that were represented. It was a classic logroll: You support me, and I'll support you. It did not take into account any interest that was based on all national needs—nor all rural needs, which were too troublesome, too high in transaction costs. That would have been too difficult. Rural policy, as a consequence, had no chance at all in the Congresses of the 1960s.

Organizationally, things then went downhill for the national—and thus for any rural—interest. The mid-1970s and after were another time of reform of this basic policymaking institution. It was a revolt against strong committee leaders. That revolt, however, did only a wee bit to reinstate central partisan leadership influence. It moved mostly toward further congressional decentralization, even greater fragmentation of that institution. The essential idea was to give greater power to the subcommittees of the standing committees.[14] Influence was further dispersed as the subcommittees gained fixed jurisdictions over what were their programs to review and recommend; these subcommittees had their own workable staffs and adequate budgets for doing so and were placed under the jurisdiction of a single subcommittee member who chaired only that one institutional subunit of Congress. The latter reform nearly ensured the attentiveness of the chair, who had no other leadership duties to serve in Congress and divide her attention. Obviously, full committees and their chairs lost power: the ability to keep some policy ideas out of sight and so out of legislation. This evolution further opened the door for a hierarchically unresponsive institutional setting within Congress. This was where Mr. Dairy-Dependent District really shined. He chaired the agriculture committee's dairy subcommittee in the House.

Yet even as subcommittees grew in number, not all policy ideas gained equal places within the new institutional structure of more than 120 such initiating subunits. Instead, these reforms addressed just one troublesome institutional problem of the committee system: the diminishing ability to compromise in committee when members represented diverse constituents. For example, it was once predicted that the agriculture committees could not eventually divide up allotted budget dollars satisfactorily among all crop interests in a single bill. An impasse would be created when each crop represented by congressional members and lobbyists insisted on greater benefits for their own kind—and when they then wanted less for others in a war of all-against-all.[15] Although that threat of impasse was real, those who feared it overlooked the institutional and interest capacities that created farmer power. Farm representatives were not about to die on the sword tip of a nondecision. Even under a single bill and with strong committee rules, as previously, farm advocates had a will to succeed and an understanding of how to do so through intercrop negotiation. Farm commodity groups met with agricultural professionals under a formally organized coalition to divide up price support and farm-income enhancement spoils. (Oops, benefits.) That is, they compromised together on the budgeted dollars—as Locke liked? Members of Congress who had crop representation responsibilities also met with these lobbyists and usually accepted their negotiated agreements.[16]

Later, when each crop had its own or its own part of a smaller subcommittee, the subcommittees shared decision making in the same general way: in committee. Why change a good and workable plan? They fought and agreed to proposals on various pieces of farm bills and farm budgets that different commodities and subcommittees could live with. Issue champions simply had more formal and more formally advanced advocacy presentations. Rural problems, however, were still crushed by a weight-of-numbers disadvantage (see chapter 2). With diffuse goals, few represented interests, and no track record of a return on previous government investment, rural policy advocates had little or no standing in what became final committee negotiations to advance any bill. There was little reason to listen to them to get a complex bill through committee. Forget that.

Examples show this institutional weight-of-numbers disadvantage for rural policy. By 1986, subcommittee governance was well established. The House Agriculture Committee divided into eight subcommittees; the Senate committee split into six. In the House, four subcommittees represented 11 types of crops and critters. One subcommittee had jurisdiction over rural policy, along with the far bigger issues of agricultural conservation and farm credit. Rural policy was handled by a single Senate subcommittee that also was responsible for the busy work of congressional oversight of agriculture and all of its investigations (evaluations, that is to say). It had only three members, all from important farm states. Its responsibilities, however, did not include rural electrification, where the interests of the best represented and wealthiest rural advocacy group (NRECA) were concentrated. Four of the other five nonrural policy subcommittees handled various aspects of established farm programs, including farm credit—which also was paired with the rural electrification interest giant, NRECA. Again, it was the diminution of general rural policy that mattered. It had a minute institutional place.

Fifteen years later, things were little different, even though subcommittee proliferation had been reined in a bit. In the House Agriculture Committee, only four subcommittees remained by 2000. None of them had *any* rural policy focus. Control over rural issues and interests was left to one subcommittee under the nebulous and thus plausibly ignored responsibilities of USDA operations and agricultural oversight. All of it! The Senate committee also had four subcommittees that year. One subcommittee dealt with rural revitalization, along with the major and frequently recurring issues of forestry and conservation. The other three subcommittees all handled farm program benefits and regulation, including research. In a decade and a half of declining farm population numbers, with periodic increases in other rural residents and industries, the institutional structure of Congress never shifted in its orientation toward its agricultural clientele. In fact, it had become more farm focused. As a result, rural policy initiatives were largely buried in the ancient institutional history of farm policy traditions. Although the institutional structure of Congress had been redesigned and fragmented, its concentrated agriculture institutional focus prevailed in lasting form. Policy shifts toward nonfarm rural interests were therefore very unlikely.

FEDERAL ADMINISTRATIVE STATE

The discussion that follows largely repeats the key points in the preceding section. There's ample evidence to draw on. USDA at one time was the subject of detailed analysis by many of an early era's leading scholars of public administration. Some argued that it was quite naturally a farm service department.[17] That was fine then, for them. Another noted that politics and administration were inseparable in USDA, presumably because of continuous farmer intervention.[18] One scholar, however, expressed more than a bit of outrage. This most prominent administrative theorist, J. Pendelton Herring, found it particularly irritating that farm interest group leaders justified the department's narrow focus on the basis of farmers' status above any other group on earth.[19] Farmers, therefore, needed—no, deserved—their own top-level federal service institution, of which they were kings. Herring, in effect, was angered by two things: the blatant expression of righteous farm group power and those interests' manipulative use of that old agrarian myth. He probably also should have been angered by the lack of program coordination in USDA.

It's somewhat more curious that these early–20th-century administrative types weren't angered that USDA did not organize as a neutral institution that balanced farmer needs and wants with those of others in society. These were, after all, highly principled people, smitten with democratic fervor.[20] Yet they probably also saw farmers as the true backbone of society. The myth must have hit them—hard, it seems. Thus, most public administration experts found the USDA of the 1930s and 1940s appropriately organized into several diverse agencies dealing with selective but quite different aspects of existing farm policy. "Let 'em go" was the management theme. One agency dealt with credit, another with soil conservation, one with commodity price supports, and so on: real fragmentation—reflecting efficient organization, of course, but not designed for comprehensive policy review. No one had institutionalized agencies with the tasks of consumer use, nutrition, food assistance, or more generically rural issues and interests than the prevailing concentration on farm enterprises. (Nor had anything similar ever been the case in the Department's pre-1930 history.) Protecting the old family farm was just fine with principles and democratic aspirations, as long as it wasn't carried to what some bemoaned as a possible but unspecified extreme.[21] Such as, perhaps, creating an entire Agricultural Establishment, unmatched in government size, that seems extraordinarily encompassing? Was that or was it not extreme policymaking? It was, at least, for the institutional traditions of U.S. government—in putting farmers first, as sorts of kings. Or unique people.

By the 1960s, and for the following decades, public administration specialists paid little attention to USDA. Their general conclusion was that it was a clientele department—that is, for farmers. So what did these specialists say when they paid any attention at all? The only question raised about USDA was about its real clients: Who were they? With small-scale farmers, big-farm operations, forestry control, food stamps, and such, USDA logically should have been having a hard time determining its precise and proper clientele.[22]

Of course, USDA was never finding that difficult. Not at all. History, through ideas and organizations, taught the lesson. USDA knew what its job was: to help farmers develop and modernize, even to expand their operations, and to produce with the greatest economy and efficiency. As another example of the department's neglect, USDA spent years ignoring organic farming, which officials until the late 1990s tended to view as backward and nonproductive. This modernization emphasis is evident in the divisions of labor within the Department of the late 1960s.[23] Five assistant secretaries directed five agencies of USDA: marketing, agricultural economics, science and education, commodity programs and trade, and—surprise—the strange and forced mix of rural development and conservation. Four of the agencies were blatantly organized for modernizing farmer clients. Together they supervised 15 bureaus, each set to serve different interests of farmers. The agency that monitored rural development efforts supervised five more bureaus: farmer cooperative services, the Farmers Home Administration, the Forest Service, soil conservation, and rural electrification. None were proponent bureaus, planning a national rural policy and working for community development. Three were mostly for operational farmers; one managed national forests and their many roads and the needs of timber companies (or lumber farmers?); the last served that single big wealthy rural interest: the rural electrification industry and NRECA.

The agency title—rural development and conservation—was a sham, a facade to serve USDA in the liberal era of the emergent American poor peoples' welfare state—perhaps trying to fool Lyndon Johnson? The only rural effort made was for all five of the affiliated bureaus to undertake some programs for poverty-ridden nonfarm rural America. These programs were to be essentially what each bureau could throw together given its talents. Where were their talents? In serving farmers, of course. Moreover, these quality-of-life programs were instigated only at the operational or bureau level of the department because of conceptual worries by each of that era's secretaries of agriculture. These secretaries, of course, were the politically appointed department leaders of presidents Kennedy and Johnson; the latter claimed to be especially moved by the poverty of his native rural Texas Hill County. Therefore, secretarial loyalties were more to the stated goals of these two politically liberal administrations than to the traditional and hierarchical ways of USDA. So they avoided the hierarchy when possible, as strange mixes of centralists and anti-institutionalists. The secretaries said things like: There was a need for a "national policy" for "smaller cities and towns," to deal with the rural crisis of "too little of everything—jobs, income, education, and services."[24] Blah, blah, blah.

Such initiatives were easier to talk about than to put into effect, however, even in coining gibberish. Institutions, you see. Reluctance to change. Bureaucracies. Neither Congress nor the career civil service professionals of USDA could see breaking from the farmers-first role of the department. Who would protect them if they did? Things were just like Herring had found them more than 30 years earlier—driven by repetitious myth and farm group influence.

Nor did the calls of these liberal secretaries of agriculture quickly (or even slowly) spur things for future USDA change. By 1990—after still another 30 years—there were 30 operational bureaus running programs under deputy and assistant secretarial units (that is, the former agencies). About 15 other bureaus conducted department business for daily management or ran bureaucratically expansive programs with other agencies such as the Navy, Energy, and the National Oceanic and Atmospheric Administration. Of the 30 USDA program bureaus, 23 operated on behalf of farm services.

Of the regulatory remainder, four ran food nutrition programs, one was for national forests, and two did the work of the former Rural Electrification

Administration. Rural programs or planning pertaining to jobs, income, education, and services were still scattered among a few bureaus with primarily farm responsibilities, such as the Economic Research Services (ERS) and the Agricultural Stabilization and Conservation Service (ASCS). The ERS did such things as research small city and rural county problems; the ASCS provided locally delivered benefits such as trees and tree planting assistance to nonfarm rural areas in erodable locations. ASCS also governed price support payments and loan guarantees—the big economic items for farmers.

There was more to the biasing problem of the federal administrative state than the infinitesimal institutionalization of rural policy within the farm-oriented USDA. By the 1990s, numerous scholars other than those familiar agricultural economists and rural sociologists were attracted to rural problems. Anthropologists, demographers, historians, human sociologists, philosophers, political scientists, and psychologists were pointing to the need for public policy attention to nonfarm rural America.[25] Some of their research had even been funded by USDA, as well as by foundations that historically funded farm research projects. Not much came of this funding, though.

Scholars apparently are not major agenda setters for the public sector. No public outcry emerged. No new rural interest groups galvanized. Few people contacted their members of Congress on behalf of renewed concern for rural life problems and needs. So elected politicians were not moved to respond to scholarly complainants. Professors rarely matter in the real world? Even the operational bureaus proved that to be the case, as no new rural programs were developed and forwarded on within the political process. So much for secretarial hopes.

By this time, however, several other federal departments were working on rural project proposals. Some, such as rural education and technology use, were already in operation. To encourage more of this, and to coordinate efforts, Presidents Reagan and Bush (the elder) maintained a Cabinet Council Working Group on Rural Communities. The Secretary of Agriculture was appointed as its chair, where jurisdiction indeed lay because of USDA's historic and institutional mission.[26]

Of course, farm, food, and trade issues were more pressing for the Secretary than rural policy. And little enthusiasm existed within USDA to support or prompt the Secretary's rural involvement. So the Departments of Commerce, Education, Energy, Labor, Transportation, and others were not further encouraged by USDA to extend their existing and proposed rural program efforts. As a consequence, there appeared to be little incentive for non-USDA departments to develop and undertake rural policy initiatives. The result, in the end, was that rural America not only gained very little from USDA; it also gained very few benefits from elsewhere within the expansive federal administrative state. Prevailing and traditional institutions were structured in other directions, for other policies, in almost all instances. Rural interests lost to long-standing interests, everywhere—and the Cabinet Working Group disappeared.

LOCAL SERVICE INSTITUTIONS

What of the local level, however? Weren't those Establishment organizations that were closest to the visible traumas of rural community life more likely to see and appreciate them? Wouldn't they do something? If seeing a problem were the criterion for instigating government action, one would guess that they would (the public interest at work?). The guess would be that research projects from the experiment stations, direct assistance from extension workers, and assorted land-grant college activities would inundate tiny little towns and desolate places. But no, that wasn't to be. Institutions, it must be remembered, operate in a highly ordered and historically formal world. Rules from above (or wherever) are followed, by golly. There never were rules, however, to coordinate and link the various bureaus that operated in local places. Quite the contrary.

All that counted was that the rules and rulemakers had been established to serve farms. These directives came from the top ranks of the administrative nation-state—the policymakers. Once policy agendas were institutionalized in this way, they were not easily reversed by local sympathizers and rational planners. Only a negligible interest emerged, then, in quality-of-life rural issues. Let's briefly review local service institutions to see why. The land-grant universities—at least a few of them—arrived on the scene first. Each, at the core, had colleges of agriculture to enhance farm development and modernization. Although many also established colleges of home economics to improve farm food and material use, none had anything resembling colleges of rural life.

Within the agriculture colleges of these universities, specialized departments proliferated. Departments of horticulture, animal husbandry, agricultural education, and agricultural economics—as well as many others— became commonplace. These departments were not to be affiliates of disciplinary science departments of biology and zoology. Nor were they to affiliate with colleges of education, or usually, social science or business school departments of economics. Farmers, the myth advised as it traveled widely, needed their own fragmented array of educational organizations for their own purposes. Fuzzy-minded folks, it seems. With few exceptions, administrators still apparently believe this, or are forced to do so, because those academic departments generally survive intact today. The importance of this independence is that the departments established curricula for students and sanctioned research options for faculty members. Not surprisingly, farming needs dominated instruction and research in the land-grant colleges of agriculture.

Even in the face of national policy initiatives such as the Rural Life Commission and rural crises such as the population migrations of the Great Depression, rural nonfarm interests mattered little. Yet the land-grant colleges and their universities did stake out claims to rural policies and problems. Furthermore, they still cling to them—mostly to avoid competition in state funding from other state university campuses. Rural sociology departments became common. There were rural resource economics departments and management departments with rural community concerns. Landscape architecture departments sometimes devised rural planning curricula. Agricultural economics departments generally were allocated one or a few faculty positions to analyze rural community economics. In time, obligatory programs were added to demonstrate land grant commitment to the broad rural mission of the Morrill Act. Rural government specialists were added at many schools to assist the amateurs of small-town politics. Rural education staff advised small school districts; rural medicine and rural public health management gained departmental status on some campuses.

Thus, although the land-grant colleges became known for their institutional rural mission, comparisons with the range of farming services demonstrated that actual commitment was once again only a facade. A new animal industries center on a campus generated far more excitement in any given year then did all of that university's nonfarm rural involvement.

That game of pretend was all but avoided by the second outreach service institution—the Agricultural Research Service (ARS). Crops and farm animals were the general topics of ARS research and development.[27] That, after all, made sense because of the specialized technical purpose of the ARS as central to farm modernization. Yet that bureau also always spoke of its rural life contributions. Faster-growing and disease-resistant trees were ARS contributions to family back yards and rural forest industries. Breakthroughs in developing better plant ornamentals for ground cover, yard brush, and floral displays also were announced with fanfare.

Yet all of the ARS's rural life rhetoric was minor patter. It was akin to the rhetoric attendant with the substantive contribution of ASCS's distribution (through the Agricultural Conservation Program) of tree plantings to non-farm residents, or its periodic efforts to fund and construct farm ponds that were used primarily for neighborhood and family recreation. By offering swimming opportunities, fishing adventures, and fanciful picnic sites, USDA's upstart commodity support agency, with county offices every-where, made the case that farm programs really benefited all Americans—urban and rural. These nonfarmer folks just didn't receive regular ASCS support checks. No big deal? Think again.

The third major outreach institution of the Agricultural Establishment made a better case for providing general community service than did the land grants or the ARS—and, of course, more than the give-away ASCS. The federal Extension Service was certainly set up to deliver new and useful in-formation to modernizing farmers. In the earliest accounts of extension agent activities, the tales were always of working directly and sympatheti-cally with farmers.[28] Yet the peculiar organization of Extension's operational structure made it behave differently than the instruction and research arms of the land-grant colleges. As a creature of national and the intentionally more influential state governments, Extension was poised and conditioned to serve varied constituencies. State-to-state differences were complex and often unique to single places (e.g., Montana, or New Jersey and its green belt).

Moreover, with Extension's operational location in each of the counties of the states, its employees were not only flexible but also especially sensi-tive to local and changing community problems. After all, they were often located in county courthouses and received some county funding. In urban areas, accordingly, it seemed strangely inadequate for Extension specialists to assist only with personal gardening needs and the operation of commer-cial greenhouses and those few remaining city farms.

The result was intriguing. State Extension offices were located on the land-grant campuses, had at least partial control of several faculty members (whose salaries they paid), and were involved in university planning and assessment of the institutional service roles of the colleges. Therefore, Ex-tension had some leverage in securing local assistance from select campus resources, including obtaining skilled faculty. In urban areas, local Exten-sion professionals increasingly saw the need for involvement in personal health, local government, and even problem areas such as sanitation and transportation. With campus support, many state Extension services moved to assist in these and other areas.

This general trend began to be observed as well, especially in nonfarm rural areas.[29] Extension offices moved to get involved in the delivery of selected county and regional services, community planning, government reorganization, and even local political reform efforts. Soon the Extension Service had a justifiable reputation for being a broadly serving community player. Nonetheless, farm services predominated in nearly all of the states—and certainly in farm regions. Despite some criticisms of meandering away from Extension's farm mission, its administrators were almost always shrewd enough to recognize that farmers had to come first when they wanted and requested services. These administrators, of course, documented that whatever service their offices performed had that old pro-farm bias, at least in theory. Farmers still came first, from any public-sector farmers' organization—or they should. At least that was the Establishment's, or the newly designed American nation-state's, expectation. Attention was to be concentrated, even when the attentive never reasoned together.

IMPLICATIONS

One could easily ask: So what? Why shouldn't farmers come first within an Agricultural Establishment? Why should services be designed as coordinated and comprehensive? Let's look first at why these troublesome developments occurred in answering those questions, for they say much about American democracy and its public policy approach.

The shifting design of the political institutions of agriculture demonstrates nothing less than the full-blown, if incomplete, creation of an American nation-state.[30] In an unprecedented way, the creation of that part of the state served and provided for farming, at least. It may be more than that mere part, however (as I argue below). What institutional design shows here is an ongoing and historical status commitment to one set of citizens, with a corresponding rulemaking neglect of another potentially competing set. That may be the key to understanding the American state as a whole. In this case, this nation-state has countenanced the creation of several specific and tangible institutions as skilled organizations that are unabashedly for-farmers-first, not for the public as a whole and not for an alternate rural clientele. That behemoth called the Agricultural Establishment (as the state) is merely an ongoing and semi-related issue area of recurring policy participant organizations that are collectively pro-farmer—when, that is, farmers are further modernizing: when the best and brightest farmers are using their greater resources in the intended way. When, for example, organic farming finds a large and growing—and quite profitable—market in the late 1990s, thereby becoming part of the modern farm sector. That, of course, was the society that had the Agricultural Establishment's ear. These organizations generally have been freed to plan for and do whatever they do best, regardless of other organizations, as long as they provided for farm interests.

The developing agricultural state as it intersected with the whole of a pro-farm society of believers of myth created a strongly pro-farm politics.[31] Let's think about previous chapter conclusions. The intersection of state and society brought a farmer-led and politically scary social movement, the eventual emergence from that movement of many powerful farm interest groups, pioneering grassroots political strategies of these groups, a resulting emphasis on constituent politics as predominant concerns of increasingly careerist elected politicians and professionalized administrators, the gravitation of political control over agriculture to Congress as the predominant constituent or grassroots institution, and the final breakdown of a once-concentrated yet diffusely supported agricultural policy by intense interests. Policy broke into a fragmented set of autonomous programs run mostly for independent members of Congress by friendly administrators on behalf of farm folks back home.

Farm politics settled into a pattern in which the whole of society let a diversified and piecemeal farm community govern itself.[32] As it wanted. Nonfarmers merely acquiesced and stayed out of the way, letting institutions meld with unstated public permission. Industry also won indirect benefits as well, of course, from railroad expansion to present-day assistance with biotechnologically altered seeds and plants. Thus, a highly skewed notion of a service state came about. In the American nation-state, it was fine for institutions to be nonneutral and nonobjective as long as no one complained too loudly about existing policy conditions. That is, it was fine as long as others let their own interests be rolled over—as consumers, as conservationists, as rural workers, and so on. In this sense, agriculture was just one sequenced set of components of an entire, decentralized American state. Illustrations abound. Mines were regulated for mine owners, at least until a huge and deadly Utah explosion created a very visible crisis and eventual public outrage. Prior to the Grange, railroad regulations served only the railroads, along with the beneficiaries of a bit of corrupt practices.

In one important sense, however, agricultural policy was different. No other American public policy area in the nation's history had ever encompassed such a large set of institutions, especially in its public organizations.[33] Moreover, these institutions as organizations were located nationwide, as were the constituents they served. So transaction costs enter as a major factor militating against reform or serious policy change (see chapter 3). Who wants to contest all this? Why bother all of these providers and beneficiaries? Don't attack them! Change is too difficult; it doesn't happen. Rural policy failure is a prime example.

Any attempt to move away from a farm modernization and development focus would have been tremendously costly from a transactions perspective—just as it would be today. First, the cost of conversion and any dismantling of institutions would have been high and fraught with organizational resistance. There was an amazing state capacity to do farm policy work and problem solving but not much else. Second, a supportive and politically attentive farm population would have been at least equally resistant. Moreover, that population was well organized. Third, these first two factors represent historical processes that have been constant over time, not short term, even as farm populations declined and farming seemed to be less socially relevant. Institutional and interest power still prevailed. Beyond those three points, a fourth high transaction-cost factor enters: The costs of learning about what to do with the wide range of rural ills would have been excessive. No one knew what data to collect (see chapter 2). The cost of convincing politicians and the public about rural policy needs as opposed to the mythic importance of saving agrarians would have been excessive as well. For all of these reasons, challenging, or new-values, interests in the late 20th century mostly sought to be let in on farm policy benefits rather than to forcefully challenge and overthrow them.

Even if farm policies were not creating situations that kept the horny-handed-sons-of-toil upon the soil, at least those policies had a direction that could be easily followed in their existing form by repetitious bureaucracies. Do more of what's done now: That was simple. Therefore, it made political sense for the American nation-state, as represented by agriculture, to stick with its farm development paradigm through thick and thin, in good times and bad times, even if widespread policy biases and failures were blatantly visible.

SUMMARY OF KEY POINTS

This chapter makes some obvious and some not-so-obvious points. All explain the prevailing power of farm policy. The obvious and less obvious follow, as does one additional point (number 7) that is based on one of the chapter's institutional observations.

1. The Agricultural Establishment has always sought to concentrate its collective attention on farmers. Services delivered have been fragmented parts of a whole, however. A centrally planned, comprehensive, and coordinated policy attention has rarely been of interest. Just deliver the capacity of what one and then another unit can do—and do it now.

2. Congress operates at center stage in federal public policymaking, as the dominant decision-making agricultural institution. Despite institutional changes or reforms over time, Congress has never been organized in ways that favor—or even call much attention to—rural policy. Committee and subcommittee governance have been organized quite well to favor farm constituents and farm policy. The institution has been organized as well to solicit farm policy proposals, or lists of new goodies.

3. Congress acts as if it prefers not to address or consider a national rural policy, independent of farm policy. Yet it has no interest in giving up its rural policy mission either. The facade of service remains jurisdictionally useful. It's a turf or territorial matter; it keeps others out of Establishment policy games.

4. USDA, as an institution that links politics and administration together, has always been organized mostly to serve existing farm programs, as well as to collect primarily farm data. Rural policy needs were always lost as parts of the maze of farmer-serving bureaus of USDA.

5. USDA never exercised bureaucratic leadership for rural policy initiatives within other federal departments. In fact, USDA's jurisdictional dominance of the quickly defunct Cabinet Council Working Group on Rural Communities discouraged rural programs by other fully capable departments, mostly through USDA disinterest.

6. Administrative organizations affiliated with USDA have long been active at the state and local level of government, particularly within counties. These local units include the operational units of the state land-grant colleges of agriculture, the ARS, the ASCS, and the Extension Service. None has been able to overcome Agricultural Establishment expectations that they serve farm needs first. Even though these institutions have observed rural quality-of-life problems most closely, they've rarely been able to service these concerns in any meaningful way.

7. The Extension Service is closest to being an exception to the rule of farmers first.[34] The reason seems apparent when one thinks of institutional rules, restraints, and expectations. Extension is operated as a multi-institutional partner, with shared support and funding by state and local governments, as well as—in this case—the less powerful USDA. Several USDA agencies participate, again fragmenting Extension accountability. Thus, from an institutional perspective, the Extension Service has greater flexibility and more supporters in servicing unique nonfarm local problems. It belongs, it seems, to more than one establishment—or at least to more than one integrated set of policy players.

8. The greatest lesson taught by farmers-first public policy is insight into the essence of the American nation-state. Despite democratic pretenses in public policymaking, neutrality and objectivity of public service apparently are not the rule or the expectation. Public officials are quite content to designate certain citizens as prime—or even the only—policy beneficiaries. Unless other factors—such as a crisis or a powerful intervening interest—enter, those conditions will be allowed to prevail institutionally. When especially strong organized interests protect existing institutions, policy change of any great magnitude is unexpected, and anything near equal service to potentially competing social types is infrequent. The state, in other words, is allowed to be notably and blatantly biased. It was, as Madison feared, at its worst, with no sense of regard for public interests. And it was far, far away from Jefferson's confidence in the rationality of wise men bringing forth wise decisions after their best reflections.

9

THE RESULTING
FRAGMENTATION *of*
POLICY

Fragmented or coordinated public policy? Let's answer the question: What's the difference between the two? The modern public sector likes to assert that its public policies are coordinated with one another (or matched) and comprehensive (or thorough) enough to deal with all of the related problems in an area of common issues. That assertion of good and proper management is no accident. Theorists of public management and policy analysis have set many standards that public officials feel obligated to meet—or, at least, to which they should aspire. None of their standards is more dear to the theorists than that of methodically and sequentially developing, implementing, and evaluating programs to ensure coordination and comprehensiveness among them.[1]

American politics, with its complex Madisonian and Jeffersonian structures, makes the dream of coordinated and comprehensive public policy improbable, no matter how dearly the ideal is held. One could say that there are too many cooks in the kitchen, with no one having control: no head chef. American government, as one experienced critic once commented, is "management without managers."[2] Because the organizational institutions of agricultural governance are so fragmented and remote from one another, what each of them does can hardly be well integrated and centrally planned. Decentralization does that. (Chapter 8 makes this point.) Of course, producing programs and their benefits as small pieces of more holistic farm and rural policies is exactly what those organizations do. This arrangement leads them to protect their turf and territory and prevents reform of the organization into a less fragmented, more cohesive whole. Thus, organizational fragmentation brings policy fragmentation. In short, the organizations are institutionalized to produce a disjointed array of services, not a logically derived and systematically understood core of services that are central to either farming or rural life. Thus, agriculture's public policy is fragmented rather than matched and thorough.[3]

As a result, rural needs more easily fall between organizational cracks within the Agricultural Establishment. Policy also meanders because each program is subject to its own routine reorganization at its own time. Thus, evaluations seldom touch on rural problems because they've been left unattended. Rationales for farm programs too often are applied after legislation passes, not as a basis for considering the proposed legislation when it's at hand. So nobody even expects a sophisticated *pre hoc* rationale for a national rural policy.

This chapter turns to the fragmentation of agricultural policy and what that fragmentation means for farm and rural understanding. The following section describes what exists. The subsequent section more specifically describes the political decision-making conditions under which fragmentation has occurred. The entire chapter makes the case that neither public administration principles nor majority-based democratic pretenses have been followed in formulating farm policy—let alone the poor stepchild, rural policy.

AGRICULTURAL POLICY IN BITS AND PIECES

One lesson: A central policy theme does not mean a central policy plan. Nor does a plan come from a central policy hope, or even from a vague wish. The central theme of farm and most rural policy has always been agrarian, and therefore national, modernization and development. Certainly the national development element has evolved; the governing notion of westward expansion was superceded by the late 20th century by the ideal of an agricultural system that would feed the world and contribute to a strong U.S. economy.[4] This was still agricultural and national development. The policy theme of modernizing the agricultural system to produce more food more economically and more efficiently has been unwaveringly straightforward. Ironically, carrying out modernization (apart from politics) can hardly be planned because so many variables—such as new farming techniques or products—enter the equation.

That observation specifically does not mean that farm policy was never directed to the same subconsciously held ends or that there was no attempt to build relationships between new and previous programs. In fact, nothing could have been less true. Let's try an analogy here: Farm policy construction was like a group of friends building a small dinner salad, which spontaneously grew as new ingredients were found all over the kitchen by diverse diners. The public policies of 1862—establishment of USDA, the Morrill Act, railroads, and homesteading—were like the salad's basic ingredients of iceberg lettuce, green onions, sweet peppers, and cherry tomatoes. As the scanning of the kitchen intensified, other somewhat complimentary ingredients found a place in the Salad Establishment: mild yellow peppers, sweet peas, julienned carrots, spinach, other baby lettuce types, arugula, purple cabbage, a bit of chipotle pepper, oyster mushrooms, chunks of asiago cheese, prosciutto, kalamata olives, shallots, anchovy filets, and minced garlic for the dressing, along with dried apricots, balsamic vinegar, olive oil, ground pepper, sea salt, and brown sugar. Bam! Or wow, what a deal—a whole meal by itself! What about the entrée, however? It's forgotten. Let's stick with what we've got.

What's the point of this odd analogy? Actually, there are three points, in addition to the forgotten purpose. First, the salad evolved in an unplanned fashion. Ingredients were added as the immediate environment was dutifully scanned. Second, the emphasis was on complementary ingredients. This approach made things work satisfactorily. No one threw in a few crushed chocolate cookies or raw catfish chunks or a freshly fried egg mixed with congealed blood sausage. Anyone who tried presumably was shouted down. Third, salad building got out of hand. What was supposed to be a simple dinner salad grew to dominate the entire meal because so many participants played a hand, collectively doing so much. Farm policy was the same: Growth prevailed when institutions responded bureaucratically as troublesome environmental circumstances were encountered; no competing institutions were added (for long, anyway) to, for instance, contract or scale back the developing farm sector; and once again things got out of hand. And the original intent was forgotten—so much so that the public sector was coming to dominate the private sector in structuring agricultural production decisions. Public policy guided planting: what, when, and how to do it.

There also were really two stages to Agricultural Establishment-building. The salad was not built all in one evening; nor was agriculture policy built entirely in 1862. The first stage resulted from an intense scan of the whole kitchen—that is, for agriculture a scan of the dominant characteristics of the entire nation. That was the period through 1914, when rather diffusely rewarding, agrarian-favoring policy benefits were brought forward.[5] Things were added. Let's consider the circumstances for providing technical education through land-grant colleges; doing applied scientific research through the experiment stations; and, when the others fail as insufficient, sending

Extension agents out to spread the gospels of science and instruction.

From an analytical or planning perspective, this was an era of considering and itemizing the widest array of environmental factors. Some internal management existed. The numerous agricultural politicians and professionals who emerged during this era considered the agrarian nature of the developing nation, that nation's presumed dependence on farming, the prospects of linking agrarian development to national development, and the likelihood of other industries—and industrialists—growing rich from the marriage of agrarian and national development. That was to be the small dinner salad. Emphasizing basic, informational farm policies and land give-aways was perfectly sensible in light of those observations. No one needed economic models to see the intrinsic logic of these policy ventures, although the individual programs did have their roots in analytical, even methodological thought.[6]

Planning for success fell far short, however, of considering every facet of what to do. Theorists of public management and policy analysis would not have been proud. No one, for example, had ordained how to get a vocational state college under way, or even where to build a New York college when its grant of land was in Ohio. No one had developed mechanisms for training applied scientists; finding a cadre of persuasive Extension workers; or mandating that education, science, and Extension professionals actually work together to logically common ends. All of these things were left to ad hoc, evolutionary chance; to serendipity and good luck; or to the emergence of a state administrative capacity. Moreover, administrative luck wasn't always good—nor was capacity building. Often there was no prosciutto in the kitchen; that is, there were no skilled or even trainable experts to employ within farm institutions. Or farmers refused to, or couldn't, pay attention to the often greenhorn "experts."

If that first stage lacked modern analytical sophistication and precision, the second stage fell even further behind in meeting optimal analytical standards. No one knew—or, seemingly, cared—if programs such as farm credit, rural electrification, and commodity payments worked together across organizations. No one cared if supposedly necessary programs, as a whole, were insufficient. People rarely asked whether government had met all the needs of all farmers.[7] These matters were simply presumed to be true, as hopes and wishes, as parts of the farm modernization and development theme. At least, such presumptions were held until new grassroots policy demands originated, as they always did.

What happened after 1914? As stage two began, the ironic condition of growing methodological sophistication was accompanied by less attention to the encompassing set of intervening farm problem variables. Programs were passed one at a time, with just one or a few goals in mind. Fix things when someone whines or cries: That was the motto of policymakers. Thus, several credit programs for farm borrowers were passed. The complex, even radical plan for a Federal Farm Board with some credit responsibilities as well as responsibility for marketing and providing farm bargaining power was experimental, short-lived, and criticized by many people for its voluntary constraints on production.[8] Rural electrification marched to its own rules, as did the AAA and the vast array of other programs within USDA agencies established between 1914 and 1938. Soil conservation, for example, initially was left to stand alone, with no institutional way to reach farmers. There was little or nothing in the way of interorganizational cross-compliance, whereby eligibility requirements for one program required a farmer's satisfactory use of another.

Indeed, interorganizational cross-compliance between programs was practically unheard of until 1985. In that year's farm bill, eligibility for commodity payments was made contingent on a farmer's successful implementation of environmental programs such as wetlands preservation.[9] Farmers, of course, howled about such nasty requirements, with one government program getting in the way of another. Shouldn't happen, they claimed. Yet both the complaints and the cross-compliance worked—and, because of the whining, policymakers later shied away from this scheme.

The analytical or methodological irony of this period of piecemeal program addition was especially intriguing. More than anything, it showed a lack of managerial or political interest in comprehensive policy attention. Nobody who mattered asked: Does this all work together on what ails American agriculture? Sector-wide performance, across programs, was not a consideration, except within some agencies through their own interorganizational cooperation. The irony? In the 1920s, agricultural analysts turned from figuring out means for better yields to also understanding the aggregate economics of the farm sector.[10] As a result, statistics became its own academic discipline. Massive data collection and improvization of better measurement instruments characterized the era, especially within USDA and through the applied problem solving of the Agricultural Establishment.

Two things happened. First, economic and other statistical analysis was used to understand the likely implications of individual programs or even sets of programs. Second, however, economic projections caused political problems. Crop estimates, for example, were blamed for commodity price declines. Too much information was suspect, too often misleading or even wrong. Farmers lost. Interest groups revolted, and Congress found proper analysis—as seen today by quantitative theorists—no longer in vogue. The result was that just as policy analysts were increasing their managerial prominence and therefore their public-sector influence, they lost favor. Their successes with bringing the AAA forward were soon forgotten in Congress, and their skills of analysis were never much used for interpreting the many components of agricultural policy. The political ground of Madisonian structure was too hot for the methodologically and logically proficient to venture across.[11] Too often they would have delivered unwanted messages, so they suffered the consequences by avoiding the pain.

This situation provided the context in which fragmented policy continued unabated. Despite the stated belief that all of USDA's program and policy analysis should be centrally integrated under the Secretary of Agriculture, and despite the later movement of the Bureau of Agricultural Economics (BAE) to staff status for the Secretary, the BAE's advocacy of holistic planning and its ability to do so were not well received.[12] Even with its history of successes for the AAAs, the BAE had lost favor.

Bureaucratic politics led to something far different after the late 1930s. Agencies and bureaus throughout USDA clamored for and won their own economists, analysts, and analytical mandates. These resources, however, were used mostly to justify their own agency programs. Analysis was used first to win and then to keep federal programs and appropriations. Analysis was a supposedly neutral means for showing program contributions to clients and for society—and at relatively low costs. Yet it became little more than a means for telling often exaggerated stories of agency successes. The descriptive old homily was quite accurate in these cases: "Figures don't lie, but liars do figure." All of this was compounded in its effect by closely allied private-sector interest groups, with all their diversity, also hiring their own economists—often as consultants from the land grants.

The result was easy to see. Just as organizational fragmentation meant policy fragmentation, the latter then led to analytical fragmentation. Institutional discredit resulted as well. Analysts and data collectors were everywhere, in far more than the few central statistical agencies and bureaus such as the restored (from BAE) Economic Research Service (ERS) and the National Agricultural Statistics Service (NASS). It was often a battle of one set of economists against another: for instance, an ERS economist disagreeing with an ASCS economist over the economic impact of marketing orders for navel oranges.

As the foregoing example shows, however, even centrally located analytical agencies such as the ERS generally still followed narrow evaluations and planning for individual programs or commodities. Seldom did they—

or were they allowed to—step into the "big picture" perspective of commenting on the whole of agriculture, the entire agricultural economy, or the total national financial effects of agricultural policy. On the rare occasions when analysts did venture there, they suffered and lost political battles.[13] They also became even more suspect as a result. Under such circumstances, there was no opportunity to produce a sophisticated study of rural problems and their relationship to farm practices and farm public policy.

WHY ALL THIS?

Fragmentation of organizations and policy persisted because serving farm needs was never easy. Governing ideals from the outset were *laissez faire*, except when corruption or social crises created incentives to resist the prevailing mood of doing little. Open and nasty political divisions characterized the nation regionally through factionally bifurcated or split political parties, idealistically by virtue of what activist level the American state should have, and between grassroots social movements facing off against ruling demands made behind closed political doors by political elites. It was often a matter of well-financed captains of industry against the relatively poor.[14]

Under such conditions, government was led for decades by strong political parties. Parties were valued as the only means for controlling the potentially explosive behavior of voters and elected congressional members, for imposing discipline on elected members who might want to respond to things other than parties and their elites as driving political forces, and for lending continuity of purpose to the institutional preserves of governance.[15] Entrepreneurial or free-agent policymakers who served themselves, their own ideals, or their own constituents too well without partisan endorsement were hamstrung. Thus, despite large numbers of farmers, agrarian values were not easily provided for under strong party government. Farmers and ranchers of the era weren't welcomed inside the tents of political bosses. They were too unruly (see chapter 6). Numbers were never enough; majoritarianism was not at work.[16]

Agrarians lacked a pleasant voice and a unified voice. Without mutual linkages, the thousands of local farm groups and farmers as individuals were ripe for those short-term forays into social movement protests, third-party electoral ventures, and assorted revolts against industry and capital.[17] Moreover, Southern farmers were Democrats; those in the North were Republican. Neither group, however, made compelling partners to be invited willingly into the political inner circles of party elites. God willing (as the policymakers saw things), they should be and were left to be served and satisfied by dispersed agricultural institutions and goodies such as rural free postal delivery. These policy gifts were intended to encourage education, civility, and political quiet among those populating the expanding nation. As chapter 6 implies, if you can't give farmers the new economy they want, give them the promise of the future for upward economic mobility through institutional support. At least the most productive, market-committed of these folks seemed to buy that line.

Thus, it was in the context of partisan disadvantage and politically weak modernizing and civilizing agricultural institutions that farm leaders sought governmental reform, especially from the strong leadership of an elitist Congress. Farmers and farm state legislators aimed for a network of their own for policy discussions and for forcing bipartisan policy decisions. That initial network was formally created as the Farm Bloc of 1921—a congressional forum organized in large part by the Farm Bureau. Its instigation was nearly simultaneous with the 1920s crash of farm prices and land prices. Its motivation was a reaction to party issues—specifically, the growing and festering farm state attitude of "let's get off the *%&#*%& tariff battle."[18]

The tariff was especially touchy to farm state legislators who saw the problems of their constituents—that is, their rebellious voters—being neglected. Attention in Congress revolved around the tariff because Democrats clearly "lost money on duties while Republicans gained."[19] At least in the general economy, the benefits of farm programs after Reconstruction were not so carefully determined or decided. Agriculture was different from the rest of the economy in that, during modernization and development, unfavorable terms of trade had caused the U.S. agricultural sector to lag inevitably behind nonagricultural sectors.[20] Therefore farmers—whether they were Democrats or Republicans—found their economic fortunes lagging further behind the rest of society. As a result, congressional representatives from farm regions wanted to escape party elite control and democratize power through committee processes—which became the basis for bipartisan networking. This development gave farm issues a temporary advantage, which persevered as the farm bloc and its interest group allies moved from six-month formal status to eventual long-term informal cooperation.

Because this process worked out so well in killing the Hoover administration's Farm Board and in passing Roosevelt's AAA, network fervor only increased. Congress became an increasingly integral part of the institutional Agricultural Establishment, remaining quite bipartisan and proactive in support of farmers. The agricultural committees were regarded as farmers' committees in the House and the Senate. Supportive farm groups, notably the Farm Bureau, became, as we saw, semi-institutionalized as expected but not mandatory policy players. So did some commodity groups. And, of course, growth-orientated agricultural service agencies and organizations—the administrative bureaucracy—cooperated with both types of groups, giving rise to the popular notion of a closed "iron triangle" dominating agricultural policy.[21] The idea was that legislators, lobbyists, and administrators ruled together and collectively by themselves, over a restricted range of issues that interested only them.[22] These issues generally kept coming back to Washington for resolution; they were regarded as increasingly commonplace to an expanding, more policy-active, yet wide-open U.S. government.[23]

Given the sheer amount of public interest in American policy and the relative ease with which nearly anyone could muck around within or outside of the process, the idea of isolated iron triangles proliferating from agriculture throughout government seems misplaced. The enemies, from party leaders to business interests, were still mucking around. How could such isolation happen? On those dimensions, iron triangles are silly concepts, even scary in their inaccuracy.[24] Returning to the literature on public management and bureaucratic decisions, however, we see that the inherent sense of the concept is also understandable. That's especially true given the emerging network furor of the congressional committee reform era of the 1920s.

Let's look directly at German theorist Max Weber's analysis of proper bureaucracy to explain.[25] Weber's ideas and network concepts show a good (if not established) philosophical fit. Political networks are regarded as creatures that bring together all relevant institutional and interest players who have a specific and common stake in some policy matter. Weber's emphasis, in brief, was on the logical division of labor within large organizations. Expertise and special knowledge should be the basis for dividing up bureaucratic tasks (see chapter 8). One set of officials should apply themselves to one project while other teams work on related other projects, programs, and policy. Through mutual respect for one another's neutral competence in administration and analysis, the sets of teams supposedly learn acceptance of the others. So there should be positive reciprocity: Nobody gets in anyone else's damned way. Designated supervisors then controlled for accountability. It's not control by the competing teams, however. They don't have the latitude to decide to go along or not. The supervisors decide what works or works together. Ah: A Hamiltonian centrist idea imposed on Madisonian decentralization. Could it work? We'll see in chapter 12.

Weber's ideal became standard bureaucratic logic, even in America's politically open institutional structure. Because reforms such as those of Congress and the resulting networking tend to be self-perpetuating and driven by the self-interest of the reformers, Weberian logic charted a quick and continuing course within the Agricultural Establishment. That course of action gave rise to the identification of those varied self-governing networks: price policy, conservation, credit, agricultural research, and the like.[26] The networks, because of their intensity of purpose, spawned even more professional service-style interest groups, such as the Soil Conservation Society.[27] Groups for water quality, marketing tactics, credit lenders, and research user firms also were soon closely allied, working to be semi-institutionalized within the Agricultural Establishment. In the main, however, the status and the concern of the professional service groups were reserved for their network roles, not for their place in all of agriculture.[28] No established network nor new group was so bold or so foolish as to venture afar as an outsider who championed a new rural policy agenda. Specialization and expertise, without doubt, entrenched myopia as well as positive intensity into national agricultural policy processes. This was "my way, my stuff" political theory—and hardly surprising, given the circumstances (and, of course, Madison's visions).

Was such network protection a needless and constantly paranoiac response, however? Certainly not, because farm policymaking was becoming even more difficult—or harder to fight for—within the Agricultural Establishment. How could these fragile networks of institutional and interest players venture into championing rural issues and policy? They were too preoccupied with protecting their own highly valued turf. There were many reasons. Farmer numbers were in constant decline; consequently, farmers represented a suffering voting bloc. Partisan politicians once again split the farming sector after World War II, and Democrats and Republicans alike were proposing to shake up farm policy. Agriculture, with its solid core of professional civil servants and advocates and its large budgets and extensive facilities, was the source of great jealousy among people who focused on other issues, from other economic sectors to good government causes.[29]

Within government, other counter-reformist trends and decentralization itself were imposing high transaction costs. People within other sets of institutions also were jealous of agriculture's resources and suggested reallocation to other policy areas—their own. Congress was less likely to be bipartisan, even on farm issues. Some congressional leaders were ambitious to return to elite control of policy agendas and proposals, particularly on what became omnibus, catch-all farm bills. And the White House, still locked in a Hamiltonian fantasyland, consistently tried to find ways to regain farm and rural policy leadership. Incentives such as these were more than sufficient to keep protective agriculture policy networks alive and, whenever possible,well—and dedicated forever to their farmer clientele.

IMPLICATIONS

What is evident is a policy process that has been ruled far more by the political needs of the moment than by careful thought or majority American opinion. Agriculture rarely sought to advertise specific accomplishments. Instead, it kept tossing out for consumption that old agrarian myth and its important Establishment service to those needy farmers. As a final irony, American agricultural modernization and development was unplanned yet intended. It was wanted, no matter how it turned out—just so it was big. Modernization and farm development also played a significant role in national expansion, bringing people and agrarian opportunities to the frontier.[30] Agricultural development hardly stabilized rural America, however (see chapters 1 and 2 again). Development was a destabilizing force as many people left farming and ranching or remained poor in modernizing and western regions, which led to community decline. That's the balanced view, rather than the extremist view. Extremists see this all as a big plot.

On the other hand, America's Agricultural Establishment was a huge success in producing a fantastic food machine. Nowhere else in the world did a comparable production capacity emerge, relying on either public or private support or some mix of the two. It was an international envy, and institutions such as Extension and research services were exported, in parts, worldwide.[31] Many American farmers and agribusinesses prospered for years, as long as they led in technological change. The food machine was flawed, however, and not kind to all: Farm exits intensified. Chronically low prices bedeviled producers. Land prices were bid unrealistically high. Eventual asset fixity in production capacity had led many people, in retrospect, to invest foolishly.[32]

The ease with which agricultural institutions were added in America explained the positives and the negatives, the goods and the bads. Moreover, their goods and bads came about in a largely nonanalytical and antimanagerial fashion—even as scientific discovery led modernization efforts by the Agricultural Establishment. Nobody really ever accurately projected which programs would succeed and which ones would probably fail. Making accurate projections in the face of so many constantly changing variables was like assembling a big jigsaw puzzle that is tedious and time-consuming to put together.

There was far more to eventual farm and rural conditions, however, than the ease with which institutions were added. Farmer politics and farm policymaking were always difficult, even with perceptions of gingerly and merry expansion the norm. Agrarians in more improved versions by then were a valued development resource; but they were not valued political allies until the 1920s. Therefore, farmers seldom got their way until Congress reformed its leadership, until Weberian logic prevailed in administration, and until issue networks played an increasingly influential role. The entire business of decentralization made it easier to protect agricultural institutions through increasingly troubling and threatening times. There was no one policy giant for enemies to target for a quick end. Yet nobody fought to add rural America to the bloody mix. One really couldn't do so and survive.

Once again, however, there were bads among the goods. Agriculture's giant food machine prospered through specialization, division of labor, and emphasis on its own expertise. Yet those same conditions fostered even greater myopia among established policy networks. Under fear and threat, the old guys of agricultural policy were less likely to innovate, voluntarily expand missions and agendas, or examine the prevailing flaws of modernization and development. So myopia led to considerable—though far from total (see chapter 10)—institutional stagnation and very limited acquisition of information about prevailing long-term farm or rural conditions. Farm policy therefore was regarded so often and by so many in politics as an antiquity of sorts after the 1960s.[33]

SUMMARY OF KEY POINTS

Let's wrap up the discussion of institutional and interest structures as they protect farm modernization and development policy. Some of the points made here are the most critical ones raised yet in this long essay. Their implications generally reflect quite negatively on the meaning of governmental capacity for the American nation-state. More and more bureaucratic capacity, we should conclude, does not necessarily produce informationally better, more understandable, or more well-liked or popular public policy.

  1. Despite the proliferation of public management theory and policy analysis, the ability and will to methodologically plan and identify likely farm and rural policy variables is severely restricted. Political

decisions dominate—as one would expect of such a complex, Madisonian and Jeffersonian American state. Things can hardly be well integrated and centrally planned for agricultural policy. No one can realistically sit back and say: Let's see what we can plan for rural America over the next 10–20 years. At least, no one in the public sector can do so and be taken seriously.

2. Agricultural programs and policy intentionally come in bits and pieces. Even as analytical methods and skills escalated, they rarely emphasized holistic analysis, as the much maligned report on the structure of the agricultural economy in the 1970s did.[34] Nobody within the sector wanted to read, as the report suggested, that big was bad—just as nobody wanted to hear about integrating rural problems into farm problem solving.

3. A combination of faith and a hoped-for common sense appears to have led to the initial development of U.S. farm policy and the Agricultural Establishment. Those conditions did not promote comprehensive or coordinated public policy efforts, however—especially policies that covered rural America. No one has ever been sure of which policies are needed in a comprehensive farm and rural policy base or which ones are sufficient for that base's existence.

4. Public policy efforts appear to have gotten out of hand with their unplanned response to complementary programs and projects. They didn't cover everything, however (for example, rural issues and interests). The intended purpose of farm policy as private-sector development seemed to be lost, however, as the public sector assumed greater dominance in assisting and even making farm production decisions.

5. Farm public policy, as it responded to farmer preferences, was not served well under strong political parties and influential political elites or politically weak agricultural institutions. Of course, rural policy would have fared no better. Such poor service to popular political demands led to considerable movement toward political reform in Congress; it also led to policy networking.

6. The emphasis on reform in Congress and the creation of broader patterns of interaction with public policymakers relied on networks of legislators, lobbyists, and institutional administrators. The presumed players merely showed a self-interest in specific types of

policy. They were hardly unanimous in their views, however, and they were never as isolated from outside-the-network political demands as iron-triangle theory would suggest.[35] Never could that be in America.

7. Networking worked so well with the congressional Farm Bloc—and later through its informal farm bloc successor in Congress—that pressure for such cooperation spread to issue areas *within* the sector.[36] Networking actually was so consistent with the respected management theories of Max Weber that it spread widely within the other structures of American public institutions, such as Congress and agricultural research.

8. Networking developed as a means of lowering what at the time were escalating transaction costs in 1920s farm policymaking. The need for easier decision making seems ironic at first. After all, more and more Agricultural Establishment institutions appear to have been easily created in the 19th century, even under *laissez-faire* conditions. Yet that ease is apparent only if one links agricultural to national development and if one links capitalist interests to the desire to educate and civilize those always suspect agrarians.[37]

9. Networking in the 20th century was merely a derivative of such transaction-cost thought, as more and more semi-institutionalized interests and institutionalized administrative personnel came to press their policy demands along with the direct voices of farmers. Farmer power, in this regard, never stood alone. It stood with the power of these others. Indeed, it was the state that mattered most as an organizing entity, in terms of what it provided and what it inspired politically within society. It was the incomplete state that, despite its capacity, left out attention to rural America. It was too costly and potentially debilitating to that existing state capacity to fight that battle, too.

10

THE IMPOSSIBLE TASK *of*
RURAL ADVOCACY

We now shift our attention away from the best friends but bad guys of rural policy: farm policy beliefs, farm institutions, farm interests, and farmer allies. Let's focus instead on the problems with the strategies of rural policy reform within the Agricultural Establishment and what's been wrong with them—often, unavoidably so. Chapters 10, 11, and 12 look at the negligible prospects for rural advocacy. Can the past be holding back the present, and the future as well? Of course it does—and it will, in all likelihood. Chapter 13 draws a contrast with a more successful agricultural policy reform effort: the environmental movement. This essay then finishes in chapter 14 with some lessons about badly disadvantaged public policies in the always challenging and often high-capacity—that is, organizationally capable—American nation-state.

This chapter turns to the essence of the rural lobbying problem. Advocacy for the rural community and its disadvantaged populations has become as near to impossible as things can be in national politics. Unless one wants very little, and (as I have emphasized often) something that is highly particularistic or selective, in all likelihood it won't be won. At the heart of today's rural advocacy dilemma lies not only the distant past. The past as it's still played out leaves rural interests extraordinarily weak in terms of the evolving let's-get-together network politics of contemporary Washington, D.C. Yet that past would leave those interests little better off were they to rely on strong partisan advocates or successful, mostly pro-farm agricultural institutions.

The following two sections explain the reasons. The first section drags up some old rock-and-roll lyrics to emphasize and paraphrase the point that rural interests "have no place to run." No stable of trusted insider-politics friends exist. Nor, as the second section reminds us, do advocates of rural issues and interests have anywhere to hide their proposed strategies. No ballistic lobbying plans can be found in dark closets. There are few secret strategies to be developed in a wide-open national politics that would rocket previously neglected issues such as these to the forefront—at least, not without the corruption of old or new and shocking crises of the present to drive them.

NO PLACE TO RUN

Everyone, particularly those with time in the political process, has friends in Washington. Wow! Life is like that. Having friends doesn't mean the same thing, however, as being able to reliably count on them, or even trust them for one's own political purposes.[1] Friends are just a first step to advocacy success. Yet, as the folk wisdom of winning friends and allies would suggest, people try it again and again as if it's the end itself. Not surprisingly, then, friendship politics has been at the center of rural reform advocacy for the past two decades—to little avail.

The conventional rule has been simple: Make influential friends who occupy the correct institutional or interest positions in your area of policy. Then use them, as leaders in advocacy in their own right.[2] No matter what positions they occupy inside or outside of government, and no matter whether they know they're to be the leader. Lobbyists can come from anywhere, but they should understand that they're leaders. Unfortunately for rural advocates, the conventional results have been as simple as the conventional wisdom. The influentials, the friends, eventually leave the reformers alone to lose. Other entangling establishment relationships and institutional tasks prove more formidable than what once seemed plausible avenues with probable leadership players for policy change. One-time sympathizers find that their responsibilities to farm services or to other, more influential, interests are so entangling that their rural sympathies lag. In reality, there is no one to run to on behalf of quick and often creative fixes. The following are the most prominent examples of failures to perceive the flawed relationship between simple rules and no less simple results since the mid-1980s.

Example 1: Look for the most experienced and hardest-driving lobbyist leader, the eminence of reform respectability. Several people with strong rural backgrounds felt they had found such a point person in the early 1990s: Susan Sechler. This foundation executive was the easy choice; she had high status from her special interest job; considerable flexibility in recommending the foundations' advocacy funding projects; a reputation as an activist in anti-farm policy efforts, beginning with the 1970s' Agricultural Accountability

Project; and experience as an outspoken ally of nearly every social cause interest group that had recently spoken badly of farm programs.[3]

Sechler's attributes included Washington's warmest personal charm—tenaciousness; widespread and loyal contacts throughout the Agricultural Establishment; good friends in USDA; and Democratic party loyalty in what was a forthcoming Clinton administration era. She had instant, widespread visibility, if supported properly. Wasn't this a modern female John Muir, early Sierra Club, heroine and dreamweaver? At first glance, yes. In personal sympathy, most certainly. In political reality, she was not a rural advocate at heart but a more general Establishment reformer: too general a rebel, chewing off too much—especially because nobody said, "We depend on you."

As a consequence, things did not work out, at least in terms of specific rural policy leadership. The respected reformer proved to be too esteemed and too valued by too many others. Her issue niche, as her source of her own political identity and the means by which others identified her as an activist, was not as a rural expert.[4] Rural interests were just part of her clientele. Moreover, rural policy and problems were hardly her background, through her education or her experiences as an attack lobbyist. "I have a goal," she once said, "of course I do; I want to change the whole damned (agricultural) system, piss them all off."[5]

This tenacity and sweeping set of policy goals led to relationships within nearly all of the social cause interests—and their sympathizers—that have sought to be included in agricultural policy change and inclusion since 1973.[6] Consumer groups, nutrition groups, child welfare groups, poverty lobbies, sustainable agriculture organizations, and even anti-biotechnology interests were her informal clientele on numerous issues. Environmental interests were particularly prominent. So too were several leftist and Democratic-leaning think tanks.[7] In addition, she took considerable advice from many respected—if not always mainstream—authorities from traditional agriculture. Grants from her foundations went in numerous directions of public policy: not just for rural interests, and not just for reformists. Advocacy was not always on her immediate agenda; plans were often being made for more long-term future Establishment assaults.

In short, the Eminent Reformer was more of a coalition leader among a not otherwise allied set of emerging social cause groups, interests, and individual policy players. Most of these players, of course, were just in the process of finding places for themselves within or opposing the Agricultural Establishment. Thus, they were in competition among themselves for reputations and operating resources. Sechler's services to too many of them were far too broad and their impact therefore too limited on any one of them. Such ineffectual advocacy made specific rural program institutions and interests unlikely to be effectively mobilized and followed—especially because she didn't know she was supposed to.

Example 2: Let's captivate the White House. So why not go to the very top? Try the presidency—in 1993, the new home of Arkansas' Bill Clinton. After all, the history of serious rural policy initiatives has been about presidents more than Congress or even administrative professionals. So let's plant ideas with the president and hope he follows their logic.

Several other more contemporary factors also made Clinton a target— one who could have been a rural policy leader. First, as Arkansas governor Clinton had acquired a reputation as a new-style southern politician who was willing to break with traditionally conservative state forces such as rice producers and their cooperatives.[8] Second, he had networked extensively with many professional policy analysts, by himself and within prestigious national forums. Observers saw him as a policy-oriented, solution-focused politico rather than one of the policy process's good old boys, playing only on behalf of personal favorites. Third, Arkansas indeed was a rural state, seemingly less focused (to Governor Clinton) on farming than on a necessary new dynamics of progressive economic development: jobs, opportunities, and more jobs. Finally, Clinton's urbane and intellectual manner made him an approachable public official. As the reasoning went, he should have been someone who would work with similar people who had positive attitudes toward policy reforms linked to social causes and liberal politics, especially in the new South.

No one, however, found rough-and-tumble Bill Clinton to be cut from the Roughrider Teddy Roosevelt model on rural issues. Even when a simple strategy evolved to commit Clinton and his administration to Agricultural Establishment reform, he never seemed to listen. The costs of doing so by new guys in town were potentially very high. Why rock a boat that's lying still? No reason; don't: Let's keep middle-class interests happy and content. Perhaps ignorance indeed was bliss in those early but novel White House years.

What was the plan? Rely on her Eminence of Reform's liberal respectability to position herself with the new administration. The match was politically sound, though ultimately suspect. The reformer and her allies were able to win for her the position as head of the Clinton administration's transition team for federal agriculture and food appointees. What was the hope? If the strategy were successful, it would have created considerable influence for her in bringing in top-level layers of politically appointed, nontraditional USDA and related agency administrators. New social-cause folks, not the old aggies that the reformer always hoped to piss off, would be in charge of much if not all Establishment reform in the remaining years of the 20th century.

What happened? Well, the initial Clinton rhetoric sounded good—progressive, democratic, open policymaking with a reform prospective for rural people. The administration's action, however, belied any intent behind such rhetoric. As talent collection procedures sought candidates for the transition team and as numerous types of influentials made recommendations for those who could become ranking policymakers, the new wave of agricultural policy reform advocates were visibly ignored. Neither other transition team members nor White House liaison appointees were taken by this reformist troop. Despite considerable efforts to compromise, the new administration appointed more of the same old types of farm policy proponents. Fewer dissenters were incorporated into USDA under Clinton than there had been in the Carter administration. Even traditional farm and agribusiness forces—and state personalities—from Arkansas won more favored positions and voices in USDA than did national policy reformers.

Without an administration that was intent on inclusion and promoting new values, the plan and the target were inoperative. In the largest sense, both were unlikely to pay out anyway. Those with institutional status had merely to pass on that status—and its accompanying responsibilities and perceived policy successes—in their recommendations for appointments. Accepting traditional recommendations was a safe course of action for a White House that for all practical purposes had no use for a high transaction cost farm and food policy war. Thus, the motto was, let's go with society's most prominent and well-to-do agricultural experts. There were too many other policy battles possible, more visible and attractive ones to fight—such as health care reform.

For the agricultural reformists who tried to instigate such a war, however, the new and now old administration seemed worse than merely timid. Her Eminence concluded, "It was all about paying attention to the old boys, the used-up ideas, the neglect of accountability. Those things were never gone. The whole bunch of them [Clinton's folks] proved their own corruption so easily and so early."[9] So institutions and interests maintained their ongoing win streaks against issues that found only the most minimal popular support. Even when farm policy activists and players agreed to a phase-out of farm price supports, Clinton expressed only reluctant support. He wasn't sure this reform would work. It was a deed of Congress—one that its members should pay for in the case of failure.

Example 3: How about an agriculture committee chair from a rural but mostly urbane and polished New England state? For a similar lesson, return to the late

1980s. Let's set the target and sights of the lobbying artillery at a symbolically slightly lower level, however—an individual (and a most influential public official) who was more likely to be convinced. Sights were set after a quick scan of what often gets called the institutional keystone of the Washington establishment—that is, the correct congressional committee.[10] The idea was to interest a single entrepreneurial agriculture committee member who could carry other members along in passing the Bush administration's aforementioned Rural Development Act.

Who would do it? After all, agriculture committee members tended to come from a variety of states and districts dependent on farm politics (except for African American members who could be advocates for food and urban poverty positions). So these members usually are old aggies, with their own institutionalization in the funding and authorization policy center of the Agricultural Establishment. This was a problem.

There were a few exceptions, however, from places that were not as farm oriented. Two such places were obvious: the rural Southeast, where many neighborhoods within districts were nonfarm and suburban, and the Northeast, where farming had largely exhausted itself. Mostly that northern region was characterized by forests, tourism, and some small, economically stressed dairy farms. Such was the very politically avoidable New Hampshire, an otherwise volatile state that is famous for its presidential primaries. Yet there also were Connecticut and Vermont, for example, which are known for their suburban and commuter nature, prestigious colleges, and upscale vacationing—as well as a few cows. Perhaps that suburbanized environment would best produce a rural congressional advocate. So it did, and one was selected: the liberal Democratic chair of the Senate agriculture committee—a man known to be frequently hostile to commodity programs that weren't always fair, in his eyes, to his state's producers. Not incidentally, he also was in need of a restored image. His previously sound partisan but very prominent senatorial (read lordly) reputation had been harmed by an indiscrete foreign policy intervention that received great publicity and brought considerable personal distress. So this guy was happy to take up the bill as his own, even though no one told him that he was to be boss leader of the whole Rural Development Act (RDA) battle.

Patrick Leahy was to be a good, sympathetic figure who could find a nonfarm following on an independent bill. And he would have an ally: A rural lobbyist who would later receive foundation financing in the 1990s, Robert Rapoza, would work as closely as possible with Leahy's office to coordinate a bill, deliver legislative and administrative support, and rouse the support of any of several lurking rural interests and coalitions. This certainly could have done Vermont proud, right down to its traditional rural values of clean air and healthy lifestyles and hoped-for respect for its national leaders. For Leahy and Vermont, it was good restorative politics, as well as good reform politics.

Neither Leahy nor Rapoza could quite deliver, though. The bill and its support would seemingly fall together, but without much enthusiasm on the Hill. Then just as easily it would collapse, without fanfare. At least some farm state interests and members of Congress were needed to pass their committees' legislation; in the end, these forces would not accept the tenets of a distinctly rural bill. "They tricked us repeatedly," said Rapoza at the end, "just lied."[11] It was something he said again in 1992, after he found more lying about the 1990 farm bill.

What "they" as institutional pieces really did was even easier than lying. What appeared to be acquiescent, even passive, RDA supporters wanted rural policy to stay within that tradition of farm policy—or the next (1985) farm bill. So the collective efforts of old farm policy institutionalists flanked Leahy and moved discussions of the RDA and its most desirable and par-ticularistic (special favor) proposals to deliberations over that pending om-nibus bill. The House of Representatives led the way, of course, quietly and quickly. In that sense, the institutionalized were thieves, not liars. Theft from Leahy, or turf management by the House, lowered the transaction costs of any sort of political battle, or words of violent disagreement that might oth-erwise have been heard.

Example 4: Let's just find some little congressman, a guy with basic legislative needs. This idea was business as usual, not engineering a miracle of superior legislative strategy. Congress, after all, operated from Washington, not Lourdes or another blessed place such as Fatima.

Therefore, numerous affected interests looked for agricultural committee members who had expressed sympathy with specific RDA proposals—the particularistic special favors—and had some reason to act on them. Several rank-and-file leaders emerged, all tying themselves (mostly) to just one type of program: their own. All of them knew they were leaders—fronting, of course, for various organized interests. The most easily understood response was by a western drylands-state congressman. His constituents were af-fected by recurring drought, groundwater decline in aquifers, and grow-ing incidents of water wells being polluted by farm chemical use.

This congressman had a perfect opportunity to promote something that was visibly and obviously of local consequence. And he did, championing centralized rural water delivery systems, or farm and rural water through big tubes. Interest support was extensive, of course. Contractors were jubilant. Local industry welcomed rural water stability. Many farmers felt relief from future problems. As a result, the Honorable Mr. Dryland Gulch found that he had lobbyists who would work hard with his staff for his cause in the pending farm bill, who could show local applications of rural water systems already in operation. They rallied supporters, raised campaign funds, encouraged press coverage, and spoke often of environmental safety as this member's rather surprising (even to him) forte. In short, Mr. Gulch, like other members of Congress, won basic legislative needs—his own, for winning reelection and for gaining a reputation in the House as a political doer.

What happened? Rural water systems became an important if small component of the pending omnibus farm bill. It was one of numerous issues that made the 1990 farm bill vehicle desirable and, for many, a progressive act.[12] Yet, in a peculiar but not surprising way, water systems did more, by restoring Establishment prominence. They were argued for, advanced, and promoted as unique and necessary extensions of farm policy. Rural water was quite like that old rural electricity: an evolving and very much needed component of the many institutions of farm modernization and development. It was popular, in effect, because water systems were regarded as important components of a continuously developing Agricultural Establishment. Therein lies the advantage of Congress playing what major league baseball players often call "small ball."[13]

Neither Mark McGwire nor some other policy star was there hitting mighty home runs on an RDA. Plenty of rank-and-file infielders were there, however, to bloop single runs home over third—repeatedly. Several players drove in others from third base. As they did so, they won small-scale policy games. The farm institutions were then friendly. Interests were all calm. Transaction costs stayed low. The efforts of 1862 continued right through the millenium, even with a difficult 1995 farm bill still to write.

NO PLACE TO HIDE

A tale such as this one sometimes, for some readers, produces the unintentional result of raising a cheering section. The idea is one team—the entrenched farm policy folks—versus an underdog rural policy team (or even all of the anti-farm policy reformers as a team). The policy game with the baseball analogy probably fosters the let's-form-a-cheering-section approach.

If it helps in understanding the policy process in agriculture, use that two-team analogy, even though it's not exact or even always very accurate in describing policy play. Why use it, then? One reason predominates: There *is* a semblance of an underdog team. It's united only around unplanned and uncoordinated goals of Agricultural Establishment and food policy reform. This isn't a solid nine, but its opposition status still evokes team imagery. Thus, members of the public who hear about various reform positions such as the environment, agricultural trade, food safety, consumer rights, and rural policy can attract a social-cause cheering section, if they're so inclined. It may be important over time. Remember political theorist E. E. Schattschneider? He warned that, in an American political battle, you should watch the crowd as the determining factor.[14] The crowd can always expand directly into the conflict, *if* it wants. It may become dominant.

To an extent, this expansion to the battling public from the backroom-inclined organized interests has already occurred.[15] Seattle, Washington, served as a major battleground when environmentally concerned protestors of various sorts blocked World Trade Organization meetings in late 1999. Similar protests and disruptions took place in Washington, D.C., in 2000. Expansion of opposition issues has at least led many citizens to be frightened of the consequences of large-scale agricultural production and the subsequent, often international handling of components of food production—from genetics to seafood inspection. For some Americans, these fears have led to the formation of a strategic question: What should be organized and done?

For a few of those who are pondering that question, the answer lies in forming a widespread social movement from a grassroots public that is increasingly supportive of opposition politics. The "them-against-us" team concept then enters. A return to grassroots silver policy and economic reform movements of the 19th century is the presumed model for such change, even though it's a horribly outmoded model.[16] More contemporary politics suggests that if such an opposition politics were applied today, it would have to be more complex, more alive with already organized and vital interests, better informed about scientific conditions, and better able to plan and carry out the provision of political incentives for those participants.[17] Nonetheless, public opposition roots and cheers for its already recognizable but still emergent dissident advocacy cohort in national politics.

Moreover, citizens logically yet naively ask: Why don't these various and assorted folks simply get together and form a sweeping agricultural policy revolt? Why not put together a well-planned and highly specific set of reforms as absolute political demands—or shut their town down? This question, of course, implies the idea of surprising the traditional agricultural institutions and the traditional agriculturists, as well as bringing unanticipated challenges to previously dominant public policy ideas, values, and beliefs. It happens—but very rarely.[18] Generally it's carried out by those who use terrorist tactics (against, for example, animal experimentation or genetically altered crops by burning the lab or destroying the crop in the field).

There also is a flaw in the two-team analogy, however: There is no all-powerful 1927 New York Yankees unit on the field, no institutional team. That Establishment is not organized as a strictly competitive unit against those who want even severe farm policy change. That's too far-fetched, totally inaccurate, and no surprise to readers of chapter 8. A better analogy than the team is that of the league. A league houses several teams, or networks as parts, all of whom routinely have some nominal overlap and interaction through the policy games they unavoidably share. They also share a self-interest in ensuring that each of the networks (teams) is sound and competitive. Social scientists, who always want their own language, have taken to calling the leagues "policy domains."[19] There's some importance in this notion, as we shall see.

America's modernizing and developing agriculture certainly has come to be such a domain in its historical evolution. As the nation's earliest policy domain, it also may be the best-integrated and most certain of its need for collective success.[20] That's true even as agriculture lacks comprehensiveness and coordinated policies and programs, or even an essence of shared policy values. Yet no domain players want the other institutionally connected networks (teams) in their league to appear inept, foolish, or less than winners. So they share ideas and information among themselves. Why? Because they also share policy space in the competitive world of government legislation, budgeting, and finance. If one loses, the others may lose as well—simply by looking weak. Yes, each network (team) organizes itself, raises its own capital, and makes its own trades, but the domain sets the schedule and hosts the World Series.

So why consider the policy domain at this point? Again, the answer lies with better descriptive reality than the weaker two-team analogy allows. The domain concept implies, first, acceptance of that common theme of an always modernizing and developing agriculture as a national goal; that is the policy space. Second, it implies that Weberian networks of specialized bureaucratic expertise are considerably free to go their own way—unless they are terribly wrong or lacking in some degree of neutral competence. That's also regarded as bureaucratic inertia. Third, the domain implies accountability not only through administrative leadership but also through institutionalized politics and the numerous and growing number of clientele interests that are allied, or semi-institutionalized, into league play. The regular players are a domain constant; they turn over and change slowly. Controversy at some level also is a domain constant, externally and more so internally as different policy values of different programs conflict. In the baseball analogy, the Cubs, for example, always claim superiority over the Cardinals, although both preach the inherent superiority of the National League and, more particularly, the Central Division.

Fourth, that latter point means that domain institutions are continuously subject to modification and alteration of what they do, the programs they operate, and even how they go about doing things. Remember, the 2000 Cubs once sought to trade Sammy Sosa. Safe and nutritious food is a policy good that recently has been appended to the core goal of farm modernization and development, for instance. No one ever thought of it in the 19th century. Fifth, the scientific traditions of the Agricultural Establishment and early commitment to even imperfect analysis encourage such inquisitive thought and recognition of the need for program and domain changes. Without that unique characteristic of adjustment, the Agricultural Establishment would never have stabilized and grown to be so influential over time.[21] Its paradigm of agrarian values would not have sustained agriculture alone, no matter how ingrained it was in American culture and how protective the Madisonian and Jeffersonian structure of interest-group government was. The myth was constantly updated at the margins.

A resulting question always permeates the agricultural policy process, then. Domain participants—the actual players on the teams—want to know how to be responsive to new information about their assigned areas of expertise. No one wants to look like a Neanderthal or have the agriculture "tribe" look like a bunch of Neanderthals. There's always guilt by association. Players then aspire to maintain their expertise and their resulting political credibility, often with coercion from other players, teams, and league leaders. They listen widely through their networking activities, and they are especially careful to hear and follow the criticisms of those who would bring competition to their unique fields of thought.

Domain participants also are at an advantage in securing information. Research staffing is extensive; research projects grow in number and purpose, with greater attention going to new-value or social-cause reform problems; information generation and collection mechanisms are superior; network opportunities are plentiful and available, and players learn about each others' strengths and weaknesses. Moreover, continuous warnings flash that agriculture is subject to great political pressure, especially public opinion.

After all, public opinion reflects consumer choices, and consumer choices are what semi-institutionalized food manufacturing and processing interests hope to cultivate. With its size and numbers, agriculture is hardly sacrosanct or free from successful political assault. This is a powerful inducement for responsible change, especially as accompanied by competing signs of administrative decline—smaller budgets, greater workloads, more difficult operational questions, more public and media criticism, less authorization for political position-taking or posturing.

So what for the dissenting team—the opposition that would reform the Agricultural Establishment? Many of these players, like the attorneys who represent agribusiness firms, are by necessity domain players as well—though it may not look that way at first glance. Without participating and gathering information from inside the domain, reformist ideas lack grounding and established conventional sense. Dissidents are known and evaluated, their ideas subject to review, their friendships often sought, and their own expertise often valued. Often, more central domain players finance their efforts. All of this lowers the long-term, or accommodative, transaction costs of dealing with the social-cause reformists—unless, of course, they're fringe status, terrorist ideologues.

Thus, at least some dissenting, new-value, reform positions are routinely incorporated into the essential work of the Agricultural Establishment, though not as quickly or as thoroughly or perhaps as diligently as the opposition would hope. Trust is still a problem for them, as well as for institutionalists who would necessarily have to give it (see chapter 7). The Braves, for instance, will never trust the Mets, but they welcome their close competition. It's good for the league, the domain of both teams. Most important for reform opponents , however, that style of incorporating new policy values into the agricultural political process prevents, in Establishment eyes, a food policy revolution. The opposition therefore must operate openly, in a public forum, in order to cultivate that fear. It must reveal its aspirations, dislikes, and goals—and its plots. Mobilization of a social cause means noise.[22] No silent armies can be brought out suddenly to overthrow much of anything. For the Agricultural Establishment's opposition, there's nowhere to hide for a secret assault, any more than there's been a secret leader for them to find who will change the policymaking equation more heavily in their favor, or in favor of rural America. Sechler, Clinton, Leahy, and even the Honorable Dryland Gulch were well known to all—and in all cases suspiciously studied. Opponents may well be in positions to move to the other team, if they wish. More likely, they'll change teams by signing onto those old farm bills.

IMPLICATIONS

The meaning of this chapter is quite clear. Better yet, that meaning can be stated succinctly. Rural advocates by the late 20th century were behaving as if they understood a basic political principle regarding their own vincibility. An alternative national rural policy apart from national farm policy appears impossible for all of the reasons cited in previous chapters. Those reasons range from institutional reluctance to farm interest politics to the political lethargy of rural residents. Yet no one in the rural advocacy community would disagree with the need for at least a limited and independent national rural policy that addresses community decline in isolated places, economic development in neglected regions, and poverty.

There is little agreement beyond that, however, in part because of the conditions noted in chapter 2. Some rural proponents insist on complete rural revitalization efforts everywhere—as a sort of reborn 1960s Great Society initiative. Big government lives in that ideal. At the other extreme, other sympathetic proponents propose a very cautious plan for rural policy. These advocates include policy professionals who would have to work directly with isolated, empty, and resourceless places. Their sense of practicality rules. Since the 1980s, rural policy proponents have joked about what they could realistically do for the "shitty little communities" (SLCs) or SLTs (towns).[23] Most have feared that program implementation would likely fail—that some places, such as the woods of New Hampshire, must be left to nature's way of adaptation.

With such divergent views and assorted middleground positions, rural lobbying has hardly occupied a political high ground. It shows in the rural lobbies' most recent strategic choices. The incentives have been to ally rural advocates with a wide range of reform interests that are highly critical of— even very angry about—the Agricultural Establishment on several counts. Unfortunately for the reformers, each interest has its own agenda and wants, and each one lives mostly in its own network within or close to the agricultural policy domain. As a consequence, there is little likelihood of a successfully broad reform movement, even as more of the public expresses food-related anxieties and anger—and even as criticisms of farm policy mount.

None of that negates the processes of policy and institutional change within the Agricultural Establishment. Reformers get attention; some reforms go on. That is to say, some social causes are called up to the major leagues. At a professional service center for those who are charged with

fostering neutral competence, new ideas and criticisms freely enter the agricultural policy process. As members of often challenged political organizations, administrators and agency experts address criticisms and respond (at
least halfheartedly) to suggestions made about their own hopeless neglect.
So does Congress. New research, new programs, new ideas, and new values then pop right up in USDA, the land grants, Extension, and agricultural
research. They simply may not pop up as highly and as visibly as traditional
issues raised by traditional farm and business interests; the more extreme
views may not—probably won't—pop up at all. Nor may any of them be
fully embraced. The controversy does encourage attention, however, and
new policy evolves. The Pittsburgh Pirates usually get a little better within
that National League Central Division every year—though not much.

Three conclusions are evident. Rural policy reform is not an independent
movement—or at least, not a very stable one. Anti-establishment reformers are not a political team that can effectively challenge the institutional
strengths, policies, and organizations that went marching nearly 150 years
ago. The criticisms brought to the Agricultural Establishment within its encompassing domain are important, however, for evolutionary change in policy and organizations. In that sense, the reformers matter because of their
noise, their public, and their press. They are no silent threat, nor are all of
their reform agendas capable of generating much of what would be called
big picture change. Most of them will win, when they win at all, through
"small ball"—that bloop hit over the shortstop's outstretched hands. Obviously, they'll win by having several players bunch hits together.

SUMMARY OF KEY POINTS

Let's stick to the lobbying basics in summarizing this chapter. The essentials
have considerable value to anyone who wishes to promote—or even understand—rural policy or the reform of farm policy or otherwise politically
but legally attack the Agricultural Establishment.

1. Rural policy victories are damned hard, with considerable odds
stacked against them.

2. Neither contemporary national network politics, nor reliance on
strong partisan leaders, nor the assistance of existing agricultural institutions do much to aid and abet rural lobbying.

3. The last two decades of the 20th century saw an interesting change
in rural lobbying. Whereas rural policy proponents once merely ad-

dressed the logical needs of poor and declining communities, attention has shifted to other strategies of finding political visibility. Friendship strategies have prevailed, as especially prominent individuals
have been used in attempts to raise the status of rural issues and generally encourage long-term Agricultural Establishment reform.

4. Such friendship lobbying has not proven to be reliable, however.
It's too simplistic to work, at least as a strategic base. Relationships
are too transient; trust is difficult to build; follow-through is difficult;
targets are also targets for other, more institutionally entrenched, political forces; and the transaction costs of dealing positively with reform demands are too high. Escalation of costs and of ongoing
battles is a mess. Farm interests still have power. Yet conflict avoid-
ance generally leaves those old farm policy hands in charge. What to
do is a good question.

5. The peculiar dynamics of high-visibility lobbying of more politically influential friends has had two effects on rural lobbying. First,
the more numerous issues of broad policy reform of the Agricultural
Establishment gain more attention because of the multitude of reform interests involved.[24] Elites of that lobby like the extra attention.
There is a downside, however. Rural policy loses some of its individual political attention as it fights for recognition with issues of the
environment, food safety, and even world food trade.[25] Second, advocates for individual and highly specific programs recognize the
need to follow a counter approach. They play small ball, waiting for
small issue openings in large bills—such as the recurring omnibus
farm legislation—to achieve small wins that still matter to people
who want their benefits. Issues get wrapped inside policy vehicles.
This approach combines to give proposed RDAs and the Fund for
Rural America relatively low political status—even at the outset of
their development. Why? Someone will dismantle them, as quickly
and quietly as possible. That's to be expected.

6. None of this means that the growing lobby of people who are
angry with agricultural institutions will not have an impact on future policy. Some interests will. The highly political nature of the
Agricultural Establishment makes institutional representatives responsive to criticism from all but the harshest reformers. Bureaucratic procedures also add to demands for an accountable review of
public opinion. For agriculture, it's imperative to evaluate and in-
vestigate new ideas, new values, new worldwide circumstances,

new ideological beliefs, and the like. Neglecting this imperative costs institutionalists their own expert credibility and thus long-term public support.

7. An oddity of structure also affects the entire agricultural reform movement. With the reform movement's many core but quite small social-cause interest groups and with its reliance on generating national and international public and press support, many advocates of reform have had to become quite involved in Agricultural Establishment networking. The two-team analogy then breaks down rapidly. It's the league that matters: the agricultural policy domain. Issues of reform expertise are most likely to be considered in those domain networks; institutionalists want to review and evaluate the reformists and their work, and reformists are dependent for their success on the superior research capabilities and information-gathering abilities of the institutions. In that sense, an environmental policy activist lives in, at least, the old soil conservation network. She shares policy space there but contests dominant policy values. The domain, as a cooperative league, has come together in important if incomplete ways. At least the domain has come together in ways that foster discussion between networks and outsiders. That also describes the evolving Agricultural Establishment pretty well.

11

THE RURAL
POVERTY MESS[1]

This chapter is about how the traditional poor peoples' focus of rural policy makes successful rural advocacy so improbable. It provides an extensive explanation of how and why players fail to relate to rural poverty and community decline. The contextual emphasis is on what policymakers think, how they learn what they think, and how their thoughts appear to affect behavior. Its point is that rural policy that has a poor peoples' purpose lacks social interest, generates no policymaking noise, and has no solid base of analytical documentation. As presently conceived, rural policy is a bore.

Were it not for the persistence of rural poverty over time, there would be next to no interest in a U.S. national rural policy. Its advocacy, perhaps unfortunately, has long been mostly about a message of social justice. Rural policy, like rural poverty, is about the politics of community decline. As chapter 2 notes, 10 percent of the U.S. population lives in remote rural places, isolated from city or urban jobs; 10–20 percent of that population lives in poverty. Overall, rural incomes fall below city or urban incomes; the lowest-paid U.S. manufacturing jobs in rural America pay more than other types of rural jobs. It's possible, therefore, to drive through the backroads of outlying rural areas and believe that poverty is more extensive than it is. It's also possible, of course, to drive through the most upscale vacation home areas of the same places and think that things are far more grand and prosperous than they are. That's even more likely, as the discussion of rural myths emphasizes.

Perhaps it's unfair to say that without poverty no one could care about rural policy. It's plausible, as this chapter emphasizes, but not entirely likely. In preparation for the 2002 farm bill, leadership of rural advocacy was shifting to the National Association of Counties (NACo), a group that historically has focused on winning rural roads and bridges. By 2000, however, a new NACo president had arrived—a southwesterner with personal roots in rural places and poverty. At least for the time being, his commitment had made NACo a player, grabbed the empty rural policy leadership ring, and focused rural interests once again on community decline. NACo's choice of an issue position was embolded by the institutional actions of a nonfarm federal department—the U.S. Department of Labor. With national employment levels unrealistically high in the millenium's beginning, the latter department had decided to concentrate on America's one area of persistent worker problems: its rural places and poor people.[2] When George W. Bush became president in 2001, he was likely soon to inherit another Country Life Report, updated by bureaucratic experts from way off the farm.

Other plausible issue choices could have been environmental degradation and the very different matter of wilderness protection. Both are of interest to people who try to define the national government's rural responsibilities. Those issues, however, are issues in their own right, with separate groups of reformists rallying around each of them. On the other hand, there is a link between each of those issues and rural community decline. With decline, what society finds is an increasing inability on the part of rural regions and places to invest in or care for local natural resources. That must be remembered for the future (post-NACo, perhaps).

This odd issue separation, accompanied by the irony of issue convergence, is what accounts for broad agricultural reformist coalitions. Although *rural* is distinct from *natural resources* in a traditional policy sense, rural problems definitely converge with natural resource problems in real life. That point is where rural activists and natural resource activists see their interests coming together. These two interests, of course, have very different types of concerns in Washington, but their advocates still see reasons to support one another. As one activist once explained, "That's not my issue, but, by being attentive to it, I can perhaps help those issues that are my own."[3]

Nonetheless, the idea of making poverty problems central to national rural policy brings forward a messy situation for rural advocates. First, initiatives that are identified as poverty programs are not particularly popular with the public, nor do many people regard them as necessary.[4] Second, a considerable amount of public disagreement exists about whether poverty programs are massive and costly failures or hidden but far-reaching successes.[5] Third, public reaction and disagreements often are provoked by acknowledgment that public officials—from legislators to analysts—have not discovered and integrated what they do know from among the many remedies needed to alleviate poverty in general.[6] Fourth, to make matters worse, rural poverty and urban poverty differ. A national poverty policy undoubtedly would leave the rural poor behind those in cities. In many ways, the problems of market and social failures in the most remote rural American places are more severe and less correctable than they are for urban places.[7]

So rural public policy failure is not the result of public officials promoting government—especially its farm policy—while acting as villains. Nor have these otherwise friendly officials done what they have out of stupidity or total ignorance. Faults—if they are that—also lie in traditions and institutions and interest conflicts in the agricultural policy domain. For much of the immediate past as well as the present, those factors have existed in a trap that advanced rural policy for its presumed yet unpopular poverty emphasis: no good, and hard for Americans to believe. Rural advocates and sympathetic policymakers now face a messy argument about what actual rural poverty needs, if any, are. Neither the information they generate, nor the analyses they do, nor the issues they select bring clarity to that determination. This situation, of course, does not bring the prospects for rural policy as poverty policy much nearer reality in rural legislation or as a major part of farm policy.

INFORMING POLICYMAKERS

Public policymakers tend to think of the acquisition of knowledge as if it exists on two distinct levels.[8] There's basic information and there's nonpartisan, objective analysis. Basic information provides reasons to support policy positions, by bringing positive or negative views to the surface of the decisional process. Because policymakers live in a political world where values comparison predominates, basic information is seldom considered to be representative of neutral or value-free public policy demands. It's all about biases. Public officials, particularly those with electoral responsibilities, wish to know who wants what, when they want it, why they want it, and what they'll do to get it.[9] Their concerns are as follows: Should government act? In what direction should the policy action be taken? How intensively should this public policy be pursued? To what end?

With such an emphasis, policymakers are hardly looking to construct their opinions from neutral data from neutral sources. Nor are they looking for data and observations that come to them only if they request it. The opposite is true: Basic information tends to come from affected or potentially affected sources, and it tends to come freely and voluntarily from angry, irritated, even happy or quite supportive sources. Rarely, however, does it come from emotionally neutral sources. As another congressman once jokingly explained, "Farmers are especially good sources of information: Unlike puppies, they never quit whining—though the pitch varies. You always know when farm problems persist or when farm conditions need to be addressed because their different verbal cues tell you when their programs aren't working."[10] He meant that members of Congress, like all policymakers, listen when the talk around Capitol Hill intensifies and takes on what seems to be a serious tone.

Farmers are not the only basic information sources within the Agricultural Establishment—though it may to many seem that way given all the whining. Other kinds of people, such as agribusiness leaders, may be such informants. And they make contact for all sorts of personal reasons. There are other frequent types of informants, however, that agricultural officials see most commonly yet are quite different from one another.[11] These sources include institutional representatives: professional administrators, White House liaisons, congressional members and their staffers. There also are the expected private-sector policy informants: interest-group representatives, grassroots political activists, community leaders, and even legislators' personal political confidants. All are supported, or undermined, by media reports, public opinion polls, and other such nonlive sources of manipulatable ideas and conclusions—or what's in a legislator's head.

Despite these varying informant types, rural policy in general and rural poverty concerns in particular are not likely to generate much commentary. Why? The answer is obvious if one thinks only a little about several possible reactions. Few if any of these sources are likely to voluntarily comment first and most dramatically on an alternative agriculture policy for rural communities. Let's see why only a small base of rural information exists. Let's look carefully at the varying contexts in which different sources of basic information sing their choruses. Then we'll judge why rural advocates suffer grave disadvantages.

Institutional Informants and Information

Consider executive branch administrative personnel first. The 1980s and 1990s were periods of contraction, not expansion, for most agencies and bureaus, even within agriculture.[12] Bill Clinton, in his 1995 State of the Union address, declared that the era of big government was over. Yet presidents from Nixon to Bush (elder and younger) have articulated the need for limits on big government. The results have been threefold. First, bureaus with new-values or social-cause programs, which are subject to criticism inside and outside of government, in an emergency are most likely to provide basic information to policymakers. These interests include environmentalists, consumers, nutrition and food safety advocates, and others with new social agendas. Poverty is old politics, handled by traditional administrative agencies. Emotional reactions to challenging ideas are many; fear probably is the biggest. Mobilization within government also creates political noise, which often resonates loudly and frighteningly throughout official Washington.

Second, bureaus with no new or recent changes in program review and operation responsibilities are most likely to shrink in size. The ERS is a good example. It has experienced almost constant cuts in past decades, even while it has been asked to do more varied analyses. The ERS and agencies and bureaus that are just as threatened simply won't have much time and energy to routinely offer basic information to others. These organizations are too bogged down in their own assignments to do friendly advisory work on any large scale. They tend, then, not to create much policy noise or to tell overheard secrets to many others.

Third, USDA as a whole has taken on a relatively remote role with regard to purposely riling policymakers outside the Establishment or at the top of USDA. Its officials appear to be neither zealous nor enthusiastic advocates for either side of any routine policy conflicts or changes.[13] On the contrary, USDA reticence seems to encourage a departmental scan of events and disagreements that are linked to its missions and jurisdictions. That's a problem. Scanners tend to look at what comes over their desks; they do not systematically study the entire environment.[14] They become aware of most issue conflicts—but more for their own preemptive reasons than to provide the informational grist of departmental policymaking. Or they just stay out of the way. "I hope to stop silly ideas," said one ARS scientist, "not get some damned congressman to take them seriously. I'm not very good at just sounding alarms."[15] That statement appears to reflect the save-only-yourself bureaucratic culture.

USDA tends to be a limited information source for opening up policymakers' eyes to new policy challengers, the reason behind such challenges, and the likely intensity of forthcoming political conflicts. That's the case, that is, unless the challengers threaten the source—who then complains all over town and country (see chapter 10). Domain players within the administration learn and become familiar with these domain institutions and people, but only those in the most challenged agencies and bureaus are frightened enough to become active informants or whiners themselves. Extension Service personnel often play the most active informant role, generally because their involvement with multiple institutions leads them to be proponents and advocates of changes within agriculture. They inform others to advance largely personal agendas that are formed, however, on behalf of favored community and grassroots clients who otherwise lack Establishment attention.

Thus, administrative professionals from agriculture are an unpredictable and generally infrequent source of routine policy information. They are particularly unlikely to address never popular or typically neglected rural policy initiatives. Rural proponents constitute little in the way of issue threats anyway, except when a new president makes a new rural policy proposal (as seems to be rather common). That gets the phone lines moving—but probably not as rapidly as when new-values, social-cause reformists rally jointly around an International Monetary Fund (IMF) protest or report, to media attention, on Third World environmental effects of IMF policy. Such largely unanticipated and publicly visible events create even a larger need to know for at least some policy proponents, as well as an expanding incentive to tell others the sorry tale of the moment. Rural ain't jazzy.

For the most part, though, USDA officials feel no great urgency to interact or to elevate their own status by sounding policy alarms (unless it's a farm issue). This reality led one newly elected congressman to conclude, "USDA certainly doesn't seem like an active political player, not even one knowledgeable enough to protect itself."[16] Although that conclusion almost certainly is incorrect, the bureaucratic quiet that led to it does seem to point that way for observers who are otherwise unfamiliar with institutional agricultural politics. In reality, for example, USDA need not openly discuss with policymakers the problems of rural economic development policy. It need only continue to ignore such a discussion in its day-to-day business to keep winning on other issues. No badgering is required.

Institutional representatives from the White House and Congress include elected officials and numerous layers of staff. Both institutions expanded their staffs many times over in the 1970s and 1980s, mostly to increase their own capacity for knowledge. The intent was to reduce congressional dependency on administrators for information and analysis.[17] Staff became of integral importance. Although many officials have staff expertise on agricultural policy, few have an abiding interest in its rural components—or much knowledge.[18] Rural poverty portions of rural policy leave most of these folks cold and disinterested. How can this issue help the boss? These people focus on elections; poverty discussions, especially involving remote places, seem less likely to be popular with the electorate. Thus, information exchanges between these partisans and with USDA seem most likely to revolve around particularistic programs such as rural water systems and reservation housing—things that count in the district back home. Apparently someone likes those benefits, even wants them. That's an important message. Now, who would that be? Why do they want them? And what would they offer for them? Good stuff to know, sometime, somewhere? Of course.

Such is most likely to be the case for rural policy information sharing, at least as it comes from dominant political institutions. Rural policy information flows when someone wants to consider development of a bill, when they want to judge what it should encompass and how much it could cost, and when they want to determine the personal political rewards and liabilities of proposing the legislation (or parts of it, as Congressman Dryland Gulch did for rural water systems). What exists are primarily reactive information sources, serving mostly one another through ongoing personal contacts. These sources build on each other.[19] What *isn't* present with frequency are politicos with a focus on the great likelihood of a major rural bill passing, an interest in the bill's essential rural poverty content, a great deal of concern for the most SL of the SLCs and SLTs, and a commitment to fight for rural legislation through political thick and thin. On these matters, officials are skeptics indeed.

Information sourcing and use, under these circumstances, involves relatively few White House and congressional players and even fewer who see a great stake for anyone in any rural bill. They see no obvious constituency that will make a clamor. The organizational structures of both institutions assign few and far-flung public officials to what seems like an obviously unappreciated and underinvolved type of public policy. Probably neither the Honorable Mr. Dairy-Dependent District nor Mr. Dryland Gulch, nor any other agriculture committee members, ever sidled up to another aggie and said, "Aren't you excited about that pending rural policy bill, and aren't we well situated to bring it about?" Of course not, and no.

Semi-Institutionalized Informants and Information

"Semi-institutionalized" means almost but not quite having made it into formal legal stature—not yet cast into law. Semi-institutionalized policy players are accorded the status of expected participants in ongoing legislative debates, at least within the battles that meet their identifiable niche or situation. Most are private-sector interests.

Everyone, for example, expects the Farm Bureau to take a position and comment on the legislative history of the Fund for Rural America, as well as nearly everything else in USDA's farm and rural policy base. A kind of protocol exists to encourage AFBF participation. To a lesser extent—partially as a result of its new-values, social-cause position—People for the Ethical

Treatment of Animals (PETA) is an expected player, though on a far more restricted basis. Legislative protocol facilitates PETA participation, perhaps through an invitation to testify at a congressional hearing. Policymakers understand semi-institutionalization as PETA's credible—indeed, legitimate— right to comment on the animal rights issues of agricultural research as covered in the farm bill or in Fund for Rural America legislation.

Obviously, PETA's history of ongoing—if often outlandish—policy involvement establishes that protocol and brings its semi-institutionalization. What is so common today is the struggle of a great many newly organized interests that are working to gain policy recognition, achieve the expectation to lobby on the political inside, and develop reputations that are greater than those of their emergent new-values, social-cause cohorts—as lobbyists with a useful or intimidating voice. There's tremendous competition over who is accorded a credible say. Not a popular say, just a credible or earned right to comment. Organized interests claim their semi-institutional status, if they get it in bloodless battles, so to speak. They're not vested or born with that status, as a newly hired AFBF lobbyist or consultant is.

All of which brings up the notion of lobbying resources. Resources are the tangible and intangible characteristics of an interest group that bring that group a reputation, issue credibility, and an advantage in being recognized. Collectively, resources equal an organization's capacity to lobby. Semi-institutionalization, with its promise of access, certainly is a major resource. There's more to resources than that, however. Political scientists have shown that the resources of organized interests are extraordinarily numerous and take on a nearly endless diversity of forms.[20] These diverse resources range from superior strategy to friends within government to the always esteemed and absolutely necessary resource of money with which to lobby. No group, in other words, needs to lobby just like all others. Resources, depending on what they are, are applied differently by each interest according to their appropriateness and the unique strengths of the organization that holds them.

The foregoing analysis leads to a key point: No rural lobby of any magnitude exists, as chapter 7 explains. It probably can't exist. Moreover, without a multiple-group rural lobby, few resources get expended in Washington. That means that no one elevates the significance of rural problems, especially poverty and economic decline. Not much campaign financing is spent. Not many media ads are made and seen. Not a great deal of scheming by rural lobbyists is reported and discussed by policymakers and staff. In short, in reality there is no rural lobby, except in disjointed pieces; as a consequence, there is no rural issue noise and presence, nothing to call widespread (or any) attention to any rural bill that's being advanced or even discussed. That's one of the important reasons for congressional and White House reluctance to take an abiding interest of their own, to fire up about what's going on—or not going on—on Capitol Hill.

With passive institutional interest in mind, let's look particularly at what conventional political wisdom has long considered the central, or key, lobbying resource: an interest group's mass membership—those who most often pay the lobbying bills and form a constituency for policymakers to try and serve. Organized interests traditionally have been regarded as groups of individuals. Groups are organized sets of like-minded joiners with a common view on some policymaking position that brings them together.[21] At least that's true in theory, if not exactly in practice. Some members may join PETA because they hate laboratory testing of beagles; others might join to protest foothold trapping of fur animals. Some might join because PETA once held a free and open concert in Washington with Grace Slick of Jefferson Airplane (later Jefferson Starship). Nonetheless, members are important as resources. A group leader probably could mobilize member opposition to the beagle issue and the trapping issue. Sympathy for both probably exists as a central, or core, PETA characteristic. And most members probably would like to be entertained live and free by Ms. Slick.

Thus, an interest group leader probably could use rural members as lobbying resources in multiple and persuasive ways, depending on their sense of camaraderie. Members can be used to demonstrate large numbers of opponents to a pending issue; to show that a particularly important class of people, such as high-status physicians, are issue opponents; to raise other resources; to engage in disruptive protests that block commerce and raise public sympathy; to write letters to Congress; to communicate with large numbers of media reporters and thus other citizens; and probably a thousand things more.

The lack of a rural lobby comes largely from what policymakers regard as an unappreciatively true and committed constituency for rural policy (unlike PETA, for instance).[22] Intellectually, public officials and their staffs understand who commands what loyalty on what matters. Politics is a combination of intellectual argument and emotional hell-raising, however. Thus, the dearth of rural interest groups, the pressure of their actual members, the noise they create, and the enthusiasm they might generate about advocacy positions all haunt rural policy information sourcing. Eventually, the policy hope itself dies. White House and congressional people don't get excited and talk about rural policy because no one else of rural stature is excited and noisy about it. Without members as key resources, the rural lobby appears to be unreal or absent. It is to be disregarded, disrespected—just dissed.

That nonreality and abstention are critical to the failure of rural policy. Policymakers of a modern era expect interest groups to champion any issue that should, from their perspective, be advanced. That's an obvious normative conclusion. "If you're here, you count," said a long-time staff associate of a former Speaker of the House; "If you're not, you don't. Who cares about you then? Nobody."[23] The reason that attitude persists is easy to see. The United States saw a quintupling of interest groups between 1920 and 1980. The country was labeled an interest-group society; having professional lobbying services was as familiar to most people as having laundry services or valet parking.[24] Moreover, group proliferation was actually more expansive than that in recent years. Forty percent of all nationally active lobbies were organized between 1960 and 1980.[25] As government took on more issues, either legislatively or through regulation, the number of new groups kept at least an even pace.[26] As a consequence, it made considerable sense for policymakers to believe that issues that were not well represented—especially by a natural constituency—didn't count. Those issues obviously lacked a credible and appreciated purpose. Believing that also made the policymaking job easier. Just support what's most well backed or popular with some special multitude. Vote the opinion polls. Low transaction costs!

There was a flaw in that representative logic, however. Somewhat surprisingly, many organized interests and active lobbies lacked members. Foundations, churches, business corporations, and even government programs offered lobbying resources to, especially, social-cause interests that failed to draw members well.[27] These were patron organizations that offered money but also organization offices, lobbying advice, lobbyist assistance, and fundraising help. Alternatively, the new groups simply did the lobbying as an extension of the patron's interest. They rallied whatever sort of public supporters of the cause that could be gathered to work with them. The Ford Foundation, for example, fathered and paid for almost all early lobbying efforts for the environmental and consumer lobbies.

Patronage was important for no group of people more than the poor, however. The poor were notorious for being ill-organized, disinclined to join, and burdened by a background that included suspicion of collective action.[28] For the even more isolated and socially suspicious rural poor, organization for lobbying purposes was even more likely to be nominal. Their declining communities also lacked internal patrons to represent poor residents. Potential institutions such as local governments had suffered financial and personnel loses during this era and could hardly support much of a lobby, even as part of a national coalition effort. Perhaps NACo could change that. Good luck.

Community interests such as the remaining churches, chambers of commerce, and service clubs often lobbied citizens on local issues. As organized interests, however, most were too far into their own numerical decline in members to be patrons for extensive community action.[29] Thus, in an interest-group society in which a premium was placed on being involved as a lobby, the rural poor were left way behind indeed. They were absolutely unimportant. They and their communities were unorganized, institutional support back home was all but gone, and no established community interests were in operation. It was messy to deal with the rural poor—self-defeating, really. In short, there was no national effort in place to excite institutional representatives about rural policy. The small size of the rural lobby and its nonmember patronage status never made declining rural communities a sound lobbying clientele.

Farm interest groups, with their long history of farm bloc networking, were far more obvious about their likely policy gains on items of importance to them. Policymakers understood how to satisfy the farm guys. With far larger membership sizes, active member participation, a nonpatronage financial dependency, political understanding, and a persistent willingness to bargain, farm interests naturally had returned to political prominence after just a brief down period in the 1940s. No surprise there either. And there's no reason to support rural programs beyond mere lip service.

Nor were there any other highly prized or otherwise prominent nonfarm private-sector sources to excite or even interest people in policy that focused on rural decline. Legislators, of course, have confidants back home to keep them locally informed.[30] And confidants are unique in that at a very early or, less frequently, a recent date, they've earned the policymaker's trust as someone who can reliably report on district or state wants and needs. That is, they provide a highly personal linkage between home and Washington about what members of Congress should do for some of their local constituents.

Rural areas, however, have seldom brought forward many influential nonfarm rural informants such as these.[31] In part, that's because remote rural places have rather obvious job and development needs. Policymakers feel they understand such simple places well. To an extent, there's not much reason to look into those local conditions for creative solutions. Questions? About what? In general, therefore, few members of Congress are moved by the plaintive pleas of local community influentials—if there are any.

In recent years, an exception has been Rep. Colin Peterson (D-MN), from an almost completely remote district in northwestern Minnesota. Peterson's staff reports that he knows everyone in his district—and talks to all of them;

he has developed the habit of requesting ideas from individual constituents about how to ease short-term jobless rates and set up exploratory public-sector jobs and training programs. Federal dollars have been used accordingly. For the most part, however, such personal legislator interests have not imposed their influence on congressional intent or on national rural policy initiatives. Apparently, most policymakers lack Peterson's initiative, neighborly commitment, and basic rural roots. They seem to have known at least the myths behind the terrain and the problems too well to be attentive and innovative at the local constituent level. Familiarity with conditions of rural poverty had more generally brought acquiescence, not public policy enthusiasm.

Thus, it seems that a lack of enthusiasm, purpose, and belief characterize rural policy information sourcing—at least from all of the conventional forms of political opinion. Rural policy initiatives simply generate little discussion across the spectrum of potential policy informants. Nobody wants to talk about them or create noise on their behalf. Certainly this disadvantages the likelihood that Congress will pass a national rural policy in the near future. Just as important, it nearly dismisses the significance, or legitimacy, of the claims of rural advocates and proponents—not to mention what it does to the unvoiced public policy needs of rural residents. It seems quite clear that the very limited focus of discussion contributes to policy neglect. Thus, if rural policy needs continue to be defined as generally unpopular issues such as poverty and decline, almost nobody will talk about or listen to them. That also makes rural lobbying even more nearly impossible, at least except for all but those particularistic issues that members of Congress champion—or get to champion.

ANALYTICAL KNOWLEDGE

Basic information is knowledge that is valued by policymakers for its simplicity, its directness, and its overtly political content. It explains what challenges exist to the stability, or equilibrium, of rural public policy. With its emphasis on who, what, when, and why, it informs them about the political need—or simply the desire—for pending public policy change. Thus, basic information is highly regarded both when it comes and when (as with rural policy) it's absent.[32]

Policymakers also appreciate the other kind of information as well, however. They also see merit in nonpartisan, objective analysis—but not as much

merit and not on a par with information they receive from trusted informants. Therefore, we need to look at the context in which objective analysis
of rural problems is provided and used. To an extent, basic information wins
because it's personal: "Somebody gives me a warning because they want
me informed; I respect that."[33] Neutral policy analysis suffers a bit because
it's not personalized. "Yes," said one member of Congress, "I understand
the importance of scientifically generated knowledge. It demonstrates
whether the relationships that we expect to hold true do hold true. And such
analysis reveals what other variables, ones that we've ignored, might be
coming into play. Congress, therefore, gets choices. We can incorporate the
logic of analysis into our deliberations, or we can go with the instincts that
we hold in our political guts when it comes time to move from debate to decision. It's obviously nice to have such choices."[34]

Other members of Congress tend to agree with that erudite Senator, at
least with regard to the meaning and contribution of neutral analysis. It
helps with but does not necessarily enter the ultimate decision. Use of that
knowledge is flexibly determined—maybe yes, maybe no. Policymakers
who are most likely to look for or accept analytical studies of rural problems
do so because of their far greater familiarity with farm policy analysis. They
know better how to use it. There's more of it around. Given the size and
scope of the Agricultural Establishment, the farm-focused analytical bulk is
astonishingly large. Reports from somewhere come daily, it seems; by the
end of any given week, agriculture policy staff may well have several inches
of farm analysis on a desk corner. It's regarded as the product of programmatic researchers "who get dirty working in the mud of everyday farming"
and a large number of economic modelers "who are more enamored with
math than they are with farm problems." Thus, some important distinctions
are made that guide the use of farm policy analysis.

Not so rural policy. Most policymakers regard rural analysis as the product of either professors or economic and social science researchers within
various government agencies. Jokingly, perhaps, they see nearly all such objective analysis as the product of pointy-headed, ivory tower intellectuals.
These are individuals whose jobs don't mandate that they think about real
political conditions. So analysts are suspect for not considering—or need-
ing to consider—the political feasibility of what their data suggests to be an
otherwise preferred public policy.[35] That charge resonates with regard to rural
policy analysis: "There have been two recent and outstanding volumes of research studies on rural problems by academics. Both provide much to think
about. Both, however, fail to help me at all see what can be done legislatively

for rural America. Both also contain studies that obscure more than they reveal about rural problems. These scholars appear to me to really understand far less than the depth of their scientific probing indicates."[36]

Thus, analysis by the objective researcher may or may not provoke a decisional reaction among policymakers. It may be insufficient to do so by its content. That, of course, is the worst of the "why nots?" Public officials and rural advocates note that analysis about rural conditions remains rare. When it's advertised as available, often it's not. "The damned stuff just doesn't cross our desks, and I'm surely not able to go around looking for it" is a typical response.[37] This bureaucratically comfortable scanner, and most of her peers, only recognized one agency for its consistent production of available analytical rural policy materials: the ERS.

Moreover, several public policymakers recognized that one administrator, Kenneth Deavers, provided the entrepenural spirit within ERS to bring such reports forward: "He's almost like a lobbyist."[38] Deavers, a highly recognized rural expert, apparently demonstrated to policymakers that high-visibility leadership matters: "He gets that material out. It's never overwhelming. It's broken into pieces that we can think about one at a time, such as rural manufacturing needs or other practical rural government problems. The stuff is always readable, with more emphasis on substance than on showing off research skills. And, most important, Deavers and even his people are always available to talk. He also doesn't preach his truths. He comes as close as any data junky can to being a politically personal source."[39]

So why does nonpartisan, objective analysis not actually promote a rural policy agenda within government? Why doesn't Kenneth Deavers get it done? Let's divide the reasons between those that are peculiar to rural analysis and those that are more generically true of the reaction to central analysis within government.

General reactions should be considered first because they probably are also true of rural policy analysis products. First, government and its policy bases are not, it's believed, really neutral—nor are they intended to be. The entire focus of this long essay establishes that point. Yet analysts intend their work to result in neutral products. They ignore political feasibility.[40] They deny subjectivity. And they promote a usually quantitatively determined objectivity in their policy recommendations. They often try to measure fairness. So it's often rather arrogantly claimed that they see themselves speaking truth to power.[41] They are preaching a bit. Public policymakers understand full well, however, that these conclusions are neither complete nor the only truths. Second, basic political information, with its values content, contains more requisite governing knowledge than does objective analysis. For instance, it more likely calls attention to when actual changes in policy equilibrium are pending and when they are not. Analysts may recognize that there's a need for a rural policy act, but informants will determine when one is likely. The latter is more useful.

There also are several other frequent complaints: Third, that the analysis comes from too many sources. Fourth, that supposedly objective review by different sources produces often vastly different results. Fifth, that analytical reports are too methodological, too steeped in unreadable language, and not substantively clear. Sixth, that unrealistic assumptions are often made. Variables are excluded, presumed to be constant in their effects, or included as possibly influential for no realistic reason. One prominent legislative staffer noted that, for those reasons, he generally "swept away and threw away the volumes of farm policy reports he acquired each week, saving one, maybe, or two."[42] None of the rest were even read during scan periods. In other words, this context reveals a knowledge gap between analysts and what are hoped to be information users.

Rural policy analysis suffered from other problems as well as these generic ones. First, there was very little of it, which led to the conclusion that the subject had minimal political value. No surprise there. At least the complaint was unique, however. Second, analysis was often trivial, with researchers failing to explain the importance of their discoveries. "I don't get this analysis at all," said a frustrated staff associate who was interested in womens' issues. "What could be done for the health needs of poor rural women? Why are those different from urban women? It's too bad I don't get it because I'm advancing a related amendment to a public health bill. In addition, there's evidently no one available to comment on the study."[43]

Third, as a balance to the previous problem, rural policy analysis often addressed too much. Apart from ERS, claimed one USDA official, rural policy experts "want to cover everything about what to do with rural America. That's particularly true of academics but also the case here [in USDA]. Why can't the experts tell us just one thing about one problem? Then we can deal with it—if they have through their expertise found something, that is." [44] Fourth, and somewhat related to the foregoing, rural analysts explain too much in terms of national conditions or within overly large-scale regions. Legislators and staffs aren't mostly interested in the whole South or even the entire Great Plains. They wish to know and identify their own state and district conditions. What about mid-Michigan? Doing something for their local constituents matters most. That has associated rewards, even votes as favors. Yet they rarely get objective analysis about things back home.

Fifth—and once again tied to the two preceding complaints—rural analysis always seems to be poverty based. True, policymakers may well have superficial reactions to rural issues. Yet they do hear about rural problems that are explained by factors other than poverty and community decline, such as the need for increased tourism and multiple land use. Issues, perhaps, are subject to an alternative spin control for such redefinitions, or reformulations. Nonetheless, many policymakers would like to take credit for positive things done for rural areas that interest a broader range of citizens than proponents of the rural poor. "Poverty doesn't sell," said one disappointed 1960s liberal congressional Democrat; "I'd like to contribute legislation that gets a new luxury tourist lodge established on the Great Divide, or that gets cattle out of famous trout streams, or that improves recreation facilities and health conditions of western rural children."[45]

What are such complaints about nonpartisan rural policy analysis really suggesting? Why does this context matter? The answer seems to be obvious and noisy. Analysis focuses far too much on what analysts and their analytical communities consider the truth to which they should first speak. That is, what *they* see as the essentials of rural American life: Rural poverty, that is. In a political world, however, that approach lacks necessary value content. Policymakers are more inclined to react to issues that are regarded as more popular, located within highly specific places, and identifiable for their highly specific content. Exactly what to do, that is, for the home folks. These things are more likely to be pursued by policymakers, even if not in ways deemed optimally correct by someone else's analytical standards.

Informants who subjectively—and perhaps mistakenly—identify such things to incorporate in rural and other public policy bases will then prove more influential than the most trusted and nonpartisan objective analysts over time. Unless a dramatic rural crisis comes forward—and actually gets recognized. Or unless someone buys off a corrupted attention to rural America's most valued resources—and gets caught. Then analysis can help right what went wrong after public opinion determines what it was. If enough analysis even and ever exists.

ISSUE SELECTION

Words of advice from the U.S. Senate: "If your issue fails to play, change your issue. But don't give up legislating."[46] Senator Mississippi Delta was pointing to what he saw as the obvious, unfortunate, and total failure of rural policy in dealing with poverty and community decline. He felt that a half-century of information-sharing and analysis proved that rural communities would never receive a sympathetic policymaking hearing by emphasizing those twin issues, no matter how accurately they described reality. In particular, Mr. Delta believed that information sources did not perceive the conditions accurately; as a result, policy analysts generally moved on to other venues in studying poverty. Why? What people talk about in politics tends to decide what others are assigned to work on in staff positions.

Mr. Delta's logic can be seen in the works of social movement theorists, especially as they relate to the actual movements that the Senator watched direct policy attention away from rural America. Social movement theory holds that joint political action can come together effectively even when previously unclustered or nonaggregated mass-level customers decide to act in concert.[47] They do, that is, but only if a common message or threat conveys common meaning to likely movement participants. Thus, in the 1960s, issues of poverty were widely discussed and analyzed. When social action scenarios of many poverty protests were observed, however, the settings were always urban and central city.[48] Poverty therefore became an urban issue, preempted from being a rural issue because cities were collectively seen as horrible ghettos while the countryside was so nice. Urban and rural didn't go together in political eyes (except for those of President Johnson).

Later, when farm protests broke out in the late 1970s and early 1980s, the same preempting of rural conditions happened. Farmers were hurt badly by inflation, high debt loads, and high interest rates, as well as low prices. Farm losses increased, a national American Agriculture Movement emerged, and protests were extended to Washington as well as to almost the entire rural countryside. Other farm groups joined or formed around the protests. Media coverage was nearly as extensive as it had been earlier for urban riots. Thus, as Senator Delta saw things, the rural decline issue became a farm issue. The policy solution then shifted to farmers, who were already considered, he believed, the prime clientele within the Agricultural Establishment.[49]

As with urban rioters, farm protest messages were stronger than those of the still nonaggregated rural communities, with their lack of a common, unifying message. Farmers emphasized the immediate economic conditions and the resulting irony of how pathos could be found in the idyllic countryside. This was a sharper and a more politically shaping message than the longstanding rural message that emphasized that such pathos was, because of remoteness, an environmentally unavoidable expectation. Thus, for a second time in 25 years, rural proponents were pushed aside as others won the right to the months of protest-inspired policy discussion about poverty and rural neighborhood decline.

As two-time losers with the political imagery that they hoped to create, rural advocates and policymaker proponents needed to get smart. So said Senator Delta: Change their issue. "To one that might better work," he added; "either that or don't lobby for very much federal support."[50] "Suck up more limited funding for particularistic but persuasive policy benefits such as rural hunger programs or migrant worker services."[51]

Could a national rural policy be addressed and won, however, by not focusing on poverty and decline? Yes. And who knows? Successfully addressing another and different theme depends on rural leaders, their advocates, and the coalitions they put together. A national resource conservation policy (as mentioned earlier in this chapter) is one possibility. Another probable response is mobilization of already generally supportive and numerous social-cause reformist groups that wish to galvanize against the Agricultural Establishment. Once again, success depends on cooperation and overcoming group differences. Can an encompassing bill that offers a little bit to environmentalists, consumers, nutrition activists, and assorted, politically diverse other interests be put together? Undoubtedly it could, if existing rural advocates and proponents would agree to be but a small piece of the total policy proposal. The middle of the puzzle perhaps. But how do you redefine basic rural issues?

The odds of such a successful political transformation of rural reality are long indeed. And the degree of difficulty for actual reform coalition groups is high. Yet the ardor for taking a whack at farm policy on a wide scale remains high as well. So a strategy like one of the two described above—especially the latter—holds promise. That promise exists for two reasons of political context. First, it might well lead to a greater degree of widespread adaptation and a more rapid evolution inside the ever-changing agricultural policy domain. Especially if federal appropriations are extensive and if new program authorizations are made or existing ones extensively modified. The greater promise, however, comes from the second reason: It gets rural advocacy and rural policy discussions out of the inherently disadvantageous rural poverty mess. It's a freshly defined start to a policy area that badly needs one, after nearly a century of neglect within its domain. If it hasn't won attention since 1909, it won't be likely to do so soon. And a coalition agreement possibly can be made to target areas of potential economic growth for the most appropriate rural communities. There is the following downside, however, to issue transformation: Is too much of reality misplaced in the redefinition? If it is, new policies will miss the necessary mark of community development for all resident types.

IMPLICATIONS

The point of this chapter is easily stated: It matters greatly how a policy domain or some subpart of it is framed or defined, even talked about. And then it matters how the issues of that policy domain or subpart are perceived and examined by others. Definition again. Rural policy after the Report of the Country Life Commission was always wrapped up in two pervasive social problems: the poor who were left behind and rural community decline. That was because those two issues were dominant yet largely ignored facts of rural life. Given the positive imagery associated with American rural life, however, those concepts were difficult to grasp—and therefore to talk about. Rural meant nice, better, languid, pleasant, not poor. Moreover, farm failure problems, which were frequently discussed, were felt to be the major issues hurting the stability of things rural. So? Help farmers first in order to aid an already rich American rural life. As conventional wisdom, that made policy sense.

What people in politics discuss about social problems then determines in large part how policymakers respond.[52] Word-of-mouth discussions within the institutions of Congress, the administration, and elsewhere in the executive branch bring confidence that problems are understood and worth being dealt with (or that there's such confusion that the problems can't be dealt with legislatively). Moreover, there's an additional confidence: It believes unambiguously that lobbyists and influential individual citizens will bring forward discussions of issues of worth. That unbridled faith explains much about the representative format of U.S. government, or why private interests matter so much—and why rural areas are neglected so often.

What happens, however, when there is no discussion? If nearly all of the expected players in a previously started policy game remain uninvolved, the game is terminated—if, indeed, it were active and vital to begin with. Such has been the case with rural policy, with its history of presidential initiation. The initiatives win no active followings. Mobilization of the likely affected has been incomplete, or imperfect, for nearly a century.[53]

The implications of this chapter have far greater importance, however, than mere neglect of rural policy. It's what's implied for all American public policymaking. First, it seems that the most flimsy and least rigorous—indeed, the most likely biased—knowledge is the most generally valued by public policymakers. Information sources such as administration and congressional personnel, as well as lobbyists and key constituents, are most likely to place their own spin, or jaded perspective, on policy events. Yet their political interpretations have importance because they identify who wants what, when, and why. Moreover, they supply what's seen as a very desirable value perspective to the workings of policy formation. That is, it's good to know that a certain class of citizen likes the policy stuff that's pending.

On the other hand, analytical information that is nonpartisan, objective, scientific, analytical, and more likely to inform about the importance of a greater number of factors is suspect. Suspicions ironically exist about methodological capability and the usefulness of the analytical data. As James Bonnen noted so emphatically, the lessons of the Enlightenment, or the Age of Reason, appear to have lost their political luster in modern American public policy decision processes.[54] Certainly policymakers and the public lack the analytical sophistication of the analysts. Thus, suspicion makes a degree of sense. In some cases, however, policymakers just don't like the answers derived from analysis. Nor do they feel that quantitative interpretations lend themselves to politically feasible, or acceptable, solutions.[55] Too few value interpretations? Anyway, so what happens? Well, the most sophisticated knowledge sources about policy needs usually are ignored in favor of the opinions of contemporaries, political cohorts, and people embroiled in serving some values but not others. Farmers first; then let's help rural community elites? Yes.

Again, however, there's contextually more. Some types of issues, such as those of poverty and particularly the rural poor, are least likely to be addressed. Policymakers feel that these "bad" issues lack popularity and public appeal for most voters. They have such notable flaws. So whatever it is that analysis shows about conditions of rural poverty gets placed aside, nice to know but not worth thinking much about, not worth doing. After all, no national rural policy bill will pass anyway, as informants keep saying. The 1972 and 1980 bills passed as anomalies, only because they advanced local community control over federal expenditures. They were part of a wider government trend toward a new type of federalism. People talked about them for reasons of that new federalism.

Thus, advocates and proponents of certain policies face a dilemma. Do they keep plugging away, or do they redefine the issues and purposes of the legislation they actually prefer? This latter prospect presents a frightening scenario. Does a rural policy bill, for example, take on the meaning and shape of a natural resources bill rather than any element of a rural poverty proposal? Such alterations in issue selection can certainly change the alignment of policy forces—the whos, wants, whats, whens, and whys of value-laden, social-cause politics.

Is refocused legislation still worthwhile, however? That's the big question. Does it meet the service requirements of the Agricultural Establishment, in this case, or does it contribute to solving problems linked to rural community needs? Refocused legislation resulting from redefinitions of relevant issues may do no good at all for any of the most needy constituents of conventional rural policy. Changing constituents in any severe way certainly is cowardly politics and probably is antithetical to analytical suggestions. It also may be good sense, however. It may be one way—perhaps the only way—to effectively address an alternative to farm policy. That's the appeal. Without considering those left behind in agricultural modernization and development, why bother? No reason at all, except to score very questionable political points.

In short, the political problems that are most likely to be solved through knowledge derived from basic information sources also are quite likely to end as major policy misses, or ultimately impossibles. So the context in which information is learned by policymakers really matters. These misses are likely to yield certain important principles and certain analytically identifiable policy needs—but too late to help. Efforts that involve trying to steer clear of the rural poverty mess of politics may totally miss the needs of declining communities. They also may lead to misguided understandings of economic social reality; in general, moreover, they may bring even longer-term neglect and even a denial of needy populations. The shifting selection of policy issues, therefore, must be approached gingerly and with caution. It fails to be an appropriate strategy for dealing at all times with the failure to pass legislation. Any old kind of policy at all really won't do—despite what basic information may suggest.

SUMMARY OF KEY POINTS

What in such a long chapter demands—or is worth—being understood? Things must be reduced. So let's go back to the notion from chapter 10 that rural advocacy is as close to impossible as things can be in American politics. That will provide a bit of a guide for comprehending the central points of chapter 11.

1. Public policymakers rely on several types of individuals to provide knowledge about policy needs and wants on any pending

legislation or regulation. Rural policy is no exception, and the usual message that policymakers receive is that no major rural legislation will or needs to come about anytime soon. That certainly makes the prospects for rural advocates quite difficult. They're periodically disadvantaged as well when they cling to a rural poverty and declining communities legislative focus in their ongoing demands.

2. The sources of knowledge that are most relied on tend to provide personal information about political prospects and the values of those who will most likely influence the policy process. Institutional players from Congress and the administration, as well as a variety of semi-institutionalized private-sector players from affected political interests, are expected to be such information sources. Yet they apparently discuss their wants and needs too quietly. Their absence from policy discussions provides cues about whether a proposed bill has any chance of passing. In this instance, absence of opinion does not make the policymaking heart for rural policy and its proponents grow progressively fonder. Quite the contrary. Rural advocates, in such—which is to say, most—instances, face a truly uphill battle in contesting conventional political wisdom.

3. Analytical information on rural policy needs tends to be thought of as the work of more distant, less personal sources. And so of less understanding people—even less politically knowledgeable ones. Such individuals view their assessments as value-free, nonpartisan, and objective. It's work that's thought to be the stuff of professors and, more typically, executive branch quantitative researchers. As a result, such knowledge provides limited information about pending policy process events and decisions. In addition, of course, it's knowledge that is less valued than that provided by personal information sources. For rural policy needs, this type of analysis also tends to be limited in its availability; which also shows the lack of policy process interest in rural issues. Poverty and community decline analyses also tend to be unpopular given the complexity and the limited popular appeal of those issues. Why bother? policymakers ask. All of this complicates and adds to the problems of rural lobbying.

4. Whatever rural advocates do, though, they must generate enough noise and discussion to capture the attention of those within institutions. Numerous individuals matter in creating this noise, in getting people excited about rural politics and their most jazzy issues.

5. Refocusing or redefining issues is one way that policy advocates and proponents can move to make their policy wants more politically acceptable. For example, rural poverty and community decline can be easily redressed. A national rural policy proposal that emphasizes local resource enhancement and the economic benefits of those efforts for specific rural places is one obvious way. The policy downside of poverty is replaced by the policy upside emphasis on increasing community prosperity.

6. A danger exists, however, in selecting new issues to replace essentially necessary and well-understood older ones. Policy purposes can be changed so radically that significant issues and problems are lost to neglect, not necessarily just refocused in their political presentation. Information sources and analytical experts can be guilty of this, causing serious policy abuse of purpose and intent. Rural policy would be especially prone to error and omission in this way. This certainly makes nearly impossible the lobbying work of those who believe in the need for correcting the problems of those left behind through farm modernization and development. That concern cannot easily be given a new and jazzy public and popular meaning. Water systems, as but a part of rural policy, don't cut it. Other tries should be made, however.

12

UNDERSTANDING
CONGRESSIONAL
ANOMALIES

Sometimes it's useful to think about how public policy decisions are made. Not just in what context and with what advocates, as the two preceding chapters laid out: The subject of this chapter is: Who makes decisions and why? Its purpose is to describe who works with whom, to the detriment of rural policy. That's an especially necessary topic to consider when terms such as Madisonian and Hamiltonian philosophies (ah yes, and Jeffersonian as well) are repeatedly thrown around, as in this essay. It's also necessary, as in this essay, when rigid structural or institutionalized factors are noted for their influence in determining future public policy. What's important to remember is that philosophies are not rigidly defined, either by their framers or by their later adherents. Nor are political structures, such as Congress or USDA, so tightly constructed of unbendable rules that they leave no room for manipulation by individuals, especially by those intent on winning interest-like favors for themselves—those willing to risk paying high transaction costs.

In other words, the usual variations in the personal behavior of politicians need be considered as well. As must the clash of competing institutions, and how conflicts are mediated. Rural advocacy is made difficult not only by philosophical or institutional limitations within the Establishment— just mostly so. The way policy players reconstruct ideas and rules also matters. So ambiguities of process, which produce institutional anomalies, are as important to rural policy proponents as are the routines of, for instance, congressional committees or the setting of White House priorities. Rural advocacy is made increasingly difficult by the need to look out for the unexpected or by different and unfamiliar configurations of allies that are out to get its proponents. They are out to defeat rural lobbyists, for no obvious reasons. Or advocacy is made more difficult by the occasional need to safely and securely join odd alliances that may serve rural interests at not too great a political cost.

Thus, rural advocates have targeted Sen. Leahy and President Clinton as possible, if not altogether likely, partners in their lobbying. In neither case would it have been generally expected that these two would become anti-institutionalists, or leaders for Agricultural Establishment reform. Nobody would have picked them out for such leadership in a professional coffee room discussion. Given their institutional positions and the ensuing high transaction costs that each would bear in a political conflict, they'd have hell to pay. For both of them, it was only the uniquely personal circumstances that mattered to rural advocates, even under the most remote circumstances. Remote, as in chances lost by default to existing institutions where all the incentives are organized with the status quo.

So what are the anomalies that most likely matter? One that has been discussed at length is the variable propensity for odd political agreements and alliances, those that make no apparent sense. Which unexpected ones will occur? And why? Organized interests and Establishment individuals do move outside their usual niches or situations. An example is the umbrella alliance of anti-Establishment groups that would like to seriously reform farm policy, and so much else as well. Most are new-values, social-cause organizations, often supported by nonprofit patronage organizations. Organized labor can be counted as their allies too, however, even if its alliance support is halfhearted. All of the alliance groups, however, think of themselves as leftist, progressive interests, more comfortable with Democrats than Republicans. So they have some common ground. Yet each set of groups has its own very different central or core issues: trade, the environment, jobs, consumerism, rural quality of life. All have their own individual policy advantages already written into law, or their own policy bases. These bases overlap only nominally. As a consequence, the interest groups are what are conventionally called "politically strange bedfellows." Their actual issue connections are vague and ambiguous vis-à-vis one another. So their alliance is a political anomaly, a deviation from a common political rule of thumb.

For the most part, this chapter turns to anomalous relationships between and within federal policymaking institutions, with more attention to odd situations of mutual support and opposition. Specifically, between-institution relationships that center on potential presidential alliances with Congress. Within-institution relationships that center on the internal dynamics of Congress are then covered. These two topics are the stuff of this chapter because they are the relationships that are most likely to affect rural advocacy, one way or another. Yet neither of the dynamics is widely understood or anticipated by advocates and political observers. The following sections stick to how and why the relationships matter for rural advocates and why they're not often anticipated. The chapter promises not to review all possible American government textbook situations.

THE PRESIDENT AND CONGRESS

A large part of the lobbying problem for rural interests revolves around the question of who matters most, in which institution? A simple and very early textbook rule can be cited: The president proposes, and Congress disposes. There is an element of truth in this otherwise perplexing and not very accurate description. Certainly for rural policy proposals over time, the office of the presidency initiates reforms for the rural poor and their declining communities. And Congress does dispose of them—usually right out the proverbial window: gone to never-never land.

So who has the strength to accomplish rural policy reform—or at least bridge the gap to it? Those are questions about whose institution has the greatest power. Some people would argue on behalf of the president. They would cite the president's emergence as a true national leader, with his political partisans and the country's media focused on this unique personality.[1] The president supposedly has *the* power. If we observe presidents of the past 75 years, we see that they liked to create that image. To an extent, this particular image is Hamiltonian, or centralist, in theory because it offers elements of true national, integrated, and hierarchical governance. Someone seems to be in charge. At least partisans hope so, and reporters appear to watchfully expect it. So do the policymakers of the most isolated and backward Third World countries. Probably, so too do presidents think of themselves as the single most important person in the world of politics.

The Madisonian alternative is not dead, however. Nor is the president *really* in charge even with his many proposals. For Congress need not listen. Its members can resist the encroachment of the executive, and of course the judicial branch may resist the encroachment of the legislature.[2] All Congress need do is legislate to its members' own minds, their own time, and their own tune. With its institutionalized tendency to decentralize issues within itself, Congress handles the specifics, or the meat, of policymaking. An old political saying suggests that "the devil is in the details." That's in what Congress decides and writes into legislation.

Congressional committees make Congress the keystone of national policymaking.[3] This is the school of thought that sees Congress having *the* power. Committees have expertise and fixed jurisdiction. Moreover, of course, to the extent that small sets of specialized players dominate distinct areas of public policy, congressional power to legislate is what holds each set of familiar bedfellows together.[4] These are folks who know the feel of each other. They're folks that Max Weber would appreciate, doing the specialized bureaucratic dance of divided labor. Observers who note such committee tendencies maintain that Congress rules, not the president. The chief executive ops out; he can't control so many congresspeople who are all going in their own directions. Thus, Hamilton's hopes are unfulfilled, dashed. All this is particularly anti-Hamiltonian because the charge is that congressional rule is especially uneven, unplanned, decentralized, and localized. It's run by committees—which, in this unfortunate case (for rural advocates), are vital parts of the Agricultural Establishment (see chapter 8).

The local component makes things even more Madisonian and especially Jeffersonian than does the decentralized, two-house committee system. As Madison understood and Jefferson preferred, individual legislators on the committees worry about incorporating local favors for their own constituents into even major legislation. This dynamic discourages revolt against congressional representatives, at least from their folks back home. The urge to please the home folks therefore is as mighty in committee rule as any desire to advance important national public policy goals—that is, the president's likely agenda on proposed rural legislation.[5] Private congressional interests are driven by personal ambition and trounce appeals to the public interest. Members of the committees have their own offices, made up of numerous staff personnel who work hard to find out what's best in a farm bill for northwest Iowa, or middle Georgia, or all of Texas. Members' offices are like small businesses or private enterprises. They certainly serve private congressional interests more than the public interest, even though they are within the public sector (according to this view, anyway).

To a great extent, then, American public policymaking takes on a tumultuous rather than orderly character.[6] Jefferson valued chaos and disorder of process; institutionally, he won a great deal of both for his new nation-state—perhaps more than he hoped—because he had abundant faith in Americans (especially agrarian Americans) to be rational. Members of Congress were not to make decisions just by casting district and state lots. Madison simply helped prescribe that chaos while he hoped for more certainty of logical and deliberate process on Jefferson's ship of state sailed by American crewmen.[7] Jefferson also would have been shocked by what he wrought.

Madison, however, might not have been much surprised because he also warned of venal politicians and a lack of deliberation regarding the common good.

The not-unexpected result has been the continual uncertainty over policy outcomes. Can we, for instance, pass the next farm bill? That's always a question that gets people talking. This dynamic also inevitably resulted in a kind of ever-flowing well of American political participation. At least it was participation in the direct action of influencing policymakers—lobbying, that is. And, of course, it was highly self-interested participation aimed at always helping, at its essence, that-who-is-me. If, that is, I think my own victory is possible. Without participation by the likely affected—the selfish—no normatively good bills would pass. So what happens with such a toothless and smallish rural lobby? Not much for nonfarm rural America. Moreover, with supportive participation—as from farm groups—even the normatively bad bills might well pass, as many charge of farm bills since the AAA.[8] Especially, in this case, by ignoring rural communities.

As we have seen repeatedly throughout these pages, strong interest participation through decentralized institutional support keys farm and ranch victory. Central authority rarely works to bring farms and allied interests and farmers-first institutions to heel. It has been, as one Madisonian scholar commented, a political process that might have worked well for the common good if only men were angels.[9] If such angels were prevalent, the United States might well have forsaken agricultural modernization and development policy years ago. The nation might well have favored a more balanced national rural policy that operated in conjunction with meeting farm and other industry needs.

There was, however, never enough of Hamilton's orderly centralization to bring chief executive support of rural people and places forward and to victory. There were not enough nationally focused virtuous people contemplating what government could do for these disadvantaged folks and their declining communities. Somebody else, it was always thought, represented these folks. Let them take care of the dregs left behind a modernizing agriculture's wake. Or, perhaps, it was felt that there were too few rural caregivers in the district or state to get organized. Let them nonetheless take care of themselves. No angels existed. Nor were there enough citizens who were willing to take responsibility for places that were not their own. And no sense of *noblesse oblige* brought great intellects, wealthy public-spirited business leaders, and the nation's cultural elite together to reflect jointly on the needs of rural people and places left behind by a transforming agriculture. So the executive branch was disarmed, weak as it was otherwise in a

Madisonian world.[10] Presidents bailed out on their rural initiatives and left the localized Congress in charge of their ultimate destruction. Why pay the high costs of losing the fight? No reason—as Theodore Roosevelt saw, as Bill Clinton saw.

So no one who followed rural policy ever thought that the presidency was as imperially equipped to rule as it was in other policy areas such as foreign affairs.[11] There was no rural equivalent to the ultimately resourceful National Security Advisor, no one to protect things that the president deemed rural from the encroachment of or capture by his Cabinet departments, especially USDA. There was no rural equivalent of the Central Intelligence Agency to gather massive amounts of information and make conceptual and observational sense of rural data. And, of course, there were no massively equipped armed forces to airlift to isolated rural places to secure local economies and their perimeters under executive order. In short, presidents always lacked counter-institutions to battle existing establishments.

Presidents were successful only when their proposals were linked to other, better-attended government goals than rural stability. Presidents Nixon and Carter—the only executive victors in the national rural policy arena—won their two rural policy acts as part of a more general, more dominant, government-wide initiative on behalf of a widely championed "new federalism." The intent and the rallying cry behind those two rural development acts was to turn more control and money over to local places and their governmental units.[12] Dispensed and decentralized localism, Jefferson as larger-than-life, prevailed. Congress liked that. It was like a parental allowance for kids who could then go raise themselves. And new federalism won not only rural legislation but also urban legislation and transportation legislation and many other bills *ad nauseum*.

Let's pretend, however, that all policy areas are equal in terms of worthy attention and that the legislative and executive branches of government are equal in power. Numerous political observers, after all, do believe in such a dubious truth.[13] Could rural policy then prevail over farm policy? Probably not. Forget about the actually unforgettable interest and institutional influences for the moment. It appears unlikely that the public, even the attentive public, would get behind such an Establishment reform. There'd be no public opinion support in the polls. Anti–big government, pro–local government, morally rigid, and accountability-yearning activists have become major citizen forces that shape and even allow what policy initiatives existing institutions will advance. Even Democrats and their traditional interest group and ethnic allies resist calls for a larger federal role in local life. It's the era of small government control (at least openly). Most

Americans regard a federal role in local life as yet another proof for yet more suspicions. Big government is hardly defendable to them because it destroys individualism, takes over as an unreachable authority, operates in secret, and goes about its business by using dishonesty and falsehoods.[14] Why, then, subject rural communities to such corruption? Forget that!

So, will a supportive farm-to-rural policy reform response be elicited under such presidential leadership conditions? Will the president who proposes be moved to act forcefully in conjunction with a Congress that favorably disposes as the executive branch intends? Even if the administration throws forward a national rural policy initiative? Probably not, for either of the big questions. And for more than just the foregoing reasons. With the power of food so prominent as a personal and selective self-interest, few citizens are sufficiently knowledgeable to willingly pull the plug on farm service institutions. Remember, moreover, that we're discussing this response without even considering the whining from predominant agricultural interests and institutions. With the wretched pitch of farm cries, citizens would be, yes, even more completely cowed.

Even without the farmers and their allies whining, however, public skepticism about significant funding for rural policy would probably continue to be high. It would be heightened even further because public policy neglect of rural issues and interests has become a century-old norm. Who isn't used to it? Despite some fool's complaint every once in a while, rural communities have always seemed like great places for those country folks to live. Remember the myth business? Why mess with these places now then? And many rural folks agree, especially when their highest premium is placed on their isolated and individualized lifestyles. Why let the federal government be part of all this? No way. Reject that idea. So, once again, even with a centrist government hypothetically poised to act, rural policy lacks a constituency. And its promise lacks natural beliefs among the public.

So what has all this wordiness, with its philosophy of governing institutions, been about? What's the point? Well, this commentary maintains that rural policy advocates are likely to be damned whatever they do. Institutionally, at the constitutional core of things, rural lobbies get screwed. Oops; that is, they remain at perpetual disadvantage no matter what their advocates' political strategy, no matter what changing local conditions they face.

Let's cut to the quick here. Presidents, especially those of the 20th century, do like to propose bills for rural people and communities. It's almost routine. It's public interest, social-cause stuff. Career administrators, other policy experts, or advocates who have worked for the executive's election have provided the initiative. There's a national need, of course, in that fabled public interest. Thus, institutional order exists: The president sends marching orders to Congress, and, in defeating that order, Congress fails to join the parade; they don't usually want to bed down with the odd fellow in the White House. Occasionally, however, Americans get a very politically astute president who looks carefully and moves around existing institutions. Lyndon Johnson did just that. Johnson should have been extraordinarily sensitive to rural poverty—and he was.[15]

Johnson knew better, however, than to fight with farm interests. They'd likely win, or at least bring gridlock (as they did with the report of his Rural Poverty Commission). He also knew better than to think that USDA, land-grant, and other farm institutions could be redirected anyway. Bureaucrats eventually would revert to their old ways and to old pressures. So LBJ probably also thought, "forget that." And he didn't count on a huge rural development bill. He simply added rural people and communities to his list of direct beneficiaries for the Great Society's welfare and public expenditure programs. Congress bought that idea, perhaps under a bit of duress. Rural people, nonetheless, got bigger and more available public policy benefits, along with everyone else. Rural places became eligible for community service assistance—from social services to education to health care to local government administration. So did every place else. And for a considerable time, in the 1960s—until the high costs of the war in Vietnam led to fiscal retreat—more money, for better or worse, was in the hands of rural residents.[16]

Johnson, of course, followed Hamiltonian logic, responding to a Democratically partisan public and a media that expected him to successfully strong-arm the rest of government. LBJ was the reputed man-on-horseback, the *macho* leader, *the* power. Actually, however, he led only by strategically circumventing traditionally influential interests and reluctant institutions. In an odd and self-created alliance, Johnson joined congressional urban and rural and even some suburban representatives of the beneficiaries of government largess with his liberal and Democratic platform. Talk about breaking from institutions and finding strange bedmates from strangely related places: Johnson did it. And this anomaly is unlikely to be repeated.

Johnson as Hamiltonian leader won only by doing a little Madisonian sidestep. Congress cooperated by passing numerous Great Society bills but no specifically rural policy legislation. Throughout, Johnson pandered to the localized wants of members of Congress. Congressfolks wanted more money in their districts, better roads at home and such. A large majority of them also wanted to avoid crossing swords with Johnson—who, from his leadership days in Congress, knew their individual weaknesses, personal flaws, character deficiencies, interest-group debts, and unique local problems and attendant policy needs. So Johnson, as not quite a fully subscribing Hamiltonian leader, led by patiently allowing for a Madisonian Congress and by otherwise refusing to realign the commitment of what would be considered his hierarchical subordinates within the administration. That is, federal agricultural institutions were left alone.

Johnson shows that success in policy leadership is possible only when the strength of central leadership recognizes the needs of a locally focused legislature and bureaucracy.[17] Political institutions can be allowed to coexist and keep plodding along, at least nominally together even when they have competing philosophies of governance. So institutional branches of government *can* be separate and, in essence, relatively equal.[18] Pleasing both, then, matters immensely for rural advocates under these unique circumstances. In similar circumstances, maybe even a small rural lobby could have won, as some people anticipated under Bill Clinton. But Clinton, desiring to be the boss of bosses, failed to understand Congress, just as he saw no reason to confront it.

One more thing matters from that discussion of philosophies and institutional structure. Congress hasn't accepted an executive's proposed national rural policy except when the legislation meant something else. An initiative quite simply has never been locally crafted to serve decentralized Madisonian and localized Jeffersonian logic. The proposals simply didn't match the norms of the congressional institution as drafted. Instead, all things are available to all places; few are designated for specific places (e.g., rural Florida, Appalachia, or Michigan's upper peninsula). Strategies for development, let alone people's wants from government, are different in all these locales. So Congress gives up. It far and away favors farm policy, with policy rewards to specific types of local and regional crop farmers. And it favors providing the greatest benefits to the largest farms, which bring forward the most numerous and resourceful political activists.[19]

Congress can assemble a list of rural policy benefits that can be put into a farm bill or even, if it wants, separate rural legislation. So what? Why do it? In the first place, no public support exists for anything more as a matter of really general public interest. No congressional ambitions would be served if it did. Congress also lacks the institutional structure of integrated committees to put together and pass on its own a national rural policy that treats all rural places equally. Agriculture committees have jurisdiction over rural policy bills.

Hamilton would have known that such an impasse would occur, and he never would have accepted such a congressional institution within his framework of government because of its likelihood. Congress occasionally may defer to a creative and even sneaky president, but not by its own design—just by dumb luck. Yet rural policy advocates face this congressional intransigence every time they lobby. They find that Hamilton's vision (let the executive do it) lives in American government, but it doesn't rule (much to their regret). As one rural lobbyist said, "These are really parochial people in Congress. None think of the public interest. Everybody asks just who back home wants such legislation. Jeez!"[20] Right: Institutional mismatches, driven mostly by one philosophy of government (Madisonian) over another (Hamiltonian), create that condition.

INSIDE CONGRESS

The national versus local split between the proposing presidency and the disposing Congress creates a kind of institutional warfare in national policymaking: one inside and outside of the Agricultural Establishment. That was intended, for the most part, in the Constitution's separation of powers and checks and balances, even though the Founders collectively hoped for greater resolution through thoughtful discussion. Fat chance, though.

Congress, however, has its own internal factionalization too—and not only because the Constitution divided it by the two houses of Senate and House of Representatives. That helps divide things, of course. As members of Congress often say, "The enemy is not of the other party, it's of the other house."[21]

A more perplexing divide exists with regard to exercising legislative leadership over policy. Will House and Senate leaders lead by promoting their favored policy initiatives? After all, the leadership plays an institutional role (although it's within the congressional establishment rather than the Agricultural establishment). Or will it be the committees, where institutional expertise and issue knowledge lie? Committees, of course, are within the Agricultural Establishment as well as the congressional establishment. This battle over institutional rule generally is decided by political era rather than by one case—or bill—at a time, but not entirely.

The early years of the 19th century were years of House and Senate leadership control over congressional agendas. When legislators revolted after Henry Clay's death, the committees won greater influence. What was legislatively proposed was each committee's jurisdictional business. From just before the turn of the century until about 1930, however, strong leaders took charge and ruled. Their abuse of individual member prerogatives led to another revolt in favor of reinstitutionalized, decentralized committee rule. In the 1970s, further revolts led to even greater decentralization of decision making to the subcommittees.[22] Given these changes over time, it should be clear that the members of Congress decide where the praxis of internal power actually lies—that is, who leads the congressional establishment: the experts or the partisan organizers. In the case of farm and rural policy, that means those of the Agricultural Establishment or those of the congressional establishment.

Yet for rural and agricultural policies, some undetermined combination of central and committee leadership seems to exist. Both play important institutional leadership roles. In the 1930s, the agriculture committees of both houses wrote legislation, while the leadership generally disapproved.[23] By the 1950s, the leadership of both houses exercised some internal control over farm and rural isues. They sent forth messages saying that farm bills were expected, but only with certain content.

This dynamic carried on the admonitions of President Franklin D. Roosevelt in the 1930s. FDR used partisan congressional leaders to carry his message: Do something, anything. When such leadership was given, it always added to farm bill support by vocally moving it onward. Leaders remained silent, however, over rural policy initiatives, even those of the Nixon and Carter victories. This rural policy silence seems to have had the same effect as it did on two farm bills on which the congressional leadership remained silent, at least in public: The Brannan plan of 1948 and the wheat bill of 1963 were both defeated, even though President Kennedy cheered on the latter.[24]

By the 1980s, things changed again as farm bills grew to omnibus stature, increasing in length (more than 700 pages) and issue coverage. Leaders of both parties sent requests to the agriculture committees regarding what they specifically wanted for themselves in farm legislation and often what they didn't want to see included. Their hopes were generally followed in good faith and with charity to the leadership's needs. In part this charity was the result of the fact that both houses' majority and minority leaders were from farm states and districts.[25]

There were two significant exceptions. Republican leaders initially wanted an extension of price supports in 1996 rather than the resulting Freedom to Farm Act, which phased out price supports. From 1973 onward, leaders of both parties, at times, opposed the inclusion of legislation desired by various social-cause groups. Farm bills weren't seen by all as the places to put such stuff.

Does this mean, then, that Hamiltonian leadership won within Congress on farm bills? Or that it was somehow necessary? That the decentralist Madisonians could have been avoided? Not quite. Farm bills, and national rural policy bills too, were written in the House and Senate committees. Both committees allowed ample time for their own consultation with other public officials, lobbyists, and individual constituents. Almost alone, the committees' staffs carefully and systematically examined data and in some cases analyzed it for themselves and their committee members,[26] along with USDA and other Establishment data sources and extensive data from interest groups. When impasses seemed to occur over such matters as environmental proposals or Food Stamps or what type of direct financial support should go to farmers, it was the committees that eventually resolved them.[27] The leadership rarely intervened other than to urge each bill's completion.

It was clear, then, from the 1930s onward, that the agriculture committees had the greatest influence over legislative content. The same was true with regard to whether a bill lived or died.[28] The leadership of both parties and both houses provided only nominal cooperation. Most important, they rallied the rank-and-file members of Congress around farm bills where they could.[29] This mattered because it was not always clear to many nonfarm state legislators why they should vote for bills that seemed outdated and largely irrelevant to their own personal ambitions.

Because of such concerns in a Madisonian and Jeffersonian Congress, the rank-and-file members must be considered as independent institutional sources of power themselves. They exist as an ambiguous force and a governing anomaly. But they're institutional members, of the congressional establishment, not the Agricultural Establishment. Why? To win votes on legislation that the committees truly wanted, congressional majorities had to be assembled. The committees often faced many recalcitrant congresspeople. A popular strategy emerged in the 1970s and continues to the present: Put something in the bill for each member who wants something and who then agrees to support the legislation.[30]

The result has been a plethora of new farm bill provisions and agricultural programs. Some members have wanted scientific, technical, or financial assistance for apple farmers, cherry growers, organic vegetable producers, western cattle ranchers in cougar country, and a myriad of other people. Other members have insisted on environmental, consumer, tourist, or farm worker assistance provisions. Still others have demanded such items as greater affirmative action attention within the ARS. All of these add-ons share one characteristic: They directly affect the petitioning member's own district or state or are otherwise thought to be highly relevant to district or state constituents.

Doesn't this work for rural policy bills? No—for three reasons. First, rural development legislation usually has been written for more national than local attention. It therefore doesn't lend itself well to Madisionian or local-ized add-ons—the things Congress likes. We might call it pork barreling. Locke wasn't right here, either. Second, even in farm bills, with their own rural policy provisions, very few members request things that would be considered nonfarm rural assistance. Almost none do, in fact.[31] Far less than for other types of issues, such as environmental protection or food safety. Third, agriculture committee members and leaders have never cared enough about rural initiatives to facilitate the drafting of bills that are more suitable to unique rural needs or that balance farm and rural needs. They haven't wanted to play that now well-institutionalized farm bill game of something for almost everyone. So rank-and-file members of Congress have never seen any particularistic reasons to join a majority around some or any national rural policy initiatives.

So what would rural advocates need to do to pass a bill in Congress? Who must they win over? And how would they do it? First, rural advocates would need to assemble a bill that could be used specifically and particularistically in many rural districts. That's true no matter what the bill's advertised intent or the identity of its sponsors. Second, the bill couldn't be frightening or punitive. That is to say, it shouldn't be regulatory in shape or fashion, nor should it direct financial resources away from any farm programs.

The bill must build an alliance of three types of strange bedfellows who can each stop the proposal from congressional passage. First, there must be a sincere and vocal leadership endorsement within Congress. Nothing half-hearted will do. Second, advocates must win over pro-farm agriculture com-mittee majorities in each house. These members, under existing jurisdic-tions, must draft any rural development initiative faithfully into the intended bill. And these legislators must remain faithful through any con-ference committee reconciliations, where House and Senate differences are resolved. Third, advocates need to muster a rank-and-file majority of mostly nonrural, nonmetropolitan members for a successful floor vote—with a lot of urban, metropolitan votes (in both houses) necessarily thrown in, how-ever. Obviously, such a massive effort requires more lobbyists and groups, more popular and constituent support, more ability to reach the media, and more attention by public officials than rural advocates have ever before rousted.[32] As we've seen, noise matters. Such is usually the final nail in the coffin of successful rural advocacy, the death of their periodic chances to break agricultural policy equilibrium. The bifurcated institutional system of leaders and committees, with its numerous anomalies of unpredictable rank-and-file participation and alliances, just demands far too much ag-gressive rhetoric to put the right pieces together.

IMPLICATIONS

What's the matter, then? Rural advocates face a perplexing pair of institutional problems. The first is the realization that the president and the Congress are unlikely to be in sync with one another on the essence of any rural development policy. The president wants to lead the Governing Establishment. It's the nature of that institution, at least within the philosophically divided structure of American governance. With Theodore Roosevelt, FDR, and Bill Clinton, leadership on rural initiatives was fostered by a small cadre of the federal government's own administrative and analytical specialists. So presidential proposals have been national in scope and purpose, often developed in the early days of an administration, and written to address mainly the national issues of rural poverty and community decline.

Those proposals, as a consequence, have been wildly unpopular—or just boring. They provide little to the private interests of all but a few of the home-focused members of Congress, nor do they appear to strike the fancy of a wider public that might cheer Congress on in passing what could be such a new-values, social-cause bill. That clearly explains why Congress sees very little value in putting together its own legislation.

The second institutional problem is the need to coax partisan house leaders of the congressional establishment and congressional committee members of the Agricultural Establishment to endorse rural legislation. One of the two is insufficient. And given the unpopularity of rural policy and the unlikelihood of a crisis or widespread political shock propelling such legislation forward, one won't successfully motivate the other.[33] Advocates must generate enough noise to do so. And this still begs the question of finding prominent and respected members of Congress who would be credible bill sponsors (and, like Leahy, stick or be stuck with it).

Which brings up the odd alliance business of winning supportive floor majorities. Advocates must write rural policy proposals that don't look like poverty bills, don't challenge peoples' visions of rural myths, won't just win legislative allies of leftist social-cause interests, and *will* distribute policy goodies widely across the nation. Anything else won't be politically feasible.

What this chapter implies, then, is clear cut: The task of targeting so many disparate governing institutions with such an explicit message may well be impossible. Rural interests have been too few and too resourceless to provide such broad political coverage. And they've been too anti-establishment in recent years to write or support politically feasible initiatives—or even think them through. Moreover, their existing interest-group alliances seem more likely to militate against working with institutional leaders and against designing a moderate and politically feasible national rural policy bill that looks a lot like good old fashioned pork barreling.

Is there a way out—a potentially successful strategy for passing legislation that could help the rural poor and their declining communities? (Other than LBJ's way, of course.) At this point in this long essay, failure to offer some such advice would be a cruel and stupid exercise. So, here goes.

To begin, rural advocates should tear themselves away from their new-values, social-cause friends—but not entirely. And they should make new and prestigious allies. Manufacturing associations, tourism interests, chambers of commerce, and the like should be actively sold on the value of low-cost labor in rural communities. They should even include agribusiness groups and milk the apparent interest of the National Association of Counties. Build that odd-fellow alliance. Arguments should then be made that community improvements in education, transportation, other infrastructure (such as roads and hospitals), and general quality-of-life needs must be made before such isolated places are ripe for business investments. Slums should be cleaned up before prosperous baby boom retirees can be attracted.

Then cooperatively put together that selective benefit, particularistic, pork-style bill, at least in its general outlines. Include tax benefits for business investments in dozens if not hundreds of designated rural areas, but only those suffering social and economic isolation. Call them something like enterprise zones. At that point, seek out those long-suffering rural experts within the Agricultural Establishment, particularity in USDA and its ERS, as well as in the land-grant colleges and the Extension Service. This strategy expands the odd-fellow alliance. Allocate new funds to all of them. Use them wisely to further flesh out a legislative initiative. Keep it modest or minimal in intent.[34] Especially keep it minimal with regard to any changes in policy content. Cheap is also good. Make it appear new stuff, not a threat to farm policy appropriations. Write the proposal into bill form in such a way as to keep it away from the agriculture committees of Congress. Link it to the jurisdictions of committees such as commerce, education, labor, small business, or natural resources. Accept even multiple committee jurisdictions and hearings, if helpful. Take advantage of the Department of Labor's rural employment initiative. Making that rural-is-farm institutional break is essential.

At this point, identify 40 or so members of Congress whose districts include the proposed enterprise zones. Include members of both parties. This strategy really plays further into the politics of strange bedfellows working together. Use your allied business lobbyists in addition to rural advocates to sell these congressfolks on the proposal's merits. Maybe add a few social-cause advocates for some liberal members who respond to such people. After the congressional sale is made, employ ranking federal rural experts and the new alliance's most prominent and visible lobbyists and advocates to promote the proposal with a relatively new presidential administration. Sell it as a public-interest bill of long-standing merit (since 1909, of course). Use history to your advantage.

At this point, a presidential initiative exists, and it has solid advocacy backing, as well as preexisting congressional support. Ride with it. And remember, more than half of the initially approached members of Congress should have bought in, joined on. Perhaps they've dragged in new supporters on their own. With luck, the other members that were initially contacted are at least neutral on the bill, if not mildly supportive. Have as many of these bipartisan members of Congress as possible work with the White House and its administration to launch the proposal—publicly, loudly, and with fanfare.

Contacts should be made with the leadership and the desired committees by advocates and allied congressional members. Multiple members should sponsor and introduce the bill, keeping its purpose as politically neutral as possible. Make sure it's viewed as neither radical nor pro-business. As the process continues, committee members and rank-and-file members should be lobbied hard by advocates and congressional members to build working majorities. Then go through the same thing again with the president's budget package and the congressional appropriations committees. Maybe then a rural development bill, by any other name, is home free. But who knows? Because it defies institutions, the not improbable killing blow is still likely to come forward at any of the many procedural steps.

SUMMARY OF KEY POINTS

This chapter concludes the essay's foray into what makes rural advocacy on behalf of disadvantaged people and places so improbable. Let's summarize previous factors: Leadership is hard to find; alliances between new-values, social-cause interests, and rural interests are not likely to be advantageous; and an emphasis on poverty and community decline detracts greatly from rural policy's appeal. Now institutional factors of governance and related political anomalies enter the picture. So what else matters in this chapter?

1. Odd political bedfellows with no previously logical connections often come together to try to influence legislation.

2. Stable institutional factors are more likely to affect decisions, however. Nonetheless, we're dealing with pressures within more than one establishment. Hence, matters of institutional stability sometimes can be circumvented as political realities and expectations change.

3. Successful rural policy legislation must go through the White House, the presidential administration. At least, this is the historical lesson. That institution operates according to hierarchical expectations, or a philosophically centralist approach to decision making. Hamiltonian processes live.

4. Congress is an unlikely starting point for rural policy for poor people and places. That institution is too decentralized, too Madisonian, and too directed to the private interests of its members. It is too dependent on society's wealthiest. Rural policy appears publicly unpopular and misunderstood and otherwise offers little or nothing for most congressional members and their goals.

5. As a result, Congress always dumps presidential initiatives that deal with rural policy, unless there's another, more popular, hook—such as Nixon's and Carter's new federalism.

6. One big reason that Congress is so difficult to penetrate by rural advocates is its own complex institutional structure. Partisan leaders, deliberative committee members, and a floor majority all must be satisfied—and in different ways. There's been too little in past rural initiatives to provide that sweeping satisfaction. Congress as a whole can't even get interested.

7. Under existing organizational conditions, the rural lobby and its fellow advocates won't be successful in passing a rural policy bill for disadvantaged people and places. Their alliances, their approaches to politics, and their messages are inappropriate.

8. A workable alternative exists, however. If rural advocates seek more modest goals, find more moderate and mainstream allies, and pander to the Madisonian and Jeffersonian expectations of taking a specifically localized and selective approach to rural policy content, they'll win—playing pork, that is.

13

THE ENVIRONMENTAL
POLICY CONTRAST

Since at least 1973, agricultural policy has had a reputation for being accommodative.[1] That means that farm interests have taken actual and potential adversaries, the policy reformers, and included many of their wants into the big picture of agricultural legislation. Those farm interests then go on to claim—with some credibility—that agriculture is more than about financial security for farmers, all because of accommodation of diverse interests. It's also about safe, nutritious food products and production, low-cost foods, food security for the poor, and on and on. Agriculture reforms itself; or so the rhetoric goes, as do many of the facts about this policy domain. Farm interests also maintain that farm policy *is* rural policy. It's holy writ as agrarian myth.

As this essay has underscored throughout, however, farm policy proponents mislead us all (in this case, anyway). Farm policy has accommodated rural issues only at the most minimal level. It's been just enough to keep rural policy under the farm policy umbrella, so some other department or agency doesn't claim it and enhance its programs at agriculture's expense through rural initiatives. It's forbidden that someone else should (oh my Lord) claim rural policy leadership and, therefore, undermine much of the essence of farm policy purpose.

One question arises: Have all other accommodated interests and issue types been given only the symbolic attention of rural problems or of lip service where no actual farm policy reform goes on? The answer is no. Food stamps for low-income citizens, as essentially a welfare program, command about the same amount of money as the total federal farm budget. Worries over consumer acceptance of food products drive at least parts of many USDA and other Establishment programs, from marketing to setting biotechnology standards. The interests of trade advocates have been wrapped up in everything from farm support price-setting to promotion of value-added or partially processed commodities. In this case, the more conservative free trade advocates have won the biggest place on the agricultural policy agenda.

In any case, the point is simple. Farm policy has continually adjusted and opened up significantly over the past several decades, if only to save itself. But why have some types of interests with certain specific types of issues, such as trade and food safety, been winners, whereas rural advocates and issues have not? To judge that, and to underscore a bit more why farm policy is not resplendent with rural issues, let's look a bit at the history of environmental policy. Let's see it before and after its fight for a place alongside and indeed inside farm production policy. This chapter turns, then, to environmental policy—one of the winners—as a reform interest.

ENVIRONMENTAL POLICY ORIGINS: THE INTERESTS

At the turn of the millennium, environmental concerns and rules to govern them have permeated almost every aspect of food production, from tilling the soil to choosing containers for food retailing. As one recent USDA undersecretary observed, "Environmental proponents are everywhere, and they include, at least in part, some of the once most recalcitrant (USDA) people. I think they're running scared. At least these individuals now ask whether or not a program can better meet environmental goals."[2] Let's name some changes that account for such attitudinal shifts.

Tillage and planting practices may be the biggest change of all, particularly in their visibility. The entire business of preparing the soil for planting once required numerous petroleum-guzzling trips through the field; root upheaval, plowing, breaking up the soil, raking the soil, and planting were all likely, depending on the crop. Today's corn and soybean farmers, who grow the largest percentage of U.S. production, now generally practice no-till planting. So do growers of some other crops. They drive a planting rig through last year's harvested and chopped fields once and punch holes in the soil, followed immediately in the same run by inserting seeds. Boom: Plowing and assorted tasks are forgotten for most years. Soil conservation is enhanced as a result, and irritating dust in the air is minimized for residential neighbors.

Decisions are now made to terrace farmland; in the past these erosion-controlling flattened land barriers were removed from rolling hills to get larger per acre crop yields. As one Iowa farmer observed of USDA, "They first paid for Dad to put in terraces, then they provided him incentives in commodity prices and supports to plow them out. Now I have to put back in better and even more expensive ones."[3] School districts and other policy beneficiaries are affected as well. School lunch programs are discouraged from using styrofoam packaging. Catsup can't be counted as a vegetable. Industrial processors, such as McDonalds and Seagrams, are paid to help promote their products overseas and to trade with foreign partners who use clean environmental practices. One bitter joke suggests that food stamp recipients lose their program eligibility if they fail to recycle. Someday that might not be so farfetched, depending on how poor people's advocates and environmentalists fight it out.

So, by what pathway did environmentalists achieve this stature? How did they gain this ability to moderate agriculture, even as it remains the leading source of U.S. land, soil, and water degradation? Why have their issues been good ones—issues that make environmental lobbying a winnable and high-profile part of the policy process? Let's look. What we'll find is that environmental successes in agriculture resulted from political patterns that have been dissimilar from rural policy. The same factors have been at work, but in reverse. A mythic ethos emerged; policy benefits were held out that were collectively and selectively useful; numerous policy initiatives were dismissed as unimportant and often as silly; and many advocates gave up their reform fights as impossible. Those factors are covered in the remainder of this section. The following section examines a very different set of bureaucratic or institutional conditions. In the latter instance, environmental advocates won because they faced no elaborate set of existing and countervailing institutions. Unlike rural advocates, environmentalists had a relatively open political situation. And they were very much instrumental in creating and strengthening policy institutions that were organized to understand and even to assist them.

In the meantime, what facilitated these origins?[4] One constant has been an environmental ethos that, as a guide, portrays its own mythic story. That story begins with the Christian emphasis on worldly stewardship, which led to a social premium being placed on conservation of natural resources. Later, as environmentalism (with its emphasis on natural ecological systems) gained attention, the stewardship and conservation ethos continued to be among the guiding beliefs of activist values. Then, too, there was the early–20th-century emergence of private conservation organizations, each with their own particularistic emphases. From the Sierra Club to Trout Unlimited and Ducks Unlimited, sportspersons sought to undertake actions that would preserve their own targeted resources of wilderness experiences, wild ducks, and plentiful fish, respectively. These groups were hardly alone; organizations of birders, prairie grasslands protectors, and historic preservationists also formed. All clustered around early federal programs to protect these resources. And they grew around the wilderness policy visions of Theodore Roosevelt, who was not able to inspire rural community legislation but who did soon see an act to establish national park preserves (the National Park Service Organic Act of 1916). Aroused interests encouraged and gave strength to federal officials, including Roosevelt.

Another important feature of the stewardship groups lies in their middle- to upper-class foundings. Class factors resulted because of economic and cost matters associated with the valued experiences. It took money to do this stuff—and to support interest groups. Group founders were not the regular folks who catfished in the Mississippi River or camped in a meadow two miles north of the family barn. Group members and vocal resource users also were from social classes that were most likely to participate in politics. That meant a greater-than-average likelihood that these middle and upper classes would be politically active and take action against policymakers. These people were accustomed to getting their way.[5] They stuck with their politics.

What followed next, however, eventually made for the actual transformation from conservation to environmental policy goals and political groups. Conservation programs to protect the wilderness, preserve species, and keep alive splendid fishing opportunities were visibly failing. Criticisms of group and public-sector actions were frequent, and the call for more extensive public policy protection mounted, at least by the early 1960s. It was clear that stocking more hatchery-raised fish in dirty waters where cattle grazed was no solution. Nor did declaring one area a national park actually keep despoilers out of that or surrounding places. More hopeful, if often seemingly odd solutions were offered by early environmental theorists such as Rachel Carson and a variety of professors.[6] By the mid-1960s, they emphasized strategies such as paying conservation attention to whole and balanced ecosystems. They avoided (at least initially) scientific jargon that might confuse or irritate possible followers. All components of natural systems, however, were valued and were marketed or "sold" as merely an extension of the stewardship ethos, the conversation myth, and the new premium placed on those mythically superior and unspoiled rural places. Save it all! Then parts of it may prosper together. Moreover, politically influential funding interests such as the Ford Foundation gave organizing funds to environmental interests. Prominent organizations such as the Environmental Defense Fund (EDF), the Natural Resources Defense Council (NRDC), and the Sierra Club Legal Defense Fund owe their origins to Ford monies.[7]

Environmentalists, in turn, had ready solutions for national ills, such as chemical bans or improved municipal water treatment. They touched on health as well as preservation. And they willingly compromised with old conservation interests as well as polluters—at first, anyway. They also directed their sustaining myths to education; teachers, school children, and eventually parents gained new perceptions of public policy needs. This expanded the environmentalists' support bases mightily, especially as more and more common citizens complained of ecological horror stories near their own homes.

Then environmentalists switched to new tactics, designed to curry more social favor and still carry forward their old conservation alliances. More and more they complained of their status as political outsiders, of being treated as the great unwashed of American politics. Their advertised enemies were powerful bad guys of political lore: big oil, big money, big mining, big manufacturing, and such. Nobody, of course, wanted to be listed, even symbolically, in the public mind with such bad guys. So as environmentalists slowly took on one set of despoilers at a time, public officials at least halfheartedly joined the causes. They had little choice. This moved federal rule making from national parks and fisheries programs to municipal water system reform, to cleaning up industrial emissions, and then to the actual governance of recreation and resource users.

With policy victories aplenty and with all but God on their side, environmentalists were resplendent with good issues. Thus, more and more groups formed, each specializing in its unique problem areas of the environment but nearly all maintaining leftist, reformist alliances (with a middle- and upper-class bias among those who believed in stewardship, however). Stewardship indeed had moved full bore toward supporting a social movement.[8] Not only did that movement gain the strength to challenge hunters, fishers, and users of federal lands—their one-time friends. The environmentalists also turned their attention to agriculture as the last unchecked bastion of ecological degradation. To many people within the Agricultural Establishment, those activists had to be accommodated. Many old aggies even silently acknowledged that environmentalists' claims were correct. Conservation programs hadn't quite panned out. Others, though, did not accept this.[9] The war was on, in at least half the agricultural field.

INSTITUTIONAL FACILITATION AND CREATION

Farming by its nature is the forceful bending of nature's tendencies—and resources—to human will. As a result, many of the destructive forces of production were evident to agriculture's own researchers, educators, extension associates, and—yes—farmers themselves. Few Establishment officials were dumb enough to believe that farming was first and foremost about land stewardship. Although most did believe that farmers wanted to be good stewards, all understood that greater destruction came with any hopes of farm and ranch profitability. The farming future had to be protected, but all producers lived in the present before they arrived at that future. Full speed ahead, then: watching water run downhill and taking all sorts of stuff with it.

With the need for some stewardship practices as a bridge to the future, however, Agricultural Establishment institutions of the 19th century innovated. Research was conducted, in essence, to minimize the effects of gravity. Indeed, that simple natural phenomenon pulled water downhill—along with topsoil, destructive elements such as early pesticides and animal manure, and often whole ravines of once-fertile fields. Of course, water was then contaminated. Extension workers, prior to the creation of the Extension Service, and land-grant educators all preached the suggestions of researchers. So there was an early institutional awareness and even a response to the environment, albeit a primitive response. But it was a response—both early and vital. And it recognized that questions of resource use were inseparable parts of farm economics and sustainability.

Yet farmers who often hopelessly sought immediate profits before attending to agrarian stewardship were far behind what Agricultural Establishment personnel understood after the first 50 years of institutional attentiveness. Only a major calamity created a will within federal policy-making centers to use knowledge and skills learned from this attentiveness. That crisis was the sustained drought and resulting Dust Bowl conditions of the 1920s.[10] Into the 1930s, whole communities of plains farmers abandoned their land plots and moved on—by the dozens, then the hundreds, and finally the thousands. All the while, Establishment institutions blamed Dust Bowl conditions on neglect of sensible stewardship practices.

As a result, the farm policy revolution of the 1930s created more than AAA price supports and loan guarantees. The Soil Conservation Service (SCS) was created as well, first as part of the 1933 AAA and again after being declared unconstitutional in 1935. The SCS was designed to encourage greater conservation knowledge and to provide incentives for producers to use government suggestions. Brought together from the small but knowledgeable Soil Erosion Service, the SCS quickly prospered as an institutional centerpiece of the Establishment. It raised awareness of what had caused a crisis, brought Establishment personnel together who collectively preached solutions, and, accordingly, then provided some degree of knowledge about the scope of the problem of stewardship failure and resource neglect. Like other bureaus in USDA, the SCS preached science.

Conservation policy within USDA proved at least as legitimate as price intervention. Indeed, public policy actions of the 1930s linked perceptions of price supports permanently to soil erosion controls. After all, the AAA and the SCS essentially arrived in tandem. One brought profits to continue farming, the other brought the wherewithal to continue farming into the future (at least in theory). Nonetheless, because of the Agricultural Establishment's tendency to decentralize program planning operations, the two were not coordinated. Independent status led to separate organizations, policy networks, and rules.[11] In consequence, the institutional road of politics for soil conservation, outside its proper network venue, was never easy over the remainder of the 20th century.[12] First the Extension Service fought and forestalled SCS initiatives to organize soil conservation programs cooperatively at the grassroots. The two never merged, despite the wishes of many local Extension workers. Second, many other agricultural policy networks had program responsibilities that ignored SCS demands to be environmentally responsive. It was the fault of the systematic division of labor within the Establishment. These unresponsive networks also ignored and made enemies of many private-sector groups that were gravitating to the SCS. Initially this went on with sports groups, many of whom worked on local conservation projects in conjunction with the SCS. When these groups later championed the Soil Bank program of the 1950s and other related programs to remove erodable lands from production, other institutional policy networks scorned them further.

After the passage and practices of the Agricultural Conservation Program (ACP) in 1936, however, things gradually changed.[13] The ACP openly stated that federal soil and water programs and projects were for farmers first, although they'd give some things to other folks. Unlike the SCS, the ACP proved it institutionally—and without doing messy old science. ACP responsibilities were given to local USDA offices and to local farmer-composed management committees. These committees were products of AAA actions, to encourage local participation in federal policymaking. This strategy allowed ACP decisions about who got what to be made locally and, of course, took conservation legitimately to the grassroots. Because erosion control measures such as providing trees, terraces, farm ponds, and the like were selective farm benefits, farm advocates and groups soon joined conservation organizations as friends of natural resource policy—at least the ACP's version, which did not always really foster conservation. Institutions thus begat interests, even as most groups already existed. They just found a home inside government's official conservation efforts.

As conservation moved to its environmental focus, however, things once again changed. Demands for more comprehensive—not to mention more costly and restrictive—attention were not easily received by anyone. And they certainly were not easily accepted. Many SCS and even ACP personnel were responsive to ideas such as avoiding a "silent spring" or a "closing environmental circle" of escalating resource loss.[14] Yet it was hard for even the most ardent SCS and ACP personnel to work such sweeping concepts very far into what amounted to rather narrow institutional charges or missions. Thus, although environmental groups found a home of sorts within the SCS, that home needed some serious reforming. At least that was the general reformist perception. What was especially irritating to environmental activists was the limited influence in USDA that the SCS had outside its own policy network. Many environmental groups were especially sensitive to this issue because different groups had different goals. For many groups, their goals had to be addressed outside the center of SCS programs. Therefore, environmentalists wanted to broaden the SCS's field of vision and give it an overlapping, broader, and more likely contentious regulatory authority in agriculture. They had, on the contrary, no respect for ACP and its inexact policies: Get rid of that waste.

These goals hardly seemed excessive to interested environmentalists. Yet they *were* intended to reverse years of institutional operation within the agricultural policy domain. And they *were* intended to disrupt the power of many established offices and officials. Big trouble! Environmental groups and activists care hardly a whit about the high transaction costs of forcing such change. No battle was too large any longer. Compromises with old ways of doing things were no longer felt to be necessary. Why? Because many of these environmental groups and reform activists were experienced in other domains (such as commerce and transportation), and they merely were bringing their issues to a new set of adversaries. They'd beaten big business, and they saw farmers as a comparatively easy mark, except for agriculture's public support.

Moreover, many—perhaps most—of these folks had records of achieving success on their issues in regulating and modifying corporate and government natural resource practices. They also were involved at the time in mounting even more major and nastier confrontations over their own omnibus legislative initiatives. These efforts included the Clean Water Act and the Clean Air Act, which were so encompassing that they had issues in them for everybody—at least for the many different environmental groups and their varied agendas, as well as variances for different industries and facilities. So these initiatives provided a nice basis for a cooperative environmental alliance, which drew these several reformist groups that much closer together. This strategy further facilitated particularistic and largely uncoordinated attention to environmental advocacy and reform: You do auto emissions, I'll do smokestacks.

The result was monumental for agriculture. Although some groups felt supportive of and even friendly toward agriculture in general because of the SCS, most did not. Instead, they saw the Agricultural Establishment as a collective pain in the ass: arrogant, aloof, backward, condescending, dishonest. Most saw USDA and Establishment researchers as so wrapped up in scientific methods of proof that they ignored obvious facts and easy observations.[15] Science as method was rarely the reformists' strong suit, although they equally disdained actions that ignored scientific data.

This attitude meant an all-out assault on farm policy whenever legislation—namely, omnibus farm bills—was imminent. Agricultural institutions tried accommodation in the late 1970s and early 1980s. But environmental interests just accepted their minor gains, such as stronger water-runoff standards and improved soil conservation techniques. Then the enviros ungraciously fought on as still-ardent reformers. "It was as if they would spit in our faces, right after achieving a notable compromise," said one surprised and angry USDA undersecretary.[16] By the time of the 1985 farm bill, the environmentalist alliance once again stuck together and won major victories—in this case, mandating cross-compliance standards whereby soil and water conservation practices were linked to eligibility for commodity payments.[17] Such victories were unprecedented and of decided value to environmentalist views.

Suddenly the burden of proof for practicing sound natural resource uses was placed on farmers and agribusinesses. Farmers had to prove that they did things correctly. It was not up to others to prove that they did them improperly. Farmers and others were guilty until they demonstrated that they were innocent. This broke the farmers-first paradigm on which the Agricultural Establishment had been built. And it thoroughly irritated most large-scale producers—who, as USDA's primary clients, saw already narrow margins of profitability eroding further.

This pattern broke any continued cooperation, of course, between mainstream farm groups and the environmentalists who had already supplanted and challenged any groups that remained old-style and mainly focused on conservation matters. Environmentalists didn't care with whom they broke. Groups such as the always-prominent Sierra Club and Trout Unlimited adapted quite willingly to "educated positions" on environmental policy. Other groups, however—such as the National Rifle Association and bear hunters—did not; they were castigated for their reluctance, for being backward.

In the midst of all this evolution, environmental activism—and its achievement of strong public support—led to additional and even radical institution building. The Environmental Protection Agency (EPA) grew in size and scope after its creation in 1970, from an amalgam of small institutions with limited rule-making authority. Unlike them, the EPA cast its authority over *all* relevant policy domains.[18] That is to say, the EPA cast its authority when it chose: if it mounted a crusade; if it targeted a change by being willing to go to court. Thus, EPA rulings potentially affected municipal governments, commerce, the military, Girl Scout camps, and, of course, farming (and everybody else, too, always putting the burden of proof on EPA's target). Thus, for all practical purposes, the Agricultural Establishment no longer governed itself and those operating under its rules, at least on agriculture's own terms. New institutions arose out of previous institutional reluctance, or just plain lagging attention, and a changing dynamics of interest group influence.

Environmental interests won their own institution and even expanded from its ideal to eventually win reformist support from the Food and Drug Administration (FDA) as well. The FDA governed more and more in the area of food safety, just as the EPA did for natural resources. By then the shifting of the burden of proof to farmers and agribusiness was really of consequence. The EPA was an environmental advocate,[19] the FDA a consumer advocate. And USDA entered a new arena of institutional dogfights. (Or cockfights, if one prefers that analogy for whatever barnyard reason.)

IMPLICATIONS

What's implied in this chapter? Easy: It takes a lot to break successfully into agricultural policy. The key to comparing environmental successes in national agricultural policy with rural failure lies not with any single factor. That's the lesson. Anyone who claims that narrow and irresponsible special interests, unrestrained and wrongheaded public opinion, or radical institutional change mattered most is sadly mistaken. The environmentalists' key was in the sequence and then the circle of events. One matter begat the other, and so on, until a circle of change occurred. It was much like the biblical "begatting" story—seemingly endless in its eventual effects.

Let's look first at the role of public opinion. When the environmental story of ecological systems became understandable to real people—especially existing interest group leaders—political progress became evident. The move from single-minded conservation interests was a real change. Many of the emergent environmental advocacy groups spent the greatest amount of their time and money back home, not in Washington. And they were "extremely adept at raising public concern."[20] Their intent was to generate increased public awareness and local financial support. From there they built activist organizations in Washington politics. Public support for controlling water pollution, controlling air pollution, spending more to improve the environment, and a stricter Clean Air Act was consistently high as these issues came up in the 1960s and beyond.[21] That support often exceeded 80 percent. By contrast, support for those fearsome corporate power plants declined greatly from 80 percent to about 30 percent—and Congress responded as a result.

The explanation for why environmentalists were effective remains intriguing. The whole system's rhetoric of environmentalists had a public interest, good-policy ring to it. "Save us all" was the perception. Even though each environmental group had its own issues to address, most could—alone and collectively—raise questions about the appropriateness of farm and other policies. In doing that for all polluters, environmental spokespersons were unencumbered in the public's mind with any negative appearance of having been organized simply to attack those jolly, well-meaning, and always necessary food growers—those sons of Jefferson. The public and, of course, policymakers were risk-adverse by nature. The greatest risk seemed to be loss of environmental security—which, carried to the extreme, meant farmers couldn't farm anymore anyway.

So, who benefited from simple, and often simplistic, political appeals? Whose rhetoric mattered most to a nation that finally was aware of its own environmental fears? Without question, it was the enviros, at least over time. Farmers had long been beneficiaries of knowledge that was imperfect in appearance and coverage. Nobody knew, in other words, if fears of food shortages were realistic. Nonetheless, those fears were the leading edge for farm policy legitimacy, along with the image of farmers as hearty stewards. Environmentalists, however, turned that advantage on its head. Questions of farm impropriety in environmental degradation, as they placed the burden of safety and proof on farm practices, meant that environmental activists never had to prove anything scientifically. They only had to raise questions, driven by an imperfect knowledge of likely events. Environmentalists, like farmers earlier, only had to appear logical in their public image—this time about matters of destruction.

Yet those environmental suppositions were supported by institutional claims and, indeed, bitter disputes over those claims within the Agricultural Establishment. That was significant to enhancing environmentalist images. Within the SCS and ACP missions were statements about the need to protect natural resources. Land-grant scientists took environmental positions. And, to solidify the appearance of a need to break from the restraints of agricultural institutions and their internal conflicts, environmentalists pointed to what might be the Establishment's most obvious flaw. Using imperfect knowledge and simple rhetoric, enviros pointed out that separate institutions—the EPA and the FDA—had to be created. These institutions were to counteract and check those that governed agriculture and its special interests, as well as other bad folks, in the other policy domains dominated by the degraders. Environmentalists, in contrast, were advocates for the public good!

Thus, environmental demands came to be at least on par with farm support demands in national politics. Neither was close to being the public's most important issue, but both mattered.[22] The public was won over by interest groups who were tied to institutional dynamics. The institutions governed in their own ways as interest groups won public support. Finally, interest groups won because of their institutional linkages and because of growing public support for their rhetoric. It was becoming axiomatic, as a proven natural law, that if an environmental interest uttered a threatening claim, personal public danger was by definition imminent. No proof was required, just a policy claim—resulting in dread and therefore in public support. At least that was how public policymakers increasingly read this non-domain-specific, all-purpose political arena.[23] And they liked environmental issues even more because legislation scored such numerous political successes.[24] Clean-ups were well documented in the media and often through personal, backyard experiences. Rural policy advocates could never create such a circle of sustained public policy support. Environmental advocates, inside and outside of government, had what rural policy proponents never commanded.

SUMMARY OF KEY POINTS

This essay has been an extended analysis of why the federal government has failed to assist the rural poor and disadvantaged. It's been about why declining and collapsing small communities have been ignored. This chapter has reviewed why the environmental policy community has succeeded where rural advocates have not. The Agricultural Establishment has purposely accommodated environmentalist policy demands. Not willingly, of course.[25] And not without some bitter disputes. Let's summarize by developing a simple litany of political advantages enjoyed by environmental interests as forces of farm policy change.

1. Interests and institutions mattered, inseparably. As a consequence of interest politics, institutions have altered their behavior.

2. Environmentalists have relied heavily on a long-established stewardship ethos. The suggestion is that natural resources need protective conservation.

3. This ethos, combined with the intense conservation concerns of president Teddy Roosevelt led to public policies that were protective of wilderness settings. Even national parks were established, soon after he left office.

4. Conservation groups proliferated in numbers for decades as public policies were passed to conserve natural resources.

5. Many conservation projects, shared jointly between federal officials and interest group activists, just failed, however. They had inadequately considered system effects, such as mixing planted trout fingerlings with contaminated water.

6. This policy failure led to conservation group interest in holistic, or system-wide environmental ideas. Most of the initial ideas were expressed by traditionally nonpolitically connected researchers (even poets).

7. Nonetheless, these environmental ideas were giving rise to adaptation by conservation groups to more encompassing policy issues. They also provided the basis for organizing more specifically environmental groups rather than conservation groups. Patronage monies from foundation sources, such as the Ford Foundation, greatly encouraged them.

8. This combination of policy failure and group emergence led to an increasingly radicalized, reformist alliance identification for environmental activists. They became part of an environmental social movement, not just a scattered, reactionary set of wannabe policy influentials.

9. Group influence grew from the environmentalists' upper- and middle-class origins, the greater propensity of these people to participate actively in politics, and their successful forays into creating broader public awareness of environmental problems.

10. Public awareness was responsive in large part because of the logic employed by environmental activists. Their messages appeared to be personally germane, deserving of attention because of their apocalyptic warnings, and inspired by a genuine public interest. For much of the public, environmentalist messages took on an axiomatic stature. They seemed to be not merely political manipulation but laws of nature.

11. Eventually, environmental groups that once were directed toward compromise became more confrontational and unwilling to yield. They therefore broke from many of the friends with whom they once cooperated: old guard conservation groups and farm interests. This break from odd alliances made environmental interests a more potent threat to agriculture, and it hastened institutional efforts to accommodate environmental concerns within farm policy.

12. This environmentalist strategy initially won only because long-established bureaucratic agricultural institutions, such as the SCS, were available as settings for negotiation.

13. Agricultural institutions eventually cooperated—some would say yielded—because of their own inherent cleavages or splits. Institution-building had encompassed conservation as a critical part of farm policy in the 1930s—simultaneously, in fact, with the creation of federal price policy.

14. Institutions such as the SCS and land retirement policies such as the Soil Bank had become friendly and supportive homes to many conservation and later environmental interests. They provided entry, at least. In so doing, these groups shared considerable interaction with no-longer friendly farm interests. Thus, the Agricultural Establishment took on something of a split identity. Sometimes it was farmers first, other times it was stewardship first. It all depended.

15. As these competing goals were articulated publicly, they led people to further question the environmental safety of existing national farm public policy.

16. The creation of the EPA and the redirection of the FDA had the same effect. These institutions also provided a counterweight to existing Agricultural Establishment institutions. They were announced advocates of interests other than farm modernization and development policy; thus, they were organized environmental and social-cause interests as well. With such institutions lying in wait to influence farm policy, old and once-dominant farmer institutions entered a race to accommodate environmental policy demands.

17. Because of the interactive, or circular, effects of the public, organized groups, and institutional changes, environmental activists came to have real political power within agriculture. To these individuals, interests, and institutions, however, rural policy problems were just an infinitesimal problem to consider. Why try? The transaction costs of eventual policy agreements were so high—so time- and budget-consuming—that all but core or central problems to rural participants entered, along with particularistic programs negotiated in political back rooms. National rural policy was further left behind as a result of these dynamics.

18. Rural policy, as preceding chapters have made clear, never could have created such a circle of sustained political influence.

14

A FINAL EXPLANATION

One interesting theory of political decisions caught fire among fledgling political scientists in the early 1970s: the theory of nondecision making, in which the mobilization of political and social bias leads to the absence of action on behalf of interests challenging the status quo. Nondecisions occur when advocates back off and give way to force, intimidation, co-optation, norms, rules, procedures, or simply fortification of the institutional embattlements by those doing the biasing.[1] Careful readers of this essay should understand that, although the concept initially appears to be similar to what's discussed here, it really is not. After all, so many presidential initiatives were advanced. Our analysis, as we've all borne it patiently, is *not* about the conscious actions of the powerful to kill a contrary ideal, or even a counter idea—at least, not mostly about that.

Instead, the recurring defeat of national rural policy was mostly a product of institutional neglect. Institutions just did business via tradition and first purpose. Moreover, defeat was accompanied by the claims of farm interest groups in their clamor for more benefits for themselves and their own. Interests were protective of the status they'd already won. Rural policy defeat usually was not a case of policy players waging war against anything as much as it was postponement of a good idea for a better time—way into the future.

That better time never came because the agricultural sector was always in such difficult economic shape. A few dollars more were always needed for farm and ranch modernization and development and, yes, even for staying alive. At the millennium's turn, exorbitant sums were being pumped by the federal government into emergency farm aid, beyond usual appropriations for budgeted agricultural institutions. Emergency payments for market losses, crop disasters, and livestock assistance in fiscal year 1999 were more than $5.2 billion and in fiscal year 2000 were nearly a whopping $12.5 billion. A national rural policy with an allocation of $3 billion would raise the roof with advocates' joy.

The point has always been that farmers-first institutions and interests could never call nonfarm rural development a bad idea. The conditions of farmers left behind and out of the sector were well known. And rural poverty, attendant social problems, and community decline also were nicely understood. So farm voices could call for rural development only through farm development and maintain that additional support for rural communities should come later, after the farm sector stabilized. That posturing lives on. In a 2000 report of an agribusiness institute, "plant-based lubricants" were praised for their "great potential for *rural economic development*. Farmers could benefit not only from increased demand for vegetable oils but also, more significantly, from collective ownership of a company manufacturing value-added products."[2] What, though, have we learned about a generalizable theory of institutions, interests, and policy neglect by the state?

INSTITUTIONS AND THE STATE

A lot, it seems. A set of intricately structured institutions eventually were created from previous institutional investments made in the modernizing of subsistence-styled agrarians. From a prideful myth that emphasized farmers' inherent worth as stabilizers of a democratic society, institutional governors eked out a strategy for enhancing national expansion and development. That strategy of national development was based on agrarian development as the means to populate the frontier. In all likelihood, there was no farsighted plan for creating further institutions. Nor, in a Madisonian world, could one have worked. Institutions emerged on variations of need, farm and ranch conditions, and prevailing political sentiment—including fear. As these institutions coalesced, they took on the identity of the legitimate nation-state, at least as it governed this economic sector.

Agrarian modernization and development were continuously refined by professional institutional representatives—knowledgeable experts on whom the state was built and depended. As a consequence, modernization was defined, in turn, as land provision, education, research, extension and farm outreach, economic protection, marketing, and, finally, direct financial support: Gifts of money. Professionals conceived of such policy approaches, debated their merits within and between institutional organizations, and set up mechanisms for the delivery of policy benefits.

As time elapsed, the broad outlines of an Agricultural Establishment were evident. Just as important, patterns of interaction within and from the Establishment were set forth. Contact between professional experts and agricultural producers were to be face-to-face and direct. Producers later were included in local-level governing committees for many agricultural programs. Producers also were anticipated and later expected to organize into groups to press their own political demands. Other policy claimants who came later were expected to do the same. As such, lobbying of Establishment personnel came to be accepted and even welcomed. Political responsiveness by the Establishment was prized.

That responsiveness eventually led to the formation of public policy networks. It was easier to structure relationships only with lobbies that routinely pressed specific officials on their items of responsibility, within their jurisdictions. Don't deal with all groups. Policy networks also were vehicles for the routine interaction of institutional representatives who shared different functional responsibilities for the same type of producer services. Specialists in the legislative, administrative, and local service units divided their labors by expertise and talked mostly with their own kind. Thus, there was a soil conservation network and networks centered around policies such as credit, Extension, and price supports.

Networks proved inadequate, however, for all Establishment interaction. Policies and problems often overlapped, information had to be shared, and efforts had to be made to make those in other networks and institutions appear more professional and expert. So the agricultural domain came into play; it was understood as a common forum for the institutionalized, the semi-institutionalized, and the public policy wannabes. Washington, D.C., as lobbyists often say, was like a small town because everyone who needed to know one another did. It really was like several small towns, then, composed of several domains. Experts and lobbies had a place, so to speak, for integrating the Establishment and making it collectively stronger—by being better prepared, in touch.

It would be wrongheaded to conclude from all this that the capacity of the state explains the expansion of public policies and their benefits to farmers. Although the Agricultural Adjustment Acts of 1933 and 1938 were put together and operated effectively only because of agricultural professionals, these individuals hardly did it all alone.[3] As comparative research on American and European state capacities has explained, the United States is a weak nation-state.[4] Its government apparatus is less developed, less legitimately powerful, and less able to twist interest-group positions to the experts' view of the public interest.[5]

Nor does it appear that institutions used their own capacity merely to reward upper social classes within the agricultural sector. Middle-class, market-orientated, ever-modernizing farmers certainly won the most from the Establishment.[6] But the intent of the modernization and development effort, after all, was to tame the yeoman animal, making agrarians more capable as likely-to-be-middle-class farmers and more satisfactory as political allies. Hansen appears to be correct when he explains that later Establishment policies of price supports and loan guarantees were the result of farm interest groups—the lobbies—finally winning institutional access.[7] That is, these groups became semi-institutionalized and freed administrators and legislators from central authority.

What can best be said of the institutional state is that it picked up fairly quickly on a strategy of winning the West and reclaiming the South. As institutions developed their own capabilities, they worked together within the policy domain enough to accept and then define the central meaning of farm and ranch modernization and development. Better-educated, better-prepared producers, with government's professional assistance and economic support, could and would develop a sound market economy. That was the mantra. The ability to stick with that well-understood assignment through numerous circumstantial changes kept the Establishment on line, its policies intact and stable, and its neglect of rural policy as an alternative strategy a constant.

INTERESTS AND SOCIETY

Organized political interests were in the business of generating discussions about westward expansion and agricultural modernization 20 years before the fourfold legislation of 1862 was passed. Business leaders, especially from the railroads, had been anxious to expand West, to the frontiers of financial profit. But would they go West from the East or from New Orleans? As economic and political conditions grew worse, the opportunities for federal support of expansion grew in Washington. So it could be said that American business as well as Lincoln and his Congress fathered the strategy of agrarian modernization and agricultural development. That was why these complex bills were passed when Republicans were otherwise caught up in winning a war.

Farm groups were not without a countervailing power to business interests, however, as the 19th century wore on. Emergent farm interests of the era were notably short term in their life cycles and dramatic in their demands for basic economic reform. Nonetheless, their protest-style upheavals and their reformist zeal scared the hell out of those who were interested in a stable but economically more prosperous middle and western America.

So business interests with their dominant positions in Congress were only too happy to listen to agricultural professionals and market-oriented producers who wanted better ways to reach farmers. The spoilsmen were at work. Promises of more productive and prosperous agrarian conditions, a growing middle class of producers who would trade and sell goods, and a quieting of rural radicalism caught business and congressional attention. It was enough to forget about *laissez-faire* principals of governance. Thus, institutionalists were persuasive voices while businesses such as railroads, lumber, banks, and merchants paved their ideas' ways.[8]

The first two decades of the 20th century saw farm and ranch interests with diminished influence as a result of increased agricultural prosperity and decreased agrarian radicalism. Farmers were listening to professionals who could help them grow more. The exceptions were those urging the continuing expression of populism and the rise of progressivism. Business interests were willing to confront adherents of both in the electoral arena, however, where their defeats usually were predictable. After all, national sentiments were bringing the century to the brink of the conservative Hoover administration. Farm interest power at that point was nominal, following institutional leaders (except for the yeomen hellraisers).

As we have seen, however, farm organizations were galvanizing and moving to Washington, as permanent lobbies in residence. Those interest groups eliminated Hoover's Federal Farm Board. And the institutionally created Farm Bureau, with its grassroots mobilization, helped greatly in organizing the congressional Farm Bloc, creating in the process the first elements of yet another agricultural institution within the Congress. By the time discussions on the AAA began, Washington farm groups from North, South, and West had helped bring Franklin Roosevelt to the presidency and won their leaders a place in the drafting of emergency farm legislation.[9] Surprisingly, farmers were voting Democratic and now were on the political inside, as partners at least in bringing forth the most prominent and best-liked farm institutions. Not only did the Farm Bureau and its lobbyists contribute to the AAA, they also took aim at and soon destroyed the administratively created Federal Security Administration (FSA). As the successor to the rural poverty-focused Resettlement Administration, the FSA sought to distribute farm support benefits to tenant farmers and away from landowners. It did—to the tune of $516 million in small farm loans.

The Farm Bureau rebelled because FSA policies failed to reflect the direction of the AAA, which distributed the greatest benefits to large-scale farmers who were already moving ahead—as did the Soil Conservation Act and the ACP. Moreover, the FSA threatened to attract a large member constituency to the Farm Bureau's more radical but nearest rival, the NFU.[10] The NFU was still mostly a yeomen's group, and it had been an initial supporter of the FSA for that reason, just as it had opposed the AAA.

The Farm Bureau won, for reasons linked to the class and society argument. It had more members who favored its policy positions. As McConnell explained, and as we have seen, larger-scale and higher economic status farmers participated in interest groups and politics more often. Lower-income farmers, the leftover yeomen, very seldom joined even the NFU.[11] That meant that for several years, the Farm Bureau, as Extension's darling, ruled the interest group politics of agriculture. In doing so, the market-oriented American Farm Bureau Federation (AFBF) was protective of existing agricultural institutions, brought considerable pressure to stabilize a policy equilibrium, and in general maintained a conservative influence—no changes, please—over sector debates. No wonder, after the FSA's demise, rural policy was in real trouble.

We've already covered the post-World War II politics of agricultural interest groups. What can be said? The AFBF continued to battle with the NFU over the core of farm policy—direct payments and loans, as well as to whom those funds were distrubuted. The AFBF generally won the upper hand by gravitating to Republicans who, after President Truman, most often controlled government and its institutions. During Democratic administrations, though, the member-declining and low income-supportive NFU exercised considerable influence while the Farm Bureau sought unsuccessfully to be bipartisan.

An amount of disgust with partisan bickering led leaders of several commodity groups to take active political positions, as cotton growers and the milk producers had earlier. Commodity groups generally had organized around the promotion of crop or breed improvement and marketing. Angus breeders, for example, aimed to make their all-black cattle the preeminent breed for taste and texture. These groups certainly operated in the spirit of modernizing agriculture, using expert advice.

Groups such as the National Association of Wheat Growers, however, which organized in 1950, and the National Corn Growers Association of 1957 grew up around the idea of taking advocacy control over price support policy away from the Farm Bureau. They wanted to be price policy's primary supporters, or first line of defense. These groups were responding to the administrative and congressional splintering of institutional attention to price and loan programs. For all practical purposes, each politically protected crop was treated differently and by different players within small networks. So it made more sense for corn or wheat advocates to interact primarily with corn or wheat decision makers. The goal was to promote their crop programs as politically neutral, apart from partisan disagreements. So they hoped to neutralize the Farm Bureau and forestall institutional infighting that might well kill the golden goose and its check-writing to farmers. As institutional followers of farm modernization and development, they succeeded nicely.

By the early 1970s, it appeared that institutional representatives of the Agricultural Establishment would write future bills by themselves. With commodity group advice and consent, of course. It was here, however, that labor allies of the agricultural domain changed the equation for determining farm power. Food stamps for the poor had been used to distribute surplus farm products from 1939 to 1943. This meant going to the county courthouse to get boxes of free food. The stamp idea stayed around in USDA; experiments for other forms of food dissemination were tested in 1961. In 1964, however, the Johnson administration maneuvered the Food Stamp Act through a reluctant Congress and hostile agricultural committees.[12] Yet that Act was only a small first start. The envisioned growth by advocates in USDA was horrifically slow. Congressional and most administrative institutional leaders maintained their reluctance.

Labor interests then entered the contest. They refused to support the 1973 omnibus farm bill unless a full-blown food stamp program was appended to it. Poor peoples' groups supported labor. This would have killed the bill because labor controlled just enough congressional votes to prevent floor majorities from organizing. So farm institutions and interests became accommodating, allowing nonfarm experts and advocates into the drafting of farm bills.

What was happening? Institutional promotion of farm policies within the Agricultural Establishment was attracting more newly organized interests into the Establishment's processes. As with commodity program governance and the Farm Bureau, institutions were begetting organized interests. The agricultural domain, or the farmers' league, was expanding. Poor people's groups and the institutions to which they responded were being given some small part within the drama of the domain. As were labor groups, whose leaders liked food stamp availability for striking workers.

Because evolving agricultural institutions were doing so many other things—from food safety to soil and water conservation—already organized interest groups, as well as brand spanking new ones, responded to USDA and land-grant work. Rural interests such as Rural America were among them because of the Establishment's always stated rural responsibilities. Consumer groups such as Public Voice for Food and Health Policy, however, had advantages that led them to be accommodated when rural interests were not. Food health scares, proliferating newspaper reports, and a gravitation of many members of Congress to support well-publicized new-values, social-cause interests got consumer groups into the domain. They were regarded as strong enough to stop farm bills from passing. Look at Ralph Nader (in those days)! Their support, as a result, gave relatively minor institutional agencies and players greater prominence.

As we've seen, the same thing happened with environmentalists: With their previous successes and respected reputations, they also were able to block farm bills. Consumer and environmental issues and interests solidly penetrated the discussion and learning forums of Washington politics. Rural policy problems did not. Their advocates were only very, very marginally accommodated—with tokens, through "small ball" strategies. Perhaps they were best seen as captured, not accommodated at all.

So the 20th century ended with a marvelous diversification of influential agricultural interests. The Farm Bureau was there but largely displaced in price and loan policy control by commodity groups. The growing institutional diversity of the Agricultural Establishment, however, led each of these groups to be there to support that Establishment. The same was soon true for other interests organized around poor people, consumers, and environmentalists.

Moreover, the game was still expanding. For example, as science and technology gave us biotechnology and genetic alteration of food, USDA was assigned to regulate its production and distribution. The land-grant colleges sponsored numerous biotechnology programs and research projects. And to question the administration and resultant congressional action, new biotechnology organizations formed. Some articulated industry positions and Establishment promotion of its products. Others, such as the Foundation for Economic Trends, became vocal institutional critics that all but demanded public bans on these products. All of the new players, by reason of the discussions and fears they generated, became determinants of the future of agricultural biotechnology as it moved from science to administration to the market.[13]

So enough's been said. In the 19th century, interests begat institutions and both begat considerable public attention—which, in turn, governed the institutions. On the other hand, the 20th century was different. As large and encompassing institutions came into being, they begat better-organized interests, and both begat some degree of public responsiveness, either to prevailing myths or to fears that could be generated among (as Schattschneider foretold) the crowds of public policymaking observers: the people who either attentively or subconsciously watched the fights.[14]

THEORETICAL IMPLICATIONS

Rural institutionalists and interests always came to promote an alternative policy vision for rural America. They always knew, of course, that farm modernization and development policy was not an acceptable policy for all of rural America. But the cluster of institutions and interests to which they were consigned by the state discouraged their advocacy and rebuffed their message. That message was too much a threat to what was always emerging as a modernizing and developing farm sector clinging to a market economy.

Any remaining yeomen farmers, or poor people left behind from agriculture, or declining communities were not worries that Establishment institutions could take to heart. To acknowledge them called into question the reasons why public policy supported an increasingly middle- and upper-class farm and ranch agriculture. That's why the FSA took such a direct assault. There also was the question of rural policy dollars being redirected from farm policy expenditures. Neither institutions nor prevailing interests wanted that. No more than environmental or consumer interests as fellow social-cause allies wanted rural communities to win funds from food safety or resource conservation programs.

All of the choices that rural advocates have had for battling such inequities were bad ones. First, the choices they had for movement leaders were severely restricted and ridden with problems. Second, the very nature of the issues of poverty and decline that they advocated were unpopular and lacked believability. And, third, the governing institution—the presidency—on which they were forced to rely for access to the political process, and power within it, was wrong. Each president's approach emphasized, as it was bound to, a Hamiltonian or centrist positioning, a national but never localized perspective, and a lack of priority commitment. All of that was inappropriate in a terribly intense, Madisonian and Jeffersonian political world. For rural institutions and interests to win in this way, the president would have had to exercise real and effective leadership—which is his only true weapon. The public would have had to be informed and brought along, the public and the Congress would have had to come to believe that they were being led to a worthy end, and—worst of all—the president would have needed to package and to sell to Congress and the public a specific agenda.[15] There was no way rural America could command or deserve such high transaction-cost attention. In no way would a president fight such an institutionally devastating battle against such powerful interests. Presidents had to move on to other things than rural policy. And, from Teddy Roosevelt to Billy Clinton, they did.

The question remains: Is this a recurring problem in American government or is the neglect of rural America an anomaly? What we want to know is whether the state creates institutions that create interest group support that, in turn, condemns more realistic—or at least alternative—public policies. My hunch is that it does: that rural policy is no rare case.

My hunch comes first from a class discussion that took me, as instructor, years to understand or sort out. It was a public policymaking class of mostly ranking military officers taught toward the end of the Vietnam war. Several of the officers were in what would be called Special Forces. They were highly trained commando types who used specialized training and weaponry to accomplish behind-the-lines mayhem. All felt discriminated against and disrespected by traditional military officers—from the infantry, from navel ship operations, and from Air Force fighter wings. The point is simple. The traditional military officers in class agreed that this dissing was exactly the case—and that doing this to these "unproven" souls was the correct response.

Military operations, the traditionalists argued, depended on accumulated brute force: Lots of soldiers running together. Lots of ships firing missiles. Waves of attack jets. War was a team game. And, they argued, the Special Forces officers weren't team players. They were loners who plotted to do the grand and most impressive nastiness, but not necessarily the most needed stuff. So the traditionalists downplayed Special Forces in their planning, their war games, their personnel requests, and budgeting. And their Pentagon superiors did the same in their congressional requests.

What impresses me now from that classroom experience was the extent to which military institutions mostly went on with business as usual. They downgraded agents of change in that business. It also strikes me as important that (at the time, anyway) interest groups of former, and sometimes present, officers organized to provide external political support for *their* institutions. Tailhook is one example. Congressional contacts were made, campaign contributions were encouraged, good publicity for their way of business was hoped for but not always gained.

Institutional resistance is even more clear if we look at specific agency behavior. The Department of the Interior (DOI) is an excellent example, especially on western water settlement disbursements. For 70 years DOI has gone about the business of distributing water rights to cattle producers and large cities such as Los Angeles. As Indian nations began to make water claims, DOI, under old procedures, just never got around to recognizing that Native American rights were legitimate.[16]

The same sort of institutional discrimination has been evident within the Agricultural Establishment with regard to public policy on migrant workers, as well as tenants. Once again, as we'd suspect by now, landowning farmers came first. And for years, laws were passed to deal with farm needs for migrant assistance. Only when work and living conditions became a subject of considerable media attention did public policy address worker needs, from education to quality-of-life to pesticide safety. Here again, however, those are the same agricultural institutions that discouraged rural policy.

So we should consider institutions other than Agriculture and the similar ones of Interior. One that comes to mind after DOI is that of civil rights. Clara Bingham's fascinating study of female congressional members leaves one clear impression.[17] The institutional structures of Congress that had supported African-American civil rights were content to rest on their laurels. They didn't extend their support to women's rights. And no interest groups that had lobbied for civil rights earlier joined the bandwagon on women's issues.

Male members of the House Judiciary Committee, for example, would introduce pro-choice abortion bills without consulting female members of the committee. For years the congressional women's caucus avoided taking a pro-choice stand because of the influence of just two senior women members. Both were Catholic, pro-life, and, most important, popular women who played roles in the House leadership. An African-American member's interest in tax credits for impoverished workers was disregarded by a senior committee member and black caucus dean in favor of his favorite issue, industrial Empowerment Zones. Poverty policies, as has been noted before, aren't popular. Nor, apparently, is deferring to a female member's concern for the poor. In all three cases, congressional institutions were major impediments to extending civil rights concerns and to women advocates in the House.

Finally, let's turn to more recent events. In the wake of Ford Motor Company's problems with rollover accidents and, perhaps, the misuse of Firestone tires on its light trucks, Congress passed new auto safety legislation. That legislation created a furor among venerable consumer groups such as Public Citizen. Consumer advocates were stunned because even with a plethora of hostile automotive media reports, the National Highway Traffic Safety Administration (NHTSA) recommended rules that would make it *harder* for consumers to secure information about automobile defects and accidents.[18] And it would make punishing any company wrongdoers on safety issues difficult.

Angry consumer advocates had one explanation for why these rules were passed. Existing congressional committees and NHTSA had worked with automotive companies for years; the companies—as interests—in turn had given public compliments to the regulators: the institutions. Do we see a pattern here?

Is there also a lesson here about what many people see as a ghastly rise in the number of interest groups in the 20th century?[19] That we are becoming an interest-group society? A guess can be ventured, even a good one. American political institutions began to emerge with some regularity in the 19th century. Probably the intent was to quell public insurrection and protest. More institutions followed in the 20th century, particularly after 1930. This gave us the modern state. And all of these institutions had their own policy bias in purpose and intent. A fair guess would be that many of the organized interests that formed and became active in the 20th century did so to advance and protect institutions that favored them. Probably they emerged with institutional support. This would explain the large number of business interest groups in America.[20] The proliferation of statist institutions, after all, preceded the proliferation of organized lobbies by several years.

What's intriguing about this second but closely related theory is that interests begat institutions in the 19th century (and undoubtedly later in some policy domains). These initiating interests probably represented only a few Americans: the power brokers, spoilsmen, and business barons of an early era of national politics. After all, organized people's lobbies were just coming out of their protest movement identities in the early 20th century.[21] So they had not yet won power or influence. Presidents and Congresses who were under the spell of business provided the brokers and barons with their own problem-solving devices: government employees and experts of the institutional state.[22] They gave us all as citizens a state capacity that later new-values, social-cause interests, the people's lobbies, would try and often fail to break. In many instances, the likelihood of winning appeared so remote that formidable lobbies never even effectively organized around some alternative policies—like rural policy.

SUMMARY OF KEY POINTS

Let's conclude with three points.

1. The statist institutions that modernized and developed American agriculture always operated with their own biased intent. As prob-

ably all statist institutions do. Rural policy, in particular, could never be within the Agricultural Establishment's favor. The institutional response was always, "That's not how we do business." Probably a great many public policy options throughout all policy domains have been similarly disadvantaged. They were disruptive to policy stability, the status quo.

2. Whereas business interests representing the few lobbied for agricultural institutions in the 19th century, the institutions reversed that pattern in the 20th century. As institutions became established, interest groups of the more numerous formed to protect their winnings within institutional bases. The result was that a combination of institutions and interests stood together with great influence against rural policy and any advocates that came forward. Of which there were few. This general pattern was, without doubt, true of the other policy domains, though probably at later dates.

3. Agents of change found considerable political hardships, particularly new-values, social-cause interests. They eventually won in agricultural policy only when statist institutions were forced to deal with new or more complex issues raised by technology and scientific discovery or by social change in some domains. Obviously, not all challenging interests won, and some outmoded and outdated public policies continue to live with us. Let's not say here what they are, however.

NOTES

PREFACE

1. For the best example, see John Mark Hansen, *Gaining access: Congress and the farm lobby, 1919–1981* (Chicago: University of Chicago Press, 1991).
2. William P. Browne, *Groups, interests, and U.S. public policy* (Washington, D.C.: Georgetown University Press, 1998), 192–208.
3. Robert L. Paarlberg and Don Paarlberg, "Agricultural policy in the twentieth century," *Agricultural History* 74 (spring 2000): 136–61.
4. Willard W. Cochrane, *The development of U.S. agriculture: A historical analysis* (Minneapolis: University of Minnesota Press, 1979).
5. Theodore W. Schultz, *Redirecting farm policy* (New York: Macmillan, 1943); Theodore W. Schultz, *Agriculture in an unstable economy* (New York: McGraw-Hill, 1945).
6. Frank R. Baumgartner and Bryan D. Jones, *Agendas and instability in American politics* (Chicago: University of Chicago Press, 1993).
7. William P. Browne, *Private interests, public policy, and American agriculture* (Lawrence: University Press of Kansas, 1988).

CHAPTER 1

1. William P. Browne, Jerry R. Skees, Louis E. Swanson, Paul B. Thompson, and Laurian J. Unnevehr, *Sacred cows and hot potatoes: Agrarian myths in agricultural policy* (Boulder, Colo.: Westview Press, 1992).
2. James T. Bonnen and William P. Browne, "Why is agricultural policy so difficult to reform?" in *The political economy of U.S. agriculture: Challenges for the 1990's*, ed. Carol S. Kramer (Washington, D.C.: Resources for the Future, 1989), 9–13.
3. Colin M. Turbayne, *The myth of metaphor*, rev. ed. (Columbia: University of South Carolina Press, 1970).
4. Thomas A. Lyson and William W. Falk, eds., *Forgotten places: Uneven development in rural America* (Lawrence: University Press of Kansas, 1993).
5. Frederick Jackson Turner, *The frontier in American history* (New York: Holt, 1947).
6. As Richard C. Wade points out, the rise of interior western cities led to frontier successes, fueled by the needed convergence of national resources. See *The urban frontier* (Cambridge, Mass.: Harvard University Press, 1959).
7. Patricia Nelson Limerick, Clyde A. Milner II, and Charles E. Rankin, eds., *Trails towards a new western history* (Lawrence: University Press of Kansas, 1991).

8. Solon Justus Buck, *The Granger movement: A study of agricultural organization and its political, economic, and social manifestations, 1870–1880* (Cambridge, Mass.: Harvard University Press, 1913).

9. Blake McKelvey, *The urbanization of America, 1860–1915* (New Brunswick, N.J.: Rutgers University Press, 1963), 61–72.

10. Alexis de Tocqueville, *Democracy in America*, volumes I and II (New York: D. Appleton, 1904; reprinted from 1835 and 1840). See also J. Hector St. John de Crevecouer, *Letters from an American farmer* (London: T. Davies, 1782).

11. John Mark Hansen, "Choosing sides: The creation of an agricultural policy network in Congress, 1919–1932," *Studies in American Political Development* 2 (1987): 195.

12. Lowell K. Dyson, *Farmers organizations* (Westport, Conn.: Greenwood Press, 1986).

13. Robert H. Salisbury, "An exchange theory of interest groups," *Midwest Journal of Political Science* 13 (February 1969): 1–32.

14. Sidney Verba, Kay Lehman Schlozman, and Henry E. Brady, *Voice and equality: Civic voluntarism in American politics* (Cambridge, Mass.: Harvard University Press, 1995).

15. Gilbert C. Fite, *The farmers' frontier, 1865–1900* (New York: Holt, Rinehart, and Winston, 1966); Fred A. Shannon, *The farmer's last frontier: Agriculture, 1860–1897* (New York: Farrar and Rinehart, 1945).

16. Cochrane, *The development of American agriculture*, 37–98.

17. Ibid., 57–77.

18. Osha Gray Davidson, *Broken heartland: The rise of America's rural ghetto* (New York: Free Press, 1990).

19. John F. Geweke, James T. Bonnen, Andrew A. White, and Jeffrey J. Koshel, *Sowing seeds of change: Informing public policy in the Economic Research Service of USDA* (Washington, D.C.: National Research Council, 1999), 13–18.

20. Murray R. Benedict, *Farm policies of the United States, 1790–1950: A study of their origins and development* (New York: Twentieth Century Fund, 1953), 76–93.

21. William P. Browne, "Challenging industrialization: The rekindling of agrarian protest in a modern era, 1977–1987," *Studies in American Political Development* 7, no. 1 (1993): 3–5.

22. Don Paarlberg, *Farm and food policy: Issues of the 1980s* (Lincoln: University of Nebraska Press, 1980), 20–28.

23. Browne, *Private interests, public policy, and American agriculture*, 72–80.

24. James T. Bonnen, "Why is there no coherent U.S. rural policy?" *Policy Studies Journal* 20, no. 2 (1992): 190–201.

25. Thomas Robert Malthus, *Essay on the principle of population* (London: J.M. Dent, 1973, reprinted from 1914).

CHAPTER 2

1. Steven J. Rosenstone and John Mark Hansen, *Mobilization, participation, and democracy in America* (New York: Macmillan, 1993).

2. William P. Browne and J. Norman Reid, "Misconceptions, institutional impediments, and the problems of rural governance," *Public Administration Quarterly* 14, no. 3 (fall 1990): 265–84.

3. John Fraser Hart, "'Rural' and 'farm' no longer mean the same," in *The changing American countryside: Rural people and places,* ed. Emery N. Castle (Lawrence: University Press of Kansas, 1995), 63–76.

4. The data source for this chapter is the U.S. Bureau of the Census.

5. Glenn V. Fuguitt, "Population change in rural America," in Castle, ed., *The changing American countryside,* 77–100.

6. Data are from the Economic Research Service, U.S. Department of Agriculture.

7. Ken Deavers, "What is rural?" *Policy Studies Journal* 20, no. 2 (1992): 184–89.

8. Dewitt John, Sandra S. Batie, and Kim Norris, *A brighter future for rural America? Strategies for communities and states* (Washington, D.C.: National Governors' Association, 1988), 67–68.

9. Robert M. Gibbs and G. Andrew Bernat, Jr., "Rural industry clusters raise local earnings," *Rural Development Perspectives* 12, no. 3 (1997): 18–25.

10. Glenn V. Fuguitt, "Commuting and the rural-urban hierarchy," *Journal of Rural Studies* 7, no. 4 (1991): 459–66.

11. Alan E. Pisarski, *Commuting in America, II* (Washington, D.C.: Eno Foundation for Transportation, 1996).

12. Calvin L. Beale and Glenn V. Fuguitt, "Decade of pessimistic nonmetropolitan trends ends on optimistic note," *Rural Development Perspectives* 6, no. 3 (1990): 14–18.

13. Fuguitt, "Population change in rural America," 80.

14. This and related statistics were provided by Chuck Fluharty, "Rural policy: Refrain or reality in today's rural and policy contexts?" Presentation to Department of Sociology, Colorado State University (April 2000).

15. Calvin L. Beale, "Americans heading for the cities, once again," *Rural Development Perspectives* 4, no. 3 (1988): 2–6; Glenn V. Fuguitt and Calvin L. Beale, "Recent trends in nonmetropolitan migration: Towards a new turnaround," *Growth and Change* 27, no. 2 (1996): 156–74.

16. U.S. Bureau of the Census.

17. Fluharty, "Rural policy."

18. National Center on Addiction and Substance Abuse at Columbia University, *No place to hide: Substance abuse in mid-size cities and rural America* (New York: Columbia University Press, 2000).

19. Gene F. Summers, "Persistent rural poverty," in Castle, ed., *The changing American countryside,* 213–28; Rural Sociological Society, *Persistent poverty in rural America* (Boulder, Colo.: Westview, 1993), 20–67.

20. Economic Research Service, United States Department of Agriculture, *Rural conditions and trends: Socioeconomic conditions* 9 (February 1999): 5.

21. Economic Research Service, United States Department of Agriculture, *Rural conditions and trends: Rural industry* 9 (May 1999): 5.

22. G. Andrew Bernat, Jr., "An update on rural manufacturing: Rural capital expenditures lagged urban in 1992," *Rural Development Perspectives* 10 (February 1995): 15–19.

23. Terry L. Besser, "Employment in small towns: Microbusinesses, part-time work, and lack of benefits characterized Iowa firms," *Rural Development Perspectives* 13 (August 1998): 31–35.

24. Dale Ballow and Michael Podgursky, "Rural schools—fewer highly trained teachers and special programs, but better learning environments," *Rural Development Perspectives* 10 (June 1995): 6–16.

25. Robert M. Gibbs, "Going away to college and wider urban job opportunities take highly educated youth away from rural areas," *Rural Development Perspectives* 10 (June 1995): 35–44.

26. Rural Sociological Society, *Persistent Poverty in Rural America*, 68–105.

27. Economic Research Service, United States Department of Agriculture, *Rural conditions and trends: Special census issue* 4 (fall 1993): 48; Mark Nord, "Overcoming persistent poverty—and sinking into it: Income trends in persistent-poverty and other high-poverty rural counties, 1989–94," *Rural Development Perpectives* 12 (June 1997): 2–10.

28. L. C. Gray, "Disadvantaged rural classes," *Journal of Farm Economics* 20 (February 1938): 71–85; M. L. Wilson, "Problem of poverty in agriculture," *Journal of Farm Economics* 22 (February 1940): 10–33.

29. William P. Browne, "Rural failure: The linkage between policy and lobbies," *Policy Studies Journal* 28 (2001), in press.

30. This indeed is the direction that nearly all rural policy advocates and analysts have favored in recent years. See, for example, Rural Policy Research Institute, *Opportunities for rural policy reform: Lessons from recent farm bills* (Columbia: University of Missouri, 1995).

CHAPTER 3

1. Browne, *Groups, interests, and U.S. public policy*.

2. Bonnen and Browne, "Why is agricultural policy so difficult to reform?" 25.

3. Oliver E. Williamson, *The economic institutions of capitalism* (New York: Macmillan and Free Press, 1985), 1–42.

4. Browne, *Private interests, public policy, and American agriculture*, 213–36.

5. Douglass C. North, *Institutions, institutional change and economic performance* (Cambridge: Cambridge University Press, 1990).

6. On the distinction between policy and programs, see William P. Browne, *Politics, programs, and bureaucrats* (Port Washington, N.Y.: Kennikat Press, 1980), 11–15.

7. Williamson, *The economic institutions of capitalism*, 52–68.

8. Ibid.; Bonnen and Browne, "Why is agricultural policy so difficult to reform?" 26.

9. See *The Federalist Papers*, number 10 (New York: New American Library, reprinted 1961), 77–84.

10. Virginia Gray and David Lowery, *The population ecology of interest representation: Lobbying communities in the American states* (Ann Arbor: University of Michigan Press, 1996), 111–36.

11. Lester W. Milbrath, *The Washington lobbyists* (Chicago: Rand McNally, 1963), 349–50.

12. Kenneth A. Shepsle, "Studying institutions: Some lessons from the rational choice approach," *Journal of Theoretical Politics* (April 1989): 131–47.

13. Baumgartner and Jones, *Agendas and instability in American politics*.

14. Paul A. Sabatier and Hank C. Jenkins-Smith, *Policy change and learning: An advocacy coalition approach* (Boulder, Colo.: Westview Press, 1993).

15. James T. Bonnen, "Observations on the changing nature of agricultural policy decision processes, 1946–1976," in *Farmers, bureaucrats, and middlemen,* edited by Trudy Huscamp Peterson (Washington, D.C.: Howard University Press, 1980), 309–29; James T. Bonnen, William P. Browne, and David B. Schweikhardt, "Further observations on the changing nature of agricultural policy decision processes, 1946–1995," *Agricultural History* 70 (spring 1996): 130–52.

16. Jeffery H. Birnbaum and Alan S. Murray, *Showdown at Gucci gulch: Lawmakers, lobbyists, and the unlikely triumph of tax reform* (New York: Random House, 1987); Browne, *Private interests, public policy, and American agriculture,* 214–52.

17. John Kingdon, *Agendas, alternatives, and public policy,* 2d ed. (Boston: Little, Brown, 1995).

18. Robert H. Salisbury, "Interest representation: The dominance of institutions," *American Political Science Review* 17 (March 1984): 64–76.

19. William P. Browne and John Dinse, "The emergence of the American Agriculture Movement, 1977–1979," *Great Plains Quarterly* 5 (fall 1985): 221–35.

20. Hansen, *Gaining access.*

21. Browne, *Private interests, public policy, and American agriculture,* 64–108.

22. Hansen, *Gaining access,* 26–97.

CHAPTER 4

1. Stephen Skowronek, *Building a new American state: The expansion of national administrative capacities, 1877–1920* (Cambridge: Cambridge University Press, 1982); David E. Hamilton, "Building the associative state: The Department of Agriculture and American state-building," *Agricultural History* 64 (spring1990): 207–18.

2. Arthur S. Link, ed., *The papers of Woodrow Wilson,* vol. 30 (Princeton, N.J.: Princeton University Press, 1979), 24.

3. Schultz, *Redirecting farm policy;* Schultz, *Agriculture in an unstable economy.*

4. Harold Seidman and Robert Gilmour, *Politics, position, and power: From the positive to the regulatory state,* 4th ed. (New York: Oxford University Press, 1986).

5. John M. Gaus and Leon O. Wolcott, *Public administration and the United States Department of Agriculture* (Chicago: Public Service Administration, 1940).

6. Wayne D. Rasmussen and Gladys L. Baker, *The Department of Agriculture* (New York: Praeger, 1972), 3–13.

7. E. Pendleton Herring, *Public administration and the public interest* (New York: McGraw Hill, 1936).

8. Alfred C. True, *A history of agricultural extension work in the United States: 1785–1923* (Washington, D.C.: U.S. Government Printing Office, 1928).

9. Arthur S. Link, *Wilson: Confusions and crises* (Princeton, N.J.: Princeton University Press, 1974), 345–49.

10. Schultz, *Agriculture in an unstable economy.*

11. Paarlberg, *Farm and food policy,* 5–13.

12. Benedict, *Farm policies of the United States,* 129–48; see also Murray R. Benedict, "Agriculture as a commercial industry comparable to other branches of the economy," *Journal of Farm Economics* 11 (May 1942): 476–96.

13. For a theoretical and applied explanation, see Robert H. Bates, *Markets and states in tropical Africa* (Berkeley: University of California Press, 1981).

14. James H. Shidler, *Farm crisis: 1919–1929* (Berkeley: University of California Press, 1957); H. Thomas Johnson, *Agricultural depression in the 1920's: Economic fact or statistical artifact?* (New York: Garland Publishing, 1985).

15. Douglas E. Bowers, Wayne D. Rasmussen, and Gladys L. Baker, *History of agricultural price support and adjustment programs* (Washington, D.C.: Economic Research Service, 1984).

16. Bonnen and Browne, "Why is agricultural policy so difficult to reform?" 17–19; James T. Bonnen, "The political economy of U.S. rural policy: An exploration of the past with strategies for the future," paper presented at International Symposium on Economic Change, Policies, Strategies, and Research Issues, Aspen, Colo. (July 1990).

17. Lyle P. Schertz and Otto C. Doering III, *The making of the 1996 farm bill* (Ames: Iowa State University Press, 1999).

18. William P. Browne, *Cultivating Congress: Constituents, issues, and interests in agricultural policymaking* (Lawrence: University Press of Kansas, 1995), 40–62.

19. Willard W. Cochrane, *Farm prices, myth and reality* (Minneapolis: University of Minnesota Press, 1958); Glenn L. Johnson, "Theoretical considerations," in *The overproduction trap in U.S. agriculture,* edited by Glenn L. Johnson and Leroy Quance (Baltimore: Johns Hopkins University Press, 1980), 22–40.

20. Kevin Goss, Richard Rodefeld, and Frederick Buttel, "The political economy of class structure in U.S. agriculture," in *The rural sociology of advanced societies,* ed. Frederick Buttel and Howard Newby (Montclair, N.J.: Allanheld Osum, 1980), 83–132; Jon Gjerde, *From peasants to farmers: The migration from Balestrand, Norway to the upper middle West* (London: Cambridge University Press, 1985).

21. Cochrane, *The development of American agriculture,* 378–95; Johnson, "Theoretical considerations"; Kenneth L. Robinson, *Farm and food policies and their consequences* (Englewood Cliffs, N.J.: Prentice-Hall, 1989), 2–18.

22. Johnson, "Theoretical considerations"; David Hamilton, *From new day to New Deal: American farm policy from Hoover to Roosevelt, 1929–1933* (Chapel Hill: University of North Carolina Press, 1991), 8–25.

23. Ibid., 88.

CHAPTER 5

1. William P. Browne, James T. Bonnen, Jan E. Mabie, and David B. Schweikhardt, "Fits of analysis: Good ones and bad ones in agriculture's public sector," *Agricultural History* 74 (spring 2000): 181–97.

2. J. Patrick Madden and David E. Brewster, eds., *A philosopher among economists: John M. Brewster* (Philadelphia: J. T. Murphy, 1970), 2.

3. William P. Browne, Jerry R. Skees, Louis E. Swanson, Paul B. Thompson, and Laurian J. Unnevehr, "Stewardship values: Still valid for the 21st Century?" *Choices* 7 (1992): 20–25.

4. John S. Pancake, *Thomas Jefferson and Alexander Hamilton* (Woodbury, N.Y.: Barrons, 1974), 139–57.

5. Mircea Eliade, *Myth and reality* (New York: Harper and Row, 1963), 1–2, 7–11.
6. Lincoln Steffens, *The shame of the cities* (Mattick, N.Y.: Amereon, 1904).
7. Bonnen and Browne, "Why is agricultural policy so difficult to reform?" 9–13.
8. Gabriel Almond and Sidney Verba, *The civic culture* (Boston: Little, Brown, 1965), 360–65.
9. Shepsle, "Studying institutions."
10. Lucien W. Pye, *Communications and political development* (Princeton, N.J.: Princeton University Press, 1963), 153–71.
11. Harry M. Johnson, "Ideology and the social system," *International Encyclopedia of the Social Sciences*, vol. 7 (New York: Macmillan and Free Press, 1968), 77.
12. Paul B. Thompson, "The philosophical rationale for U.S. agricultural policy," in *U.S. agriculture in a global setting: An agenda for the future*, ed. M. Ann Tutwiler (Washington, D.C.: Resources for the Future, 1988).
13. Turbayne, *The myth of metaphor*, 55–77.
14. William P. Browne, "Mobilizing and activating group demands: The emergence of the American Agriculture Movement," *Social Science Quarterly* 64 (March 1983): 19–34.
15. W. Russell Neuman, *The paradox of mass politics: Knowledge and opinion in the American electorate* (Cambridge, Mass.: Harvard University Press, 1986).
16. Howard Margolis, *Patterns, thinking, and cognition* (Chicago: University of Chicago Press, 1988).
17. Murray Edelman, *Constructing the political spectacle* (Chicago: University of Chicago Press, 1988); Charles Press and Kenneth Verburg, *American politicians and journalists* (Boston: Scott, Foresman, 1988).
18. John M. Brewster, "The relevance of the Jeffersonian dream today," in *Land use policy and problems in the United States*, edited by H. W. Ottoson (Lincoln: University of Nebraska Press, 1963), 86–136.
19. Joseph S. Davis, "Agricultural fundamentalism," in *Economics, sociology, and the modern world*, edited by Norman E. Hines (Cambridge, Mass.: Harvard University Press, 1935), 3–22; A. Whitney Griswold, *Farming and democracy* (New York: Harcourt, Brace, 1948); Luther Tweeten, "Sector as personality: The case of farm protest movements," *Agriculture and Human Values* 4 (winter 1987): 66–74; David B. Danbom, "Romantic agrarianism in twentieth-century America," *Agricultural History* 65 (fall 1991): 1–12.
20. These are derived from the main points made by Browne et al., *Sacred cows and hot potatoes.*
21. Ronald N. Johnson and Gary D. Libecap, *The federal civil service system and the problem of bureaucracy: The economics and politics of institutional change* (Chicago: University of Chicago Press, 1994).
22. Paul H. Appleby, *Policy and administration* (University: University of Alabama Press, 1949).
23. Clarence D. Palmby, *Made in Washington: Food policy and the political expedient* (Danville, Ill.: Interstate Printers, 1985).
24. Ross B. Talbot and Don F. Hadwiger, *The policy process in American agriculture* (San Francisco: Chandler, 1968), 15.
25. Theodore J. Lowi, *The end of liberalism: The second republic of the United States*, 2d ed. (New York: Norton, 1979), 69–77.

26. Ibid., 71–75.

27. William P. Browne, "Farm organizations and agribusiness," in *Food policy and farm programs,* edited by Don F. Hadwiger and Ross B. Talbot (New York: Academy of Political Science, 1982), 198–211; Browne, *Private interests, public policy, and American agriculture,* 41–63.

28. Browne, "Mobilizing and activating group demands," 28–29.

29. Browne, *Groups, interests, and U.S. public policy,* 62–83.

30. Martha Derthick and Paul J. Quirk, *The politics of deregulation* (Washington, D.C.: Brookings, 1985), 237–58.

31. Browne et al., *Sacred cows and hot potatoes,* 16.

32. James T. Bonnen and David B. Schweikhardt, "The future of U.S. agricultural policy: Reflections on the disappearance of the 'farm problem,'" *Review of Agricultural Economics* 20 (spring/summer 1998): 2–36.

33. Thanks for this observation to the too easily forgotten but wonderful movie, *Lone Star.*

34. Pancake, *Thomas Jefferson and Alexander Hamilton,* 158–87.

CHAPTER 6

1. Guy Benveniste, *The politics of expertise,* 2d edition (San Francisco: Boyd and Fraser, 1977), 139–59; Richard Stillman II, *The American bureaucracy: The core of modern government,* 2d ed. (Chicago: Nelson Hall, 1996), 219–77.

2. Elisabeth S. Clemens, *The people's lobby: Organizational innovation and the rise of interest group politics in the United States, 1890–1925* (Chicago: University of Chicago Press, 1997), 273–317.

3. Browne, *Private interests, public policy, and American agriculture,* 14–40.

4. Hansen, *Gaining access,* 17–19.

5. Based on personal conversations with the strange old man who raised peacocks in his yard in my neighborhood—paraphrased, I'm sure, from many childhood conversations.

6. Shidler, *Farm crisis;* Bonnen and Browne, "Why is agricultural policy so difficult to reform?" 13–15.

7. Dyson, *Farmers' organizations,* 233–52.

8. Buck, *The Granger movement,* 33; Theodore Saloutos: *Farmer movements in the South, 1865–1933* (Lincoln: University of Nebraska Press, 1960), 51; Allen Weinstein, *Prelude to populism: Origins of the silver issue, 1867–1878* (New Haven, Conn.: Yale University Press, 1970), 351.

9. Richard L. McCormick, ed., *The party period and public policy: American politics from the age of Jackson to the progressive era* (New York: Oxford University Press, 1986), 106–08.

10. Saloutos, *Farmer movements in the South,* 23–24, 57–87.

11. Richard Hofstader, *The age of reform* (New York: Knopf, 1953), 109.

12. Saloutos, *Farmer movements in the South,* 187; Theodore Saloutos and John D. Hicks, *Agricultural discontent in the middle west, 1900–1939* (Madison: University of Wisconsin Press, 1951), 114, 154.

13. Hansen, *Gaining access,* 27–28.

14. William J. Block, *The separation of the Farm Bureau and the Extension Service* (Urbana: University of Illinois Press, 1960).

15. Christiana McFadyen Campbell, *The Farm Bureau and the New Deal* (Urbana: University of Illinois Press, 1962); John L. Shover, *Cornbelt rebellion: The Farmers' Holiday Association* (Urbana: University of Illinois Press, 1965); Hansen, *Gaining access*, 26–77.

16. Hamilton, *From new day to New Deal*, 170–94.

17. Browne, *Private interests, public policy, and American agriculture*, 89–108.

18. Dyson, *Farmers' organizations*, 21–22.

19. William P. Browne, "The fragmented and meandering politics of agriculture," in *U.S. agriculture in a global setting: An agenda for the future*, edited by M. Ann Tutwiler (Washington, D.C.: Resources for the Future, 1988), 136–53.

20. John Ferejohn, "Logrolling in an institutional context: A case study of food stamp legislation," in *Congress and policy change*, edited by Gerald C. Wright, Jr., Leroy N. Rieselbach, and Lawrence C. Dodd (New York: Agathon, 1986), 239–45; Browne, *Cultivating Congress*, 22–39.

21. Louis E. Swanson, "Rural development dilemma," *Resources* 96 (1989): 14–17.

22. Browne, *Cultivating Congress*, 81–83.

23. William P. Browne and Louis E. Swanson, "Living with the minimum: Rural public policy," in *The changing American countryside: Rural people and places*, edited by Emery N. Castle (Lawrence: University Press of Kansas, 1995), 481–92.

24. Hansen, "Choosing sides," 183–229.

25. Bonnen and Browne, "Why is agricultural policy so difficult to reform?" 7–33.

26. Ibid., 13–16.

CHAPTER 7

1. See, for example, Harrell R. Rodgers, Jr. and Gregory Weiher, eds., *Rural poverty: Special causes and policy reforms* (Westport, Conn.: Greenwood Press, 1989); Thomas A. Lyson, *Two sides to the Sun Belt: The growing difference between the rural and the urban South* (New York: Praeger, 1989); Cornelia B. Flora and James A. Christenson, eds., *Rural policies for the 1990s* (Boulder, Colo.: Westview Press, 1991).

2. Rural Sociological Society, *Persistent poverty in rural America*, 292.

3. Rasmussen and Baker, *The Department of Agriculture*.

4. Browne and Reid, "Misconceptions, institutional impediments, and the problems of rural governments," 265–84.

5. *Report of the Country Life Commission*, Senate Document 705, 60th Cong., 2nd sess. (Washington, D.C.: U.S. Government Printing Office, 1909).

6. Richard S. Kirkendall, "Farm politics and the New Deal," in *Agrarianism in American history*, edited by L. H. Douglas (Lexington, Mass.: D.C. Heath, 1969), 148–53.

7. John D. Black, *Agricultural reform in the United States* (New York: McGraw Hill, 1929); Gray, "Disadvantaged rural classes;" Wilson, "Problem of poverty in agriculture."

8. John C. Culver and John Hyde, *American dreamer: A life of Henry A. Wallace* (New York: W. W. Norton, 2000).

9. Nick Kotz, *Let them eat promises: The politics of hunger in America* (Garden City, N.Y.: Doubleday, 1971).

10. National Advisory Commission on Rural Poverty, *Rural poverty in the United States* (Washington, D.C.: U.S. Government Printing Office, 1967).

11. Kingdon, *Agendas, alternatives, and public policy.*
12. Personal interview, September 1992.
13. Hansen, *Gaining access,* 28.
14. Dyson, *Farmers' organizations,* 233–52.
15. Bonnen, "Why is there no coherent U.S. rural policy?" 190–201.
16. Robert C. McMath, Jr., *American populism: A social history, 1877–1898* (New York: Hill and Wang, 1993).
17. R. V. Scott, *The reluctant farmer: The rise of agricultural extension to 1914* (Urbana: University of Illinois Press, 1970); Bonnen, Browne, and Schweikhardt, "Further observations on the changing nature of national agricultural decision processes," 130–52.
18. Benedict, *Farm policies of the United States,* 375–86
19. Lowi, *The end of liberalism,* 66–77.
20. Lynn M. Daft, "The rural poor," *Policy Studies Review* 2 (August 1982): 65–71.
21. Niles M. Hansen, *Rural poverty and the urban crisis: A strategy for regional development* (Bloomington: Indiana University Press, 1970).
22. Browne, *Private interests, public policy, and American agriculture,* 136.
23. Browne, *Cultivating Congress,* 68–85.
24. E. E. Schattschneider, *Politics, pressures and the tariff: A study of free private enterprise in pressure politics as shown in the 1929–30 revision of the tariff* (New York: Holt, Rinehart, and Winston, 1935).
25. Browne, *Groups, interests, and U.S. public policy,* 192–208.
26. This starts with David Truman, *The governmental process* (New York: Knopf, 1951); it goes on to Laura R. Woliver, *From outrage to action: The politics of grassroots dissent* (Urbana: University of Illinois Press, 1993).
27. Hank C. Jenkins-Smith and Paul A. Sabatier, "Evaluating the advocacy coalition framework," *Journal of Public Policy* 14 (April 1994): 175–203.
28. Milbrath, *The Washington lobbyists.*
29. Rural Sociological Society, *Persistent poverty in rural America.*
30. Grant McConnell, *Private power and American democracy* (New York: Knopf, 1966); Lowi, *The end of liberalism,* 66–77.
31. John Gaventa, *Power and powerlessness: Quiescence and rebellion in an Appalachian valley* (Urbana: University of Illinois Press, 1980).
32. Schattschneider, *Politics, pressures and the tariff.*
33. William J. Nagel, "Federal organization for rural policy," in *Toward rural development policy for the 1990's: Enhancing income and employment opportunities,* 101st Cong., 1st sess., S. Print 101-150, edited by Congressional Research Service and Joint Economic Committee of Congress (Washington, D.C.: U.S. Government Printing Office, 1990), 231–38.
34. Swanson, "The rural development dilemma," 14.
35. Browne and Swanson, "Living with the minimum," 481–92.
36. Kevin W. Hula, *Lobbying together: Interest group coalitions in legislative politics* (Washington, D.C.: Georgetown University Press, 1999).
37. Paul A. Sabatier, "The acquisition and utilization of technical information by administrative agencies," *Administrative Science Quarterly* 23 (September 1978): 369–417.
38. Browne, *Cultivating Congress,* 26.

39. Ronald T. Libby, *Eco-wars: Political campaigns and social movements* (New York: Columbia University Press, 1998).
40. Rural Sociological Society, *Persistent poverty in rural America*, 292.
41. Gaventa, *Power and powerlessness*.

CHAPTER 8

1. Glen O. Robinson, *American bureaucracy: Public choice and public law* (Ann Arbor: University of Michigan Press, 1991), 13.
2. Ibid., 13–14.
3. Request made to author on a tour of a member's district in 1994. The author was with the member addressing constituent groups on the flaws of logic in agricultural policy.
4. Same member, same tour, off-handed remark between stops.
5. Browne, *Politics, programs, and bureaucrats*, 11–15.
6. Kenneth A. Shepsle, *The giant jigsaw puzzle: Democratic committee assignments in the modern House* (Chicago: University of Chicago Press, 1978).
7. Richard F. Fenno, Jr., *Congressmen in committees* (Boston: Little, Brown, 1973), 192–279.
8. Hansen, *Gaining access*, 31–33.
9. Ross K. Baker, *House and Senate* (New York: W. W. Norton, 1989), 57–63.
10. Talbot and Hadwiger, *The policy process in American agriculture*, 163.
11. Ibid., 163–72.
12. Ibid., 161.
13. Morris P. Fiorina, *Congress: Keystone of the Washington establishment*, 2d ed. (New Haven, Conn.: Yale University Press, 1989), 58–63.
14. John P. Heinz, "The political impasse in farm support legislation," *Yale Law Journal* 71 (April 1962): 952–78.
15. Garth Youngberg, "The National Farm Coalition and the politics of food," paper presented at Fourth Annual Hendricks Public Policy Symposium, Lincoln, Neb. (1979).
16. Gaus and Wolcott, *Public administration and the USDA*; Griswold, *Farming and democracy*.
17. Appleby, *Policy and administration*.
18. Herring, *Public administration and the public interest*, 258–59.
19. Griswold, *Farming and democracy*, 175.
20. Jess Gilbert, "Eastern urban liberals and midwestern agrarian intellectuals: Two group portraits of progressives in the New Deal Department of Agriculture," *Agricultural History* 74 (spring 2000): 162–80.
21. James W. Davis, Jr., *An introduction to public administration: Politics, policy, and bureaucracy* (New York: Free Press, 1974), 53.
22. Rasmussen and Baker, *The Department of Agriculture*, 53.
23. Ibid., 119–20.
24. Neil Schaller, compiler, *Proceedings of phase I workshop: Social science agricultural agenda project* (Minneapolis: Spring Hill Conference Center, 1987).
25. Browne and Reid, "Misconceptions, institutional impediments, and the problems of rural governments," 277.
26. Ernest G. Moore, *The Agricultural Research Service* (New York: Praeger, 1967).

27. Gladys L. Baker, *The county agent* (Chicago: University of Chicago Press, 1939).

28. Paul Henderson and David Francis, eds., *Rural action: A collection of community work case studies* (Boulder, Colo.: Pluto Press, 1993).

29. Theda Skocpol, *Social policy in the United States* (Princeton, N.J.: Princeton University Press, 1995), calls this the "Tocquevillian" approach to state building. States are considered as sets of institutions rather than as autonomous..

30. Peter Evans, Dietrich Rueshemeyer, and Theda Skocpol, eds., *Bringing the state back in* (Cambridge: Cambridge University Press, 1985).

31. Browne, *Private interests, public policy, and American agriculture* and Browne, *Cultivating Congress* illustrate all this. See also Jess Gilbert and Carolyn Howe, "Beyond 'state vs. society': Theories of the state and New Deal agricultural policies," *American Sociological Review* 56 (April 1991): 204–20.

32. Palmby, *Made in Washington*.

33. Cochrane, *The development of American agriculture*.

34. Paul H. Appleby, *Big democracy* (New York: Knopf, 1945); Philip Selznick, *TVA and the grass roots* (Berkeley: University of California Press, 1949); Norman I. Wengert, *Valley of tomorrow: The TVA and agriculture* (Knoxville: Bureau of Public Administration, University of Tennessee, 1952).

CHAPTER 9

1. Laurence E. Lynn, Jr., *Designing public policy: A casebook on the role of policy analysis* (Santa Monica, Calif.: Goodyear Publishing, 1980), 4–5; and Laurence E. Lynn, Jr., *Managing the public's business: The job of the government executive* (New York: Basic Books, 1981), 23–48.

2. Lynn, *Managing the public's business*, 3–22.

3. Benedict, *Farm policies of the United States*, xii–xiii.

4. Robinson, *Farm and food policies and their consequences*, 48–87.

5. Bonnen, Browne, and Schweikhardt, "Further observations on the changing nature of agricultural policy decision processes," 130–52.

6. Browne et al., "Fits of analysis," 181–97.

7. Herring, *Public administration and the public interest*; Clarence C. Davis, "The development of agricultural policy since the end of the world war," in *Farmers in a changing world: The yearbook of agriculture, 1940* (Washington, D.C.: U.S. Government Printing Office, 1940), 297–336.

8. Hamilton, *From new day to New Deal*, 59–64, 230.

9. Katherine Reichelderfer and Maureen Kuwano Hinkle, "The evolution of pesticide policy: Environmental interests and agriculture," in Carol S. Kramer, ed., *The political economy of U.S. agriculture: Challenges for the 1990s* (Washington, D.C.: National Center for Food and Agricultural Policy, 1989), 156–57.

10. A. Hunter Dupree, *Science in the federal government: A history of policies and activities* (Cambridge, Mass.: Harvard University Press, 1957); Geweke et al., eds., *Sowing seeds of change*.

11. James T. Bonnen, "Providing economic information in an increasingly difficult policy environment," *Review of Agricultural Economics* 22 (fall/winter 2000): 500–518.

12. Browne et al., "Fits of analysis."

13. The most infamous case is the structure of the agricultural economy report with its extensive criticism of size and income growth in farm numbers. See Economics, Statistics, and Cooperatives Service, U.S. Department of Agriculture, *Structure issues of American agriculture* (Washington, D.C.: U.S. Government Printing Office, 1979), Agricultural Economic Report 438.

14. Clemens, *The people's lobby*. For more vintage looks at that nasty politics of elites versus the poor, see Lowi, *The end of liberalism*, 3–28; James A. Morone, *The democratic wish: Popular participation and the limits of American government* (New York: Basic Books, 1990).

15. Walter Dean Burnham, "The changing shape of the American political universe," *American Political Science Review* 59 (March 1965): 7–28; Walter Dean Burnham, "Party systems and the political process," in *The American party systems: Stages of development*, edited by William Nisbet Chambers and Walter Dean Burnham (New York: Oxford University Press, 1967), 277–307; McCormick, ed., *The party period and public policy*.

16. William P. Browne and Won K. Paik, "Farmers and the U.S. Congress: Rethinking basic institutional assumptions about agricultural policy," *Agricultural Economics* 11 (December 1994): 125–41.

17. Buck, *The Granger movement*; Saloutos and Hicks, *Agricultural discontent in the middle west*; Grant McConnell, *The decline of agrarian democracy* (Berkeley: University of California Press, 1953); McConnell, *Private power and American democracy*; Shidler, *Farm crisis*; Saloutos, *Farmer movements in the South*; Weinstein, *Prelude to populism*.

18. This controversy dominated policy and party politics for nearly a decade, putting other issues aside. Schattschneider, *Politics, pressures and the tariff*.

19. John Mark Hansen, "Taxation and the political economy of the tariff" *International Organization* 44 (autumn 1990): 527–51.

20. Kim Anderson, "On why agriculture declines with economic growth," *Agricultural Economics* 1 (June 1987): 195–207.

21. J. Leiper Freeman, *The political process: executive bureau-legislative committee relations* (New York: Random House, 1965), fathered the triangle metaphor. Ernest S. Griffith, *The impasse of democracy* (New York: Harrison Hilton, 1939), pioneered the concept academically, however, in calling these triangles "whirlpools of activity"; Douglass Cater, *Power in Washington* (New York: Random House, 1964), did the same popularizing among journalists by using the term "subgovernments." Charles O. Jones, "Representation in Congress: The case of the House Agriculture Committee," *American Political Science Review* 55 (June 1961): 358–67, indicated that such representation appears true of agriculture; see also Michael S. Lyons and Marcia Whicker Taylor, "Farm politics in transition: The House Agriculture Committee," *Agricultural History* 55 (January 1981): 128–46.

22. Randall B. Ripley and Grace A. Franklin, *Congress, the bureaucracy, and public policy*, 5th ed. (Pacific Grove, Calif.: Brooks/Cole, 1991). For agriculture, see Campbell, *The Farm Bureau and the New Deal*.

23. The emphasis on recurrence is from Hansen, *Gaining access*. Hansen is not an advocate for the overly simplistic triangle metaphor, however.

24. Browne, *Groups, interests, and U.S. public policy*, 211–15. The silliest application is the "how-to-do-policy" model by Neil Meyer and William T. Dishman, *Power clusters:*

How public policy originates (Moscow: Cooperative Extension Service, College of Agriculture, University of Idaho, 1984). No policy ideas, it seems there, exist or are of value from outside the triangle.

25. Max Weber, "Bureaucracy," in *From Max Weber: Essays on sociology,* edited by H. H. Gerth and C. Wright Mills (New York: Oxford University Press, 1958), 196–244.

26. Lowi, *The end of liberalism,* 110–12.

27. Browne, *Private interests, public policy, and American agriculture,* 109–49.

28. Don F. Hadwiger, *The politics of agricultural research* (Lincoln: University of Nebraska Press, 1982).

29. Weldon V. Barton, "Food, agriculture, and administrative adaptation to political change," *Public Administration Review* 36 (March/April 1976): 148–54. Don F. Hadwiger, "The old, the new, and the emerging United States Department of Agriculture," *Public Administration Review* 36 (March/April 1976): 155–65; Theda Skocpol and Kenneth Finegold, "State capacity and economic intervention in the early New Deal," *Political Science Quarterly* 97 (summer 1982): 255–78; Hamilton, "Building the associative state."

30. Turner, *The frontier in American history.*

31. Glenn L. Johnson, "Disciplines, processes, and interdependencies related to the problem-solving and issue-oriented work of agricultural economists," in *Beyond agriculture and economics,* edited by A. Allen Schmid (East Lansing: Michigan State University Press, 1997), chapter 9.

32. Johnson, "Theoretical considerations," 22–40.

33. Robert P. Weber, "Home style and committee behavior: The case of Richard Nolan," in *Home style and Washington work: Studies of congressional politics,* edited by Morris P. Fiorina and David W. Rhode (Ann Arbor: University of Michigan Press, 1989), 71–94.

34. Economics, Statistics, and Cooperatives Service, U.S. Department of Agriculture, *Structure issues of American agriculture.*

35. Quantitative analysis by political scientists never found such patterns as triangles, except in isolated types of very minor issues. Thomas L. Gais, Mark A. Peterson, and Jack L. Walker, Jr., "Interest groups, iron triangles, and representative institutions in American national government," *British Journal of Political Science* 14 (March 1984): 161–85; John P. Heinz, Edward O. Laumann, Robert L. Nelson, and Robert H. Salisbury, *The hollow core: Private interests in national policy making* (Cambridge, Mass.: Harvard University Press, 1993).

36. Arthur Capper, *The agricultural bloc* (New York: Harcourt Brace, 1922).

37. James A. Montmarquet explains the need for civilizing farmers. See *The idea of agrarianism* (Moscow: University of Idaho Press, 1989).

CHAPTER 10

1. Even as contemporary lobbying has moved to differentiate between advocacy among good-old-boy networks of familiar and often indebted forces, on one hand, and issue-management networks of intense policy interests, on the other hand, one thing stays the same. Lobbyists need to position themselves, first, with those who are willing and able to respond to specific requests. Friends, most obviously, do this. Browne, *Groups, interests, and U.S. public policy,* 137–67.

2. John Kingdon repeatedly shows how advocacy roles shift situationally through the policy process. That is, one legislator is the lobbying target at a moment in time. Then, from that person's institutional position, she becomes the primary advocate as colleague commitments are sought and legislation drafted. See *Agendas, Alternatives, and Public Policies*, 1st ed. (Boston: Little, Brown, 1984).

3. The Agricultural Accountability Project was one of the earliest research efforts to lay out a systematic attack on modernizing and developing U.S. food production. See Jim Hightower, *Hard tomatoes, hard times* (Cambridge, Mass.: Schenkman, 1973). As an active project participant, Susan Sechler demonstrates well how even dissident entrepreneurs come to play out extended roles in a specific policy domain and within a broader policy process. What they primarily develop is longevity, the expertise to focus criticism, and broad friendship networks.

4. William P. Browne, "Organized interests and their issue niches: A search for pluralism in a policy domain," *Journal of Politics* 52 (May 1990): 477–509; William P. Browne, "Issue niches and the limits of interest group influence," in *Interest group politics*, 3d ed., edited by Allan J. Cigler and Burdette A. Loomis (Washington, D.C.: Congressional Quarterly Press, 1991), 345–70.

5. Personal discussion, fall 1992.

6. Browne, *Private interests, public policy, and American agriculture*, 130–49.

7. Ibid., 138–43.

8. Diane Blair, *Arkansas politics and government: Do the people rule?* (Lincoln: University of Nebraska Press, 1988).

9. Personal discussion, spring 1993.

10. Fiorina, *Congress*.

11. Personal interview, fall 1985. Across the board, this attitude was shared by the liberal to centrist Democratic Leadership Council and other social-cause leaders. They were angered and frustrated by Clinton staff appointments. Very few of their populist favorites found places. The new administration, upon arrival, was transforming itself from a proponent of big government on behalf of the powerless to one of middle-class proponents. Jonathan Cole, "Mr. populism returns: Play it again Stan," *The New Republic* 223 (September 11, 2000): 18–19.

12. Browne, *Cultivating Congress*, 40–62.

13. Lobbyists often talk of playing "small ball" as a first priority. When they play out that strategy, they want just one run, little publicity, and the more likely probability of scoring on a bloop single rather than a majestic home run.

14. E. E. Schattschneider, *The semi-sovereign people: A realist's view of democracy in America* (New York: Holt, Rinehart and Winston, 1960), 1–4.

15. The vocal reaction against genetically altered foods is the best example. More than 250,000 individuals contacted USDA in favor of very strict organic agricultural standards in 1999–2000. See *Organic Gardening* 47 (May-June 2000): front and back cover pages.

16. Weinstein, *Prelude to populism*.

17. Jeffrey M. Berry, Kent E. Portney, and Ken Thomson, *The rebirth of urban democracy* (Washington, D.C.: Brookings Institution, 1993).

18. Again reaction to genetic alteration of foods is the best example. But public concern

was expected by agribusinesss firms. William P. Browne, "Bovine growth hormone and the politics of uncertainty: Fear and loathing in a transitional agriculture," *Agriculture and Human Values* 4 (winter 1987): 75–80.

19. Browne, *Cultivating Congress*, 31–34.

20. This applies in one four-domain comparison. See Heinz et al., *The hollow core*.

21. William P. Browne, "Agricultural policy can't accommodate everyone who wants in," *Choices* 4 (first quarter 1989): 9–11.

22. Rosenstone and Hansen, *Mobilization, participation, and democracy in America*.

23. This was very much the oft-repeated fear among rural policy experts in the middle 1980s. Personal conversations from my office within the Agricultural and Rural Economic Development branch, Economic Research Service, United States Department of Agriculture, Washington, D.C., fall 1985. I thank ERS for the funding, the office, and the staff assistance.

24. Ron Eyerman and Andrew Jamison, *Social movements: A cognitive approach* (University Park: Penn State Press, 1991), foresaw such a strategy.

25. The grassroots, nonfarm political activist groups apparently reflect this broad reform orientation because they are targeted by so many national group leaders. At least, campus activists say that's the case. An example at my home campus reinforced this point by appearing after this chapter was completed. Students claimed that their new publication, *Voices of Dissent*, focused on—or perhaps unfocused on—"concerns for CMU's administrative policies, global warming, animal cruelty, equality, free speech, and many other social issues." *The Campus Progressive* 1 (April 2000): 2. Why so much issue diversity? "It's the way to show how terrible things are, bombard possible members with *all* the bad news, mobilize *everyone* in what's a small town situation," said a student leader in a personal interview.

CHAPTER 11

1. This chapter is the product of several years of work supported by numerous grants from sources interested in Congress and social policy. These sources include the Ford Foundation and the Rural Economic Policy Program of the Aspen Institute. In addition to the grant from Ford, financial support was provided by the ERS for preliminary work on the project, as well as later for data analysis. Resources for the Future's National Center for Food and Agricultural Policy also assisted by providing office and clerical assistance in Washington, through its visiting fellows program. Central Michigan University contributed through its Research Professors program and the Institute for Social and Behavioral Studies; these two programs provided five semesters of released time. The Everett McKinley Dirksen Congressional Leadership Research Center also provided financial support. Preparation of this manuscript was supported in part by grants from the W. K. Kellogg Foundation and the Regional Centers for Rural Development.

2. Fluharty, "Rural policy."

3. Anonymous interview, environmental lobbyist; see Browne, *Private interests, public policy, and American agriculture*, xiv–xvi, for interview information.

4. This is a result of the neoclassical political regime orientation whereby unhindered

market mechanisms are expected to provide for social policies. Poverty programs therefore are unpopular with policymakers because they generally are held in low esteem by society. Gosta Esping-Andersen, *The three worlds of welfare capitalism* (Princeton, N.J.: Princeton University Press, 1990).

5. The failure view is held by Charles Murray, *Losing ground: American social policy, 1950–1980* (New York: Basic Books, 1984). In contrast, the success view is held by John E. Schwarz, *America's hidden success: A reassessment of twenty years of public policy* (New York: W. W. Norton, 1983).

6. Working Group on the State and Rural Poverty, "The state, rural poverty, and rural policy," in *Persistent poverty in rural America*, ed. Rural Sociological Society Task Force on Persistent Rural Poverty (Boulder, Colo.: Westview, 1993), 292–326.

7. Isabel V. Sawhill, "Poverty in the U.S.: Why is it so persistent?" *Journal of Economic Literature* 26 (September 1988): 1073–1119.

8. Bonnen, "Providing economic information in an increasingly difficult policy environment," 500–518.

9. Borrowed from Harold D. Lasswell's classic work, *Politics: Who gets what, when, and how* (New York: Meridian, 1936, reprinted in 1958).

10. Information for this section comes from a personal project on Congress that followed from my interest group research (cited in note 3 to this chapter). The conclusions rely most extensively on anonymous random interviews with legislators and staff in 113 House of Representatives and Senate offices. Several other staff and Washington policy participants involved with rural policy provided background information. The Ford Foundation and other organizations cited in note 1 to this chapter supported that research. The rationale for the latter project can be seen in Browne, *Cultivating Congress*, 223–31, 242 for interview information.

11. Ibid., 109–30.

12. See, for instance, Charles O. Jones, *The presidency in a separated system* (Washington, D.C.: Brookings Institution, 1994), or reviews in *National Journal* volumes from that period.

13. Anthony Downs, *Inside bureaucracy* (Boston: Little, Brown, 1966).

14. Harold Wilensky, *Organizational intelligence: Knowledge and policy in government and industry* (New York: Basic Books, 1967).

15. Anonymous background interview, Agriculture Research Service scientist; see Browne, *Cultivating Congress.*

16. Anonymous interview, freshman member of Congress, elected midterm; see Browne, *Cultivating Congress.*

17. Michael J. Malbin, *Unelected representatives: Congressional staff and the future of representative government* (New York: Basic Books, 1980).

18. Browne, *Cultivating Congress*, 237–39, 242–43.

19. Edward O. Laumann, *Bonds of pluralism: The form and substance of urban social networks* (New York: John Wiley, 1973), 111–30.

20. Truman, *The governmental process*, 537–44.

21. Salisbury, "Interest representation."

22. Nagel, "Federal organization for rural policy," 231–38.

23. Anonymous interview, staff member to former Speaker of the House; see Browne, *Cultivating Congress*, 227.

24. Jeffrey M. Berry, *The interest-group society*, 3d ed. (New York: Longman, 1997), 241–55.

25. Jack L. Walker, Jr., *Mobilizing interest groups in America: Patrons, professions, and social movements* (Ann Arbor: University of Michigan Press, 1991), 35–40.

26. Robert H. Salisbury, John P. Heinz, Edward O. Laumann, and Robert L. Nelson, "Who works with whom: Interest group alliances and opposition," *American Political Science Review* 81 (December 1987): 1217–34.

27. Berry, *The interest-group society*; Walker, *Mobilizing interest groups in America*; Salisbury, "Interest representation."

28. Jeffrey M. Berry, Kent E. Portney, and Ken Thomson, "The political behavior of poor people," in *The urban underclass*, edited by Christopher Jencks and Paul E. Peterson (Washington, D.C.: Brookings Institution, 1991), 357–72.

29. Bonnen, "Why is there no coherent U.S. rural policy?" 190–201.

30. Browne, *Cultivating Congress*, 115–19.

31. Ibid., 207–13.

32. Ibid., 150–58.

33. Anonymous interview, House agriculture committee member; see Browne, *Cultivating Congress*.

34. Anonymous interview, U.S. Senator; see Browne, *Cultivating Congress*.

35. David J. Webber, "Analyzing political feasibility: Political scientists' unique contribution to policy analysis," *Policy Studies Journal* 14, no. 3 (1995): 545–53.

36. Anonymous interview, House agriculture committee member; see Browne, *Cultivating Congress*.

37. Anonymous interview, congressional staff associate; see Browne, *Cultivating Congress*.

38. Ibid.

39. Anonymous background interview, Secretary's office; see Browne, *Cultivating Congress*.

40. William P. Browne, "Political feasibility: Institutional limits on environmental regulation," in *Flexible incentives for the adoption of environmental technologies in agriculture*, edited by Frank Casey, Andrew Schmitz, Scott Swinton, and David Zilberman (Norwell, Mass.: Kluwer, 1999).

41. Aaron Wildavsky, *Speaking truth to power: The art and craft of policy analysis* (Boston: Little, Brown, 1979). Wildavsky updates this old term to explain the task and meaning of policy analysis.

42. Anonymous background interview, Congressional rural policy staff proponent; see Browne, *Cultivating Congress*.

43. Anonymous interview, Congressional staff legislative director; see Browne, *Cultivating Congress*.

44. Ibid.

45. Anonymous interview, veteran congressman; see Browne, *Cultivating Congress*.

46. Anonymous interview, southern U.S. senator; see Browne, *Cultivating Congress*.

47. James Q. Wilson, *Political organizations* (New York: Basic Books, 1973); Charles Tilly, *From mobilization to revolution* (Reading, Mass.: Addison-Wesley, 1978).

48. Nick Kotz and Mary Lynn Kotz, *A passion for equality: George Wiley and the movement*

(New York: W. W. Norton, 1977); Frances Fox Piven and Richard A. Cloward, *Poor people's movements: Why they succeed, why they fail* (New York: Pantheon Press, 1977).

49. Browne, *Private interests, public policy, and American agriculture*, 89–108.
50. Anonymous interview, midwestern congressman; see Browne, *Cultivating Congress*.
51. Or avoid diffuse, collective benefit policy demands. As long as expressed interests are particularistic, even idealized policy demands seem acceptable to many members of Congress. See also Eyerman and Jamison, *Social movements*.
52. Richard S. Kirkendall, *Social scientists and farm politics in the age of Roosevelt* (Columbia: University of Missouri Press, 1966).
53. The question, however, is, has it been this imperfect? Schattschneider, *Politics, pressures and the tariff*.
54. Bonnen, "Providing economic information in an increasingly difficult policy environment."
55. Browne, *Cultivating Congress*, 133–60.

CHAPTER 12

1. John Kenneth White and Daniel M. Shea, *New party politics: From Jefferson and Hamilton to the information age* (Boston: Bedford/St. Martins, 2000), 27–30.
2. Gary Rosen, *American compact: James Madison and the problem of founding* (Lawrence: University Press of Kansas, 1999).
3. Fiorina, *Congress*.
4. Lowi, *The end of liberalism*.
5. Browne, *Cultivating Congress*.
6. Richard K. Matthews, *The radical politics of Thomas Jefferson: A revisionist view* (Lawrence: University Press of Kansas, 1986).
7. Jean Yarbrough, *American virtues: Thomas Jefferson on the character of a free people* (Lawrence: University Press of Kansas, 1998).
8. Willard W. Cochrane and C. Ford Runge, *Reforming farm policy: Towards a national agenda* (Ames: Iowa State University Press, 1992), 3–7.
9. Richard K. Matthews, *If men were angels: James Madison and the heartless empire of reason* (Lawrence: University Press of Kansas, 1995).
10. Karl-Friedrich Walling, *Republican empire: Alexander Hamilton on war and free government* (Lawrence: University Press of Kansas, 1999).
11. Arthur M. Schlesinger, Jr., *The imperial presidency* (New York: Houghton Mifflin, 1973).
12. Michael D. Reagan and John G. Sanzone, *The new federalism*, 2d ed. (New York: Oxford University Press, 1981).
13. Charles O. Jones, *Separate but equal branches: Congress and the presidency* (Chatham, N.J.: Chatham House, 1995), 20.
14. Gary Wills, *A necessary evil: A history of American distrust* (New York: Simon and Schuster, 1999).
15. Doris Kearns, *Lyndon Johnson and the American dream* (New York: Harper and Row, 1976).
16. Daft, "The rural poor," 65–71.

17. David W. Sears and J. Norman Reid, "Rural strategies and rural development research: An assessment," *Policy Studies Journal* 20, no. 2 (1992): 301–09.
18. Jones, *Separate but equal branches*, 23–36.
19. Gilbert and Howe, "Beyond 'state vs. society,'" 218.
20. Personal interview, November 1992.
21. Personal interviewee's remark, November 1991.
22. David W. Rohde, *Parties and leaders in the postreform House* (Chicago: University of Chicago Press, 1991), 1–16.
23. Hansen, *Gaining access*, 75–76.
24. Don F. Hadwiger and Ross B. Talbot, *Pressures and protests: The Kennedy farm program and the wheat referendum of 1963* (San Francisco: Chandler, 1965).
25. Browne, *Cultivating Congress*, 7, 227.
26. Ibid., 9, 18, 19, 35, 36.
27. Ferejohn, "Logrolling in an institutional context."
28. Jones, "Representation in Congress," 358–67.
29. Ibid.
30. Browne, *Cultivating Congress*, 83–84.
31. Ibid., 236.
32. Baumgartner and Jones, *Agendas and instability in American politics*.
33. William P. Browne, "Some social and political conditions of issue credibility: Legislative agendas in the American states," *Polity* 20 (winter 1987): 296–315.
34. Browne and Swanson, "Living with the minimum," 481–92.

CHAPTER 13

1. Browne, "Agricultural policy can't accommodate all who want in," 9–11.
2. Personal interview, May 1986.
3. Personal interview, December 1999.
4. Browne, *Groups, interests, and U.S. public policy*, 176–78.
5. Rosenstone and Hansen, *Mobilization, participation, and democracy in America*.
6. Jeffrey M. Berry, *The new liberalism: The rising power of citizen groups* (Washington, D.C.: Brookings Institution, 1999), 71.
7. Ibid., 71.
8. Libby, *Eco-wars*.
9. Charles S. Hyneman, *Bureaucracy in a democracy* (New York: Harper, 1950).
10. Lester R. Brown, *Building a sustainable society* (New York: W. W. Norton, 1981).
11. Lowi, *The end of liberalism*, 72, 74–75.
12. Talbot and Hadwiger, *The policy process in American agriculture*, 292–93, 300.
13. Rasmussen and Baker, *The Department of Agriculture*, 94–95.
14. Rachel Carson, *Silent spring* (New York: Houghton Mifflin, 1962); Barry Commoner, *The closing circle: Nature, man and technology* (New York: Knopf, 1971).
15. Hadwiger, *The politics of agricultural research*, 150–68.
16. Personal interview, May 1986.
17. Katherine Reichelderfer, "Environmental protection and agricultural support: Are tradeoffs necessary?" in Kramer, ed., *The political economy of U.S. agriculture*, 9–13.

18. Walter A. Rosenbaum, *Environmental politics and policy*, 3d ed. (Washington, D.C.: Congressional Quarterly, 1995).

19. Christopher J. Bosso, *Pesticides and politics: The life cycle of a public issue* (Pittsburgh: University of Pittsburgh Press, 1987), 153.

20. Rosenbaum, *Environmental politics and policy*, 34.

21. Benjamin I. Page and Robert Y. Shapiro, *The rational public: Fifty years of trends in Americans' policy preferences* (Chicago: University of Chicago Press, 1992), 154–56.

22. Ibid., 117–71.

23. Richard E. Cohen, *Washington at work: Back rooms and clean air* (New York: Macmillan, 1992).

24. Marian R. Chertow and Daniel C. Esty, eds., *Thinking ecologically: The next generation of environmental policy* (New Haven, Conn.: Yale University Press, 1997). See also Ronald G. Shaiko, *Voices and echoes for the environment: Public interest representation in the 1990s and beyond* (New York: Columbia University Press, 1999).

25. Paarlberg, *Farm and food policy*, 19.

CHAPTER 14

1. Peter Bachrach and Morton S. Baratz, *Power and poverty: Theory and practice* (New York: Oxford University Press, 1970), 42–46.

2. Jessica Nelson, "Harvesting lubricants," *The Carbohydrate Economy* 3 (fall 2000): 5.

3. Skocpol and Finegold, "State capacity and economic intervention in the early New Deal," 255–78.

4. Skowronek, *Building a new American state*.

5. Heinz et al., *The hollow core*, 308.

6. Gilbert and Howe, "Beyond 'state v. society,'" 204–20.

7. Hansen, *Gaining access*.

8. John K. Galbraith, *American capitalism* (Cambridge, Mass.: Riverside, 1952), 113–15.

9. James T. Young, "The origins of New Deal agricultural policy: Interest groups' role in policy formation," *Policy Studies Journal* 21, no. 2 (1993): 190–209.

10. Theodore Salutos, *The American farmer and the New Deal* (Ames: Iowa State University Press, 1982), 267.

11. McConnell, *The decline of agrarian democracy*, 149–50.

12. Jeffrey M. Berry, *Feeding hungry people: Rulemaking in the food stamp program* (New Brunswick, N.J.: Rutgers University Press, 1984), 21–38.

13. William P. Browne, "Agricultural biotechnology, law, and social impacts of agricultural biotechnology," in *Encyclopedia of Ethical, Legal, and Policy Issues in Biotechnology*, ed. Thomas J. Murray and Maxwell J. Mehlman (New York: Wiley, 2000), 46–56.

14. Schattschneider, *The semi-sovereign people*, 1–3.

15. Jonathan Rauch, "Our greatest modern president: Father Superior," *New Republic* 222 (May 22, 2000): 25.

16. Daniel McCool, "Indian water settlements: The prerequisites of successful negotiation," *Policy Studies Journal* 21, no. 2 (1993): 227–42.

17. Clara Bingham, *Women on the Hill: Challenging the culture of Congress* (New York: Random House, 1997).

18. Telephone interviews, October 2000.
19. Browne, *Groups, interests, and U.S. public policy,* 19–27.
20. Kay Lehman Scholzman, "What accent the heavenly chorus? Political equality and the American pressure system." *Journal of Politics* 46 (November 1984): 1006–1032.
21. Clemens, *The people's lobby.*
22. Matthew Josephson, *The politicos* (New York: Harcourt, Brace and World, 1963), 61–99.

INDEX

Food and Drug Administration (FDA),
    184, 186
food stamps, 69, 196
Ford Foundation, 144, 178
Ford Motor Company, 200
Foundation for Economic Trends, 197
Freedom to Farm Act, 168
frontier, the, 2–6, 37
FSA. *See* Federal Security Administration
Fund for Rural America, 142

Gillette, Guy, 62
Grange, the. *See* National Grange of the
    Patrons of Husbandry

Hamilton, Alexander, 28, 59, 161, 166–67
Hansen, John Mark, 193
Herring, J. Pendleton, 93
Homestead Act, 39

ideas, power of, 50, 57–58
information
    institutional sources and uses of,
        138–41
    interest group sources and uses of,
        141–46
    policy analysis, 109–11, 146–50
    sources and uses of, 137–38
    valued by public policymakers, 153–54
institutions
    bias of, 27–28, 34–35, 201–02
    Congress (*see* Congress, U.S.)
    constitutional structure of government,
        28–29
    evolution of agricultural, 191–93
    interest groups and resistance to policy
        change, 199–201
    local, 97–100
    organization of agricultural, 86–87,
        100–102 (*see also* Agriculture Depart-
        ment, U.S.)
    reform of and transaction costs, 28–32,
        35–36, 102
    as rules, 25–27, 35
    See also nation-building
interest groups. *See* special interests
interest theory, 25–26
Interior Department, U.S., 199–200
iron triangles, 113

Jefferson, Thomas, 35, 61, 161
Jeffersonian democracy, 50–51. *See also*
    agrarian myth
Johnson, Lyndon, 75–76, 95, 165–66

Kingdon, John, 217n2

Labor Department, U.S., 136
land-grant universities, 97–98
Leahy, Patrick, 124–25, 159
Locke, John, 90
Louisiana Farmers Union, 64

Madison, James, 28, 34–35, 51, 161–62
McConnell, Grant, 195
media, reinforcement of mythic public
    knowledge, 53, 58
metropolitan, definition of, 15
money supply, 63
Morrill Land Grant Act, 39
myths
    agrarian (*see* agrarian myth)
    persistence of, 51
    political uses of, 52, 57–58
    See also rural life, misperceptions about

NACo. *See* National Association of
    Counties
National Advisory Commission on Rural
    Poverty, 76
National Association of Counties (NACo),
    82, 135–36, 172
National Association of Wheat Growers, 195
National Board of Farm Organizations,
    66–67
National Corn Growers Association, 195
National Farmers Alliance (NFA), 5, 64
National Farmers Union (NFU), 5, 64–66, 195
National Grange of the Patrons of Hus-
    bandry, 5, 33, 63–64, 66–67, 71, 77
National Highway Traffic Safety Administra-
    tion, 200–201
National Milk Producers Federation, 67
National Rifle Association, 184
National Rural Electric Cooperatives Associ-
    ation (NRECA), 80, 92, 95
National Rural Health Association, 80
National Rural Housing Coalition (NRHC),
    79–80